Justin Mueller revivifies the discussion of political obligation by drawing on the temporal philosophies of Bergson and Deleuze. He creates novel concepts to show how traditional theories of political obligation seek to bind us to existing forms of social and political order. His aim is not to deny the role that obligations play in our political and everyday lives, but to point to the ever-present possibility of their modification or transformation. The concluding chapter is a *tour de force* that sketches some of the ways in which this temporal perspective might transform other problems in political philosophy such as the nature of freedom and the understanding of anarchism. This book will be of interest to scholars of political obligation and to anyone interested in the possibilities of productive engagement between political theory and contemporary European philosophy.

Paul Patton, *The University of New South Wales, UK*

This is an elegant and pellucid account of a core political concept. Mobilizing his late mentor Michael Weinstein's method of "love piracy," Mueller assembles an array of unusual suspects – Henri Bergson, Gilles Deleuze, Justis Buchler, Max Stirner – to confront the blind spot at the heart of both apologists and critics of political obligation-temporality: the political subject's lived experience of time. At once an exhaustive typology, a cogent refutation of the extant theoretical impasse, and an enactment of the critical freedom it advocates, *The Temporality of Political Obligation* affirmatively recasts modern and postmodern discussions of political authority.

Diane S. Rubenstein, *Cornell University, USA*

The Temporality of Political Obligation

The Temporality of Political Obligation offers a critique and reconceptualization of the ways in which our political obligations – what we owe to political authorities and communities, and the reasons why we ought to obey their rules – have been traditionally conceptualized, justified, and contested.

Drawing from theories of time and temporality, Justin Mueller demonstrates some of the unacknowledged assumptions and theoretical blind spots shared among these ostensibly opposed positions, and the problems and contradictions that this neglect of time poses. Enriching the literature on the philosophers Henri Bergson and Gilles Deleuze, Mueller demonstrates how their theoretical frameworks on time can be used to analyze a political problem that is usually confined to the concerns of normative liberal democratic theory. Politically, this book provides readers with the means to better identify and analyze the diverse temporalities they encounter in everyday life, and better understand their experiences of them.

The Temporality of Political Obligation is a welcome and timely read which will be of interest to scholars involved in recent efforts to engage with the social and political dimensions and consequences of time and temporality.

Justin C. Mueller received his PhD in Political Science from Purdue University, and currently lectures at Northeastern University. His research interests include the intersection of time and politics, particularly surrounding questions of obligation, obedience, belonging, and freedom.

Routledge Innovations in Political Theory

1 **A Radical Green Political Theory**
Alan Carter

2 **Rational Woman**
A Feminist Critique of Dualism
Raia Prokhovnik

3 **Rethinking State Theory**
Mark J. Smith

4 **Gramsci and Contemporary Politics**
Beyond Pessimism of the Intellect
Anne Showstack Sassoon

5 **Post-Ecologist Politics**
Social Theory and the Abdication of the Ecologist Paradigm
Ingolfur Blühdorn

6 **Ecological Relations**
Susan Board

7 **The Political Theory of Global Citizenship**
April Carter

8 **Democracy and National Pluralism**
Edited by Ferran Requejo

9 **Civil Society and Democratic Theory**
Alternative Voices
Gideon Baker

10 **Ethics and Politics in Contemporary Theory**
Between Critical Theory and Post-Marxism
Mark Devenney

11 **Citizenship and Identity**
Towards a New Republic
John Schwarzmantel

12 **Multiculturalism, Identity and Rights**
Edited by Bruce Haddock and Peter Sutch

13 **Political Theory of Global Justice**
A Cosmopolitan Case for the World State
Luis Cabrera

14 **Democracy, Nationalism and Multiculturalism**
Edited by Ramón Maiz and Ferrán Requejo

15 **Political Reconciliation**
Andrew Schaap

16 **National Cultural Autonomy and Its Contemporary Critics**
Edited by Ephraim Nimni

17 **Power and Politics in Poststructuralist Thought**
New Theories of the Political
Saul Newman

18 **Capabilities Equality**
Basic Issues and Problems
Edited by Alexander Kaufman

19 **Morality and Nationalism**
Catherine Frost

20 **Principles and Political Order**
The Challenge of Diversity
Edited by Bruce Haddock,
Peri Roberts and Peter Sutch

21 **European Integration and the Nationalities Question**
Edited by John McGarry and
Michael Keating

22 **Deliberation, Social Choice and Absolutist Democracy**
David van Mill

23 **Sexual Justice/Cultural Justice**
Critical Perspectives in
Political Theory and Practice
Edited by Barbara Arneil,
Monique Deveaux, Rita Dhamoon
and Avigail Eisenberg

24 **The International Political Thought of Carl Schmitt**
Terror, Liberal War and the Crisis
of Global Order
Edited by Louiza Odysseos and
Fabio Petito

25 **In Defense of Human Rights**
A Non-Religious Grounding in a
Pluralistic World
Ari Kohen

26 **Logics of Critical Explanation in Social and Political Theory**
Jason Glynos and David Howarth

27 **Political Constructivism**
Peri Roberts

28 **The New Politics of Masculinity**
Men, Power and Resistance
Fidelma Ashe

29 **Citizens and the State**
Attitudes in Western Europe and
East and Southeast Asia
Takashi Inoguchi and
Jean Blondel

30 **Political Language and Metaphor**
Interpreting *and* Changing the
World
Edited by Terrell Carver and
Jernej Pikalo

31 **Political Pluralism and the State**
Beyond Sovereignty
Marcel Wissenburg

32 **Political Evil in a Global Age**
Hannah Arendt and International
Theory
Patrick Hayden

33 **Gramsci and Global Politics**
Hegemony and Resistance
Mark McNally and
John Schwarzmantel

34 **Democracy and Pluralism**
The Political Thought of
William E. Connolly
Edited by Alan Finlayson

35 **Multiculturalism and Moral Conflict**
Edited by Maria Dimova-Cookson
and Peter Stirk

36 **John Stuart Mill – Thought and Influence**
The Saint of Rationalism
Edited by Georgios Varouxakis and Paul Kelly

37 **Rethinking Gramsci**
Edited by Marcus E. Green

38 **Autonomy and Identity**
The Politics of Who We Are
Ros Hague

39 **Dialectics and Contemporary Politics**
Critique and Transformation from Hegel through Post-Marxism
John Grant

40 **Liberal Democracy as the End of History**
Fukuyama and Postmodern Challenges
Chris Hughes

41 **Deleuze and World Politics**
Alter-Globalizations and Nomad Science
Peter Lenco

42 **Utopian Politics**
Citizenship and Practice
Rhiannon Firth

43 **Kant and International Relations Theory**
Cosmopolitan Community Building
Dora Ion

44 **Ethnic Diversity and the Nation State**
National Cultural Autonomy Revisited
David J. Smith and John Hiden

45 **Tensions of Modernity**
Las Casas and His Legacy in the French Enlightenment
Daniel R. Brunstetter

46 **Honor**
A Phenomenology
Robert L. Oprisko

47 **Critical Theory and Democracy**
Essays in Honour of Andrew Arato
Edited by Enrique Peruzzotti and Martin Plot

48 **Sophocles and the Politics of Tragedy**
Cities and Transcendence
Jonathan N. Badger

49 **Isaiah Berlin and the Politics of Freedom**
"Two Concepts of Liberty" 50 Years Later
Edited by Bruce Baum and Robert Nichols

50 **Popular Sovereignty in the West**
Polities, Contention, and Ideas
Geneviève Nootens

51 **Pliny's Defense of Empire**
Thomas R. Laehn

52 **Class, States and International Relations**
A Critical Appraisal of Robert Cox and Neo-Gramscian Theory
Adrian Budd

53 **Civil Disobedience and Deliberative Democracy**
William Smith

54 **Untangling Heroism**
Classical Philosophy and the
Concept of the Hero
Ari Kohen

55 **Rethinking the Politics of
Absurdity**
Albert Camus, Postmodernity,
and the Survival of Innocence
Matthew H. Bowker

56 **Kantian Theory and Human
Rights**
*Edited by Reidar Maliks and
Andreas Follesdal*

57 **The Political Philosophy of
Judith Butler**
Birgit Schippers

58 **Hegel and the Metaphysical
Frontiers of Political Theory**
Eric Lee Goodfield

59 **Time, Memory, and the Politics
of Contingency**
Smita A. Rahman

60 **Michael A. Weinstein**
Action, Contemplation, Vitalism
*Edited by Robert L. Oprisko and
Diane Rubenstein*

61 **Deep Cosmopolis**
Rethinking World Politics and
Globalization
Edited by Adam K. Webb

62 **Political Philosophy, Empathy
and Political Justice**
Matt Edge

63 **The Politics of Economic Life**
Martin Beckstein

64 **The Temporality of Political
Obligation**
Justin C. Mueller

65 **Epistemic Liberalism**
A Defence
Adam James Tebble

66 **Democracy, Dialectics, and
Difference**
Hegel, Marx, and 21st Century
Social Movements
Brian C. Lovato

67 **Ideologies of Experience**
Trauma, Failure, and the
Abandonment of the Self
Matthew H. Bowker

68 **The Temporality of Political
Obligation**
Justin C. Mueller

The Temporality of Political Obligation

Justin C. Mueller

NEW YORK AND LONDON

First published 2016
by Routledge
711 Third Avenue, New York, NY 10017

and by Routledge
2 Park Square, Milton Park, Abingdon, Oxon, OX14 4RN

Routledge is an imprint of the Taylor & Francis Group, an informa business

© 2016 Taylor & Francis

The right of Justin C. Mueller to be identified as author of this work has
been asserted by him in accordance with sections 77 and 78 of the
Copyright, Designs and Patents Act 1988.

All rights reserved. No part of this book may be reprinted or reproduced or
utilised in any form or by any electronic, mechanical, or other means, now
known or hereafter invented, including photocopying and recording, or in
any information storage or retrieval system, without permission in writing
from the publishers.

Trademark notice: Product or corporate names may be trademarks or
registered trademarks, and are used only for identification and explanation
without intent to infringe.

Library of Congress Cataloging in Publication Data
Mueller, Justin C. author.
The temporality of political obligation / Justin C. Mueller.
Includes bibliographical references and index.
Political obligation. | Time–Political aspects.
JC329.5 .M84 2015 DDC 320.01–dc23
2015023359

ISBN: 978-1-138-91550-3 (hbk)
ISBN: 978-1-315-69020-9 (ebk)

Typeset in Times New Roman
by Wearset Ltd, Boldon, Tyne and Wear

Contents

Foreword		xii
MICHAEL A. WEINSTEIN		
Acknowledgments		xv
Introduction: Time and Political Obligation		1
1	Time and Temporality	14
2	Modernity and Political Obligation	56
3	Vertical Time-binding	97
4	Horizontal Time-binding	128
5	Chronarchy and Obligation	151
	Index	173

Foreword

Michael A. Weinstein

"Obligation" bids fair to be the central concept of contemporary Anglo-American political philosophy and, to a lesser extent, Continental European political thought.

The supposed "modern" "individual," gifted with their own autonomous judgment, encounters a problem when political authority issues orders concerning behaviors that, for one reason or another, they do not want to obey, including refraining from behaviors. Why should the individual not do what they want if they can get away with it, regardless of what political authority says? What, indeed, if the recalcitrant individual is motivated by a "higher" religious or moral law that (for them) trumps political law? Assailed by licentiousness from below and transient principles from above, the "modern" "individual" is in a quandary about political authority.

Into the breach comes "obligation," which addresses the question: Why should the modern individual with their own judgment obey political authority? Each theory of obligation answers that question in its own way, the aggregate of them being composed in an argumentative structure that Justin Mueller has elegantly, precisely, and insightfully described and critiqued in the following pages. Mueller has attempted to exhaust all the extant justifications of "obligation," put them in relation to one another, and then subject them to internal and external criticism grounded in an appreciation of each one. Simply as a comprehensive and an analytically cogent critical-typology of the arguments concerning obligation, Mueller's discussion makes a key contribution to contemporary political philosophy by bringing its dominant discourse into order. One can say that Mueller has offered an incisive comparative dissection of theories of obligation, an autopsy that identifies pathologies where they appear, as they often do.

Yet Mueller is after more than an exhaustive critical-typology of theories of "obligation." Apart from all the twists and turns of attempts to justify obedience to authority, Mueller has identified a gaping absence in the discourse as a whole: the received justifications of obedience leave out the dimension of time; they are atemporal.

Political "obligation" is a way of what the political theorist Robert MacIver called "binding time," that is, of holding an individual's/subject's dispositions and behaviors constant over a period of time. For MacIver, the human being is the "time-binding" animal who makes promises, signs contracts, and generally

Foreword xiii

makes commitments, and pledges loyalty and devotion, or opposition. All the theories of political "obligation" that Mueller has identified have taken time-binding for granted, constructing arguments that assume that it is justifiable or, more deeply, possible to hold people (or have them hold themselves) constant for the purpose of enforcing an "obligation" on them to obey political authority.

Only a minority of theorists of "obligation" have gone as far as advocating an obligation to obey any existing authority under which the individual has fallen at any time. As part of "modern" "moral" discourse, theories of political "obligation" have been occupied in specifying the conditions under which it is morally justified/obligatory to obey political authority. Mueller discusses all of those arguments carefully, but, at the end, they all share a refusal to confront temporality.

Mueller's major contribution to contemporary political philosophy is to have placed the extant discourse of political "obligation" in play with the discourse on time that was initiated by Henri Bergson at the turn of the twentieth century and has been continued by postmodern/post-structuralist thinkers, notably Gilles Deleuze.

Mueller finds that if one assents to the vitalist-pragmatist-phenomenological-postmodernist understanding of time as lived duration – the experience of "continuous change" (Bergson) in a "drop of experience" (William James) – then the consequences for extant theories of political "obligation" are devastating. Most importantly: Who is the subject of a putative obligation? As the mid-twentieth-century American pragmatic naturalist, Justus Buchler, put it, the human being is a "summed-up-self-in-process," never altogether the same subject from one moment to the next. Yet the received theories of political "obligation" have posited a stable subject – sometimes a universal human subject – who can be bound to (self-)imposed commitments. The temporal subject, for the concept of lived time, is momentary. Parmenides must yield to Heracleitus.

It does not do justice to Mueller's complex and nuanced critique to pretend that it is exhausted by an affirmation of the mutability of the subject. Mueller has a rich understanding of the heterogeneity and diversity of experience, which resists simple reduction. Yet the self's continuous change is at the heart of Mueller's interpretation and it is sufficient for bringing out that the "subject" of received theories of political "obligation" is unequivocally a fiction, most precisely one of those countless "legal fictions," this one most often in the guise of a "moral fiction."

One of the major and significant directions in which Mueller takes the temporal critique of extant theories of political "obligation" is to show how the latter support systems of political domination, what he calls, precisely, "chronarchy." It is vital to understand that, especially when one acknowledges that such domination is based on a fiction that distorts, indeed, falsifies, lived experience. Theories of political "obligation" play their prominent parts in ideological warfare and thereby take on an inevitable seriousness. Yet it is also possible to take a complementary perspective that theories of political "obligation" have set themselves an insoluble problem, which renders them absurd to begin with. How does one go about justifying limiting the judgment of the "individual" when one has already made that concept one's starting point?

xiv *Foreword*

The simple answer is that it cannot be done. The theorists of political "obligation" are attempting to persuade human beings whom they have already transformed into constructs, what Bergson called the (spatialized) conventional ego. They are addressing a fiction of their own creation, not human beings. They have set up a paper puzzle that, again, has no solution.

Justin Mueller has presented a genial corrective to the "spirit of seriousness" that attends discussions of political "obligation," which take on a serio-comic aspect when the persuaders are themselves persuaded of their cogency.

Acknowledgments

While there are innumerable influences in one's life whose effects may be difficult to measure, I would like to thank several people (in no particular order) for their distinct contributions to the fruition of this project. Without their conversation, thoughtfulness, care, and time, it would never have been produced.

I would like to thank Mike for being a wonderful mentor, colleague, and friend, for the many talks, for the most memorable and mind-jolting seminars, for introducing me to Bergson, and for helping me become a better thinker and person. I truly would not be the summed-up-self-in-process that I am today were it not for our time together, and for that I am thankful.

I would like to thank Robert for the excellent conversations, commiserations, suggestions, encouragement, and assistance in getting this project (and other past and future projects) in motion for publication. You are a good friend, and do me honor.

I would like to thank my parents, Dan and Darla, for raising me to value reading, learning, critical thinking, and curiosity. It may have made me insufferable at times, but let's just blame that on past-Justin.

Finally, thank you Rachel for being my companion and intellectual partner. I haven't the foggiest clue where we will be or what we will be doing in the coming years, but I look forward to our future telic entanglement.

Introduction

Time and Political Obligation

William James once argued that habit was the "enormous fly-wheel of society," the great conservative force keeping our behavior within the bounds of normalcy and the law, and the poor from rising up against the "children of fortune" (1890, 121). It is through our tendency to accept and adapt ourselves to the demands of the familiar that cultures persist, institutions endure, governments rule, and societies reproduce themselves. We are not automatons, however, and the survival of any of these aggregate bundles of order is far from assured. Regimes can be toppled, cultures transformed, and the entity we call society is a patchwork of bodies constantly in the process of being hewn and stitched together on one end whilst unraveling on the other. Disobedience and dissent are not only possible, but are in essence the ontologically default state of things. This is not because they are the norm of human behavior – habit and its channeling production of desire, perception, and activity is the prevailing motor of apparent social cohesion and continuity. Rather, it is because the threat of disobedience and disruption, of the center failing to hold, looms constantly behind all dreams of order and projects designed to bring that order about. This is the ever-renewed entropic force against which all successful schemes of continuity and unity must both struggle and use as material for their construction.

For most theorists of order and philosophers of state going back to Plato, habit has not been enough. It is a powerful inertial force, but even habit must be buttressed, renewed, and secured. Machiavelli advised the wise Prince to pursue, lacking a better option, the instillation of fear as a reliable check upon disloyalty. Similarly, it is the "incomprehensible" figure of the executioner that Joseph de Maistre saw as the ultimate guarantor of political authority and all social bonds.[1] Terror is one face of sovereignty, certainly, but as Georges Dumézil's (1988) classic analysis of Indo-European sovereignty myths reveals, sovereignty appears again and again with two faces.

Take, for instance, the two mythic "fathers" of the Roman state, Romulus and Numa. It was Romulus who founded Rome through conquest and war. He made himself king by leaving a wake of corpses (including his brother, Remus), and ruled through a constant violence (supported by the *Celeres*, his personal guards) that in turn generated its own hostility and counter-violence from the Roman Senate, ultimately leading to his own destruction. He is an exemplar of aggression, ambition, deception, and martial virtue. His successor, Numa, however,

2 Introduction

was his antithesis. Numa was appointed to rule by the Senate, but assented to the position only with great regret and hesitation. He curtailed the warlike foreign policies of Rome and maintained peace and a system of alliances throughout his reign. He was without passion, instead pursuing only justice and faithfulness. He admonished violence and banished the *Celeres*, replacing them with the "sacred fire" of the "triple *flamonium*," the major cultural and religious institutions that were the "the entire community's source of energy and solidarity." While Romulus refused to acknowledge the boundaries of the city of Rome and thus his rule, Numa sets out the boundaries of the city in order to "[fetter] lawless power" and protect the peace. While Romulus' cult of Jupiter celebrates personal conquest in battle, Numa cherishes Fides, the god of faith and fidelity, both in the state and between individuals (Dumézil 1988, 47–56).

In the figure of Numa, then, we see the maintenance of social cohesion through the force of wisdom, justice, and the ubiquitous recognition of proper action. With a purported wisdom that is unanimously celebrated by his contemporaries, Numa becomes an archetype whereby simple obedience to terror is transformed. In its place, the justice and *rightness* of his rule and rules is recognized by those citizens who live under them. Rather than terror alone, it is this second, transformative face of sovereignty that modern theorists of order have pursued, seeking to transubstantiate terror into legitimate authority, and the problem of securing obedience into the problem of "political obligation."

What is political obligation? Consider these cases:

> Although there are examples of it dating back to at least the 18th century, the practice of "fragging," whereby an unpopular officer would be killed by lower-ranked soldiers in their unit, increased in frequency among U.S. soldiers during the Vietnam War as it dragged on. Officers imposing harsh discipline and giving overly dangerous and costly orders were especially prone to being fragged.[2]

> Reporting from the postwar trial of the Nazi SS leader, Adolf Eichmann, Hannah Arendt famously argued that Eichmann was not a crazed monster or extreme psychopath. Rather, he was impressively normal and average in almost all respects, was not driven by an overwhelming hatred, and was even considered to be a loyal family man. He (and many other loyal German subjects) "did his *duty* ... he not only obeyed *orders*, he also obeyed the *law*" (Arendt 2010, 133). Nevertheless, it was the "banality of evil" entailed in uncritically fulfilling his duties that led to mass killing in pursuit of the Final Solution to the Jewish Problem.

> In opposition to the legal racial disenfranchisement of apartheid in South Africa, the Umkhonto we Sizwe, the militant wing of the African National Congress, engaged in an insurgent campaign against the white government. This insurgency included protests, sabotage, bombings, and executions.

> In 1953, Julius and Ethel Rosenberg were executed by the United States government after being convicted of conspiracy to commit espionage. They were (controversially) implicated in attempts to pass secret information regarding nuclear weapons to the Soviet Union.

Introduction 3

While walking through my neighborhood earlier this week, I walked up to a road, saw no vehicles coming, and jaywalked.

There are a variety of differences between the above cases in terms of context and consequences. They bear a family resemblance to each other, though, in raising a cluster of shared dilemmas pertaining to the rule of law, the legitimacy of authority, the cultivation of obedience and disobedience, the generation of political order, the internalization of social discipline, and the normalization and proscription of different uses of force; in other words, to questions of "political obligation." While that term might not appear frequently in everyday contemporary political parlance, it addresses phenomena that lie at the heart of political life and raise practical ethical questions that are both urgent and ubiquitous.[3] Modern theorists of political obligation frequently portray it as a "problem." In doing so, they suggest that it is something that can be provided with a solution or an answer. As observed by Hanna Pitkin, this problem actually rests on several distinct, yet interrelated questions regarding the limits of obligation ("When are you obligated to obey?"), the locus of sovereignty ("Whom are you obligated to obey?"), the difference between legitimate authority and coercion ("Is there any difference? Are you really obligated?"), and the justification of obligation ("Why are you ever obligated to obey?") (1966, 1). Theorists of political obligation are broadly concerned, then, with answering the question of why, and under what conditions and circumstances, we ought to adhere to the law, obey political authorities, or follow social demands placed upon on us, *because* (though not necessarily exclusively) they command us, rather than because of the content of their commands alone.

Political obligation only emerged as a distinct problem of political life and philosophical inquiry with the onset of modernity (we will discuss this more in Chapter 2). Although Socrates used language that bears some striking resemblance to later contract theorists and modern ideas of consent, his context and goals were very different. He resided in a participatory, semi-direct democracy (dependent as it was upon exclusions, slavery, class inequalities, and patriarchy) that generally presumed the capacity of all full citizens to co-govern, and not a modern nation-state with a separate body of rulers that required justification for their special position of ruling. In the *Crito* dialogue regarding Socrates' potential evasion of a death sentence, Plato describes Socrates' primary concern as that of piety and virtue, the fulfillment of his oracular mission, and adherence to the voice of his personal *daimon*. It is not that of developing a legitimating justification for generalized obedience to a distant body of authority by reference to an individual's independently-held moral judgment. Indeed, this modern way of thinking would have been quite alien to Socrates and his contemporaries, who had traditionally conceived of political duties in terms of socially-embedded and particularistic loyalties and allegiances involving the expectation to "help one's friends and harm one's enemies" (Blundell 1991, 1).

Similarly, while there were medieval sources of inspiration for modern political obligation theorists, there are key differences between these periods. While there was certainly political disobedience and social unrest in medieval Europe,

4   *Introduction*

until the middle of the second millennium there was rarely a serious existential challenge *within* Christendom to the authority held by God and manifested in the Church.[4] The idea of the Great Chain of Being gave its theological authority a metaphysical foundation and a worldly social and political expression. The authority of temporal powers was secured by the ultimate authority of God,[5] and insofar as "rulers were seen as part of God's Divine order in the world, general questions about political authority were, literally, inconceivable" (Pateman 1985, 100). To be justified, disobedience to a worldly ruler was sometimes framed as an opposition to their sinful or impious nature, or at least that of their commands, a claim that ultimately reinforced the authority of and obligations demanded by God (ibid.). It is only with the collapse of a taken for granted belief in this overarching, unifying, and ostensibly eternal metaphysical framework, Nietzsche's "death of God," that political obligation in its modern sense could be articulated.[6] Indeed, it is with that collapse that justifying such obligations took on a new urgency.

Although they did not always specify it by name, the problem of political obligation became a central, even primary theme in the social and political works of modern philosophers. The goal of Hobbes' "civil science," as he discusses in *De Cive* (1949), was to "make a more curious search into the rights of states and the duties of subjects" necessary for securing political order, comparing such rights and duties to the components required for the successful operation of a timepiece (10–11). As Bhikhu Parekh argues, in spite of their many differences with Hobbes, "Pufendorf, Locke, Bentham, Kant, the two Mills, Hegel and others … were all agreed that the problem of political obligation was the central question for political theory and that it was about why one should obey the civil authority" (1993, 236). By the latter half of the twentieth century, there had emerged a discrete, cohesive discourse regarding political obligation with fairly consistent kinds of normative concerns, frames for posing problems, and parameters for offering or contesting solutions to those problems.[7]

Within this discourse, there is a division between two major camps: the apologists for political obligation and the philosophical anarchists. Apologists for political obligation have, for the most part, attempted to describe and defend the ways in which political obligations can be said to be owed by political subjects to "legitimate" political orders, regimes, or authority. These efforts have been primarily comprised of appeals to principles of consent, social contract, fairness, natural duties, group membership, divine requirements, and most recently by pluralistic combinations of the above.[8] Disagreement between these positions has been generally confined to which of the above principles ought to be considered primary, and in what kinds of practical circumstances our political obligations ought to apply. All obligation apologists are united, however, in their desire to develop the most compelling and comprehensive defense of our having some moral obligation to obey some authorities at least some of the time.

The philosophical anarchists (whom we will discuss in more depth in Chapter 4) are the principal critics within the contemporary literature on political obligation, and reject the primary arguments put forth by the obligation apologists. They argue against the possibility (or at least assert the extreme difficulty) of

Introduction 5

justifying political obligations, primarily by appealing to the importance of individual autonomy and consent. At minimum, they assert the failure of existing states to meet the conditions required for legitimate consent to binding political obligations to be possible. At most, they reject the possibility of establishing political obligations a priori and argue that no states or communities could ever legitimately lay claim to political obligations on anyone. Consequently, they claim that existing theories of political obligation fail. This failure may be considered a logical failure (a theory of obligation is incoherent), a normative failure (a theory of obligation holds a mistaken view of which values are most important), a practical or empirical failure (a theory of obligation may be successful in the abstract but all existing or possible states to which those obligations would be owed fail to meet that theory's ideal standards or conditions), or all of the above. The consequence of this failure is a lack of political obligations being owed by political subjects to established authorities. While this stance may initially appear to exempt them from the general criticisms of political obligation theorists that I will be advancing, and force us to limit our gaze to the political obligation apologists, that is – unfortunately – not the case. While philosophical anarchists like A.J. Simmons and Robert Paul Wolff are certainly committed to contesting the claims made by obligation apologists, the means by which they do so leaves them open to many of the same charges. They may contest the aims of the apologists, and disavow a variety of the apologists' defenses of more conventionally coercive control, but they retain some of the foundational theoretical assumptions and parameters of framing obligation's problematisation that allow the apologists to cogently advance their positions in the first place. Recent contributions to this political obligation literature have not altered these parameters of debate in any significant way.

There are a variety of problems with the conventional approach to framing how we think about political obligations, some of which will have to be specified later as the argument in this work unfolds. The most important initial criticism that I will offer is quite simply stated, even if its implications are not. I argue that we have conceptualized political obligations in highly spatialized terms, and that this spatialization poses both theoretical limitations and practical problems.[9] The principal theoretical limitation that spatialization imposes is the masking of time. In spite of their ostensible differences and divisions, both the apologists of political obligation and the philosophical anarchists can only maintain their existing parameters of argument through the theoretical move of spatializing time. It is in this sense that the traditional dichotomy posed between the two positions – and thus the contours of this discourse as such – obscures their commonalities, shared assumptions, and shared blind spots. Many obligation theorists have, for instance, presented political obligations as formal, stable representations of an idealized vision of political order. These representations contain an implicit or explicit axiological hierarchy, extrapolate an account of desirable political arrangements, and posit a stable and unified conception of human subjectivity that is primed to bring that order about. Practically, when brought to bear against people in order to produce certain behaviors, perspectives, or political outcomes, they function as a particular kind of disciplinary

6 *Introduction*

construct. While masking time, these disciplinary constructs nevertheless function through the use of time (structured in particular ways), and by binding people as individuals and groups. In so far as we uncritically accept this regular displacement of time from our conceptualization of political obligation, we will be resigning ourselves to an incomplete account of its functions and uses, accepting a limited and politically circumscribed account of ourselves, and risking reifying the symbolic and confusing it with the real.

Consequently, in this project I will attempt to provide a basic reconfiguration and reconceptualization of political obligation in order to identify and move beyond these limitations, as well as to reinvigorate a long-standing debate regarding a particularly important facet of human experience and political life that I believe has become unnecessarily ossified. I argue that rather than conceiving of political obligations in terms of competing spatial representations of proper political order, we can more productively think about them in terms of time, and more specifically in terms of the lived experience and perception of time (also referred to as "temporality").[10] To this end, I will take up the philosophical concepts for framing and investigating temporality that Henri Bergson and Gilles Deleuze offer in order to provide the basic theoretical tools for this approach. Bergson's concept of "duration" and method of "intuition" are especially pertinent, helping us see how we regularly transform the flow and flux of time into perceptions of space, often habitually and without realizing that we are doing so. Time and space are not simply background features of the universe in this account, but are immanent, flexible elements of our experience of the world that we transform in order to give direction, purpose, and solidity to our actions and content to our understanding; in other words, in order to live. Deleuze radicalizes Bergson's initial insights regarding time in a variety of ways, developing a complex account of temporal experience and the projection of temporal structure, a machinic theory of social and individual processes, and a novel way of conceptualizing the force of time as the continual emergence of the new. On both of their accounts, time is not simply a flat, homogeneous given, steadily unfolding by the discrete, quantifiable tick of the clock, even though this is how it is conventionally understood. The diachronic image of the future coming at one's self, which is always in the present (and a cohesive and unified whole), and the present then falling into the past and oblivion becomes problematic on several counts. On the one hand, it poses obstacles for conceptually coming to terms with the decentered "multiplicity" of subjects, especially our character as tenuous bundles of convergent processes, and the manner in which our sense of self is built and rebuilt over time. On the other hand, it ignores variations in the experience of time (both for a single person and between different cultural contexts), and thus hides the fact that temporality is something heterogeneously felt, imaginatively perceived (even if implicitly), and socially constituted.

Rather than subscribe to this conventional image, both Bergson and Deleuze posit a more heterogeneous, dynamic, and flexible image of temporality. The past, present, and future are not only diachronic, for them, but also synchronic, existing simultaneously and co-constituting each other. This observation leads to two especially pertinent conclusions. First, ontologically, we are complex,

Introduction 7

multiplicitous, processual creatures; we are continuously constituted by our experiences and bear the cumulative weight of our past lived experiences in the present and into the future. Second, how we understand and contextualize ourselves and the world around us is always in relation to an explicit or implicit set of temporal projections and narratives; an interpretation or story of one's perceived past and origins, how one has become what one is, what projects and goals define one's aims, what shared timelines one occupies with others in broader socio-political discourses, and how one feels bound across time in relation to others in these discourses.

By thinking in terms of time and temporality, the parameters of conceptualization and terms of debate over obligations change dramatically. At the broadest level, this shift allows us to pay greater fidelity to the complexities of lived human experience and highlight a dimension of perception and social life that political obligation theorists have generally neglected. Several traditional problems and assumptions within obligation theories are also transformed. Rather than conceiving of individuals as autonomous subjects (with a pre-selected slate of preferences and values), or idealized obligation-bearing members of an imagined distribution of social roles, we can now think of them as concrete, complex beings undergoing processual development and change within a variety of overlapping social contexts, power relationships, and discourses. Rather than asking if obligations "exist" or follow from presumed value hierarchies, we can ask how perceived obligations are internalized, felt, and imagined by individuals in relation to the mutable projects and frames through which they interpret, understand, and direct their lives. Rather than asking what kind of state can legitimately compel obedience through the assertion of political obligation claims, we can ask how it is possible that states can be seen as "legitimate" at all. Rather than asking if an individual truly consented to an obligation, we can now ask if consent can even be discussed intelligibly as something one does at all, or if it is rather necessarily always something attributed or posited *by others* onto an individual who is then compelled (potentially internally and externally) to comply with this attribution over time.

Conflicts over perceptions of political obligation carry consequences beyond the realm of scholarship. Political regimes stand or fall in part on their ability to justify and inculcate belief in their claims to legitimately rule over their subject populations, and thus to rightly prescribe political obligations and enforce corresponding demands of obedience. The theoretical framework developed in this project provides conceptual tools for both understanding political obligations, as well as for exposing them as contingent, constructed, alterable, and rendible. It offers stronger ground for developing a philosophical anarchism, as well as tools for enabling an applied disbelief in the foundations of formal political obligation claims, opening practical possibilities for the cultivation of critical dispositions and practices. At the same time, it provides theoretical space for affirming and cultivating new obligations (of a particular sort).

This contest over perceptions of political obligation broaches fissures and tensions at the heart of political theory as a discipline and form of inquiry. The existing debates over political obligation have attempted to engage with the

8   Introduction

problems and complexities of obedience and disobedience in political life. As suggested, their failure to incorporate the dimension of time, both as a process and dimension of human perception, has severely limited the potential scope and value of their inquiries. This project's goal of integrating temporality and contemporary theorizations of political obligation can revive those debates by shifting the basic parameters of discussion and making new questions pertinent and possible.

In Chapter 1, I discuss the concept of temporality and relate it to conventional conceptions of time and space. I present what it means to think in terms of temporality, and what a temporal analysis can help us understand in social and political theory generally and the problem of political obligation in particular. In doing so, I provide a comprehensive overview of the theory and methods of conceptualizing temporality offered by Henri Bergson and Gilles Deleuze, the two main sources guiding the inquiry, and suggest how we can use their ideas on temporality to understand political obligation in ways that they themselves did not explore.

In Chapter 2, I then look more closely at the concept of political obligation itself. I argue that we must situate contemporary theories of political obligation within the context of the emergence of modernity, both in order to understand these contemporary theories as well as to clarify the ways in which they actually differ from their pre-modern counterparts. Modernity produced a sense of rupture with the past and shattered the time perspectives that knit together premodern social orders. I argue that contemporary theories and practical discourses of political obligation can be usefully understood as efforts to reconsolidate the personal and social unities that the time perspectives of the pre-modern world had underwritten. I also argue that political obligation theories are a means of exerting control, both as practical political tools and disciplinary constructs, but also in the psychological and phenomenological manner discussed by Bergson; as a way to create the perception of continuity, order, purpose, and structure within one's world in order to facilitate certain kinds of action in one's life. Theories of political obligation can be seen as a form of what I refer to as "timebinding," a process which structures our perceptions of time and of our conventional selves (the representations, personal history, and identities which constitute the symbolic dimension of our overall "self") across time in order to facilitate compliant behavior in relation to some social or political ends.

In Chapter 3, I elaborate on this by arguing that there is a distinct process which we can call "vertical time-binding" that is implicitly used as a means of grounding several theories of political obligation, especially forms of religious political naturalism, and theories of natural duty, membership, and fairness. These vertical time-binding theories function by creating a universalizing, homogenizing, and atemporal conception of political obligations. In doing so, they produce stratified images of properly distributed roles, institutions, axiologies, behaviors, sensibilities, and burdens. They then attempt to bind one's conventional self to this stratified image in order to produce desired forms of political obedience.

In Chapter 4, I identify a second form of time-binding – "horizontal timebinding" – that is primarily deployed by consent and social contract theorists, as

Introduction 9

well as philosophical anarchists. Rather than trying to squeeze people into a stratified social image, horizontal time-binding theorists attempt to bind a subject's embodied self to and through their conventional self across time. This is achieved through a multi-stage process of extracting, crystallizing, and extending a real or hypothetical moment from a person's life, and using it as a disciplinary tool to justify and compel the compliance and obedience entailed in a particular obligation claim.

In Chapter 5, I develop an alternative means of conceptualizing political obligation and freedom that attempts to move beyond the limitations of conventional theories, and that keeps the dimension of temporality front and center. I introduce the concept of "chronarchy" to characterize how the many processes of time-binding that comprise a public situation can produce and sustain social stratifications and structures of rule. I also introduce the complementary concept of "anachronarchy" to characterize the processes by which the ossifying, ordering forms of time-binding can be loosened, disrupted, and undermined through both the negation of those time-binding projections, and the creation of alternative temporal projects. I compare these two countervailing tendencies, discuss the new paths they open up for theorizing political obedience and obligation alongside a form of "critical freedom," and address the possible practical dangers and limitations that accompany this interpretation.

It is worth noting that we will be restricting our discussion of anarchism in this project to the "philosophical" anarchists. This has little to do with any judgment regarding the value of the broader tradition of more militant "political" anarchism (as it has frequently been called, though the juxtaposition can be confusing given political anarchism's thorough engagement with all manner of philosophical questions) for thinking about political obligation. Nor does this suggest that the various strands of the broader anarchist tradition would somehow be exempt from the temporal analysis we will be developing here. An analysis of the methods of time-binding used within the broader anarchist tradition would provide for a thought provoking comparison with our current study. Here, we will be restricting our analysis of the anarchist position to philosophical anarchism by virtue of the fact that it is effectively the only anarchism that makes any serious appearance within the discourse of the dominant contemporary literature on political obligation. An extensive engagement with political anarchism on the part of contemporary obligation theorists is almost entirely absent.[11] When not dismissed by silence, it is frequently defined out of the purview of consideration by virtue of a preemptive declaration that relevant parties must cater to the desires of modern liberal democratic subjects with idealized modern liberal democratic wishes as a litmus test for discursive entrance. When it does make a more extended appearance, that engagement often suffers from serious flaws of interpretation, misrepresentation, or a clear lack of familiarity with that body of thought as a whole.[12] Since one of the principal aims of this project is not only to analyze what political obligations are, but also how they have been understood within a particular modern body of literature, any substantial coverage of temporality within the many strands of political anarchism will have to wait.

10   *Introduction*

Ultimately, this study provides a comprehensive critique of the parameters through which political obligations have been traditionally conceived, and philosophically justified and contested. By prioritizing temporality, we can trace the ways in which particular conceptualizations of political obligation are made possible or meaningless, both collectively and within individual experience. We can also understand how political obligations function as disciplinary constructs and mechanisms of control. This control can be understood in terms of conventional sovereign coerciveness as well as Foucaultian senses of the term, certainly, but also in existential and deeply personal ways.

I have three overarching goals in this project. First, rather than closing off prior debates over political obligation, I believe that the theoretical framework developed here can reinvigorate them. My own commitments lead me to hope that this will provide a more robust alternative position for advancing an anarchist critique of political obligations. In spite of this (or rather, because of), the theoretical approach I develop does not deny the existence of political obligations, but instead re-frames the way in which we can understand them. Consequently, it may also prove beneficial to obligation apologists who are more open to moving beyond the limits of conventional liberal democratic political theory. Second, within contemporary literature on temporality and its relationship to politics, particularly in work inspired by the Deleuzian and Bergsonian traditions, there has been little sustained, focused engagement with modern theories of political obligation as such.[13] This project is a corrective to this.

Bergson's own later work on obligation in *The Two Sources of Morality and Religion* (1991) suffers from several problems (which I will address more fully in Chapter 1) that limit its usefulness for our present efforts. Deleuze occasionally provides limited comments on modern obligation theory, particularly regarding the social contract tradition, but, as Paul Patton observes, his overall work is marked by a general non-engagement with most of the major questions and concerns of Anglo-American and traditional liberal political theory (Patton 2000, 1). When he does provide commentary, it is usually through the temporally-inspired, but largely spatial analysis of his later collaborative work with Félix Guattari. This leads me to the third goal of this project, which is to re-emphasize the role and importance of temporality, especially in terms of our active and passive *perceptions*, for the Deleuzian analytical toolbox. Deleuze's mature shift to theorizing social life, power, individuation, and change through more spatial terms (territorialization, lines of flight, striated space, molarity, strata, etc.) was certainly valuable, and in its own way retained the temporal insight developed in his earlier work. One unfortunate consequence of this shift, though, was a relative neglect of the more directly temporal subjects and concepts of his early work. I consider this to be a loss for our efforts to theorize the political. Our project at hand can also be read, then, as an attempt to bring the temporal analysis of Deleuze's earlier work into closer contact with the more spatial analysis of his later, more overtly political work, by way of Bergson.

Introduction   11

Notes

1 "All greatness, all power, all subordination rests on the executioner; he is both the horror and the bond of human association. Remove this incomprehensible agent from the world, and in a moment order gives way to chaos, thrones fall, and society disappears" (Maistre 1993, 20).
2 See George Lepre's *Fragging: Why U.S. Soldiers Assaulted Their Officers in Vietnam* (2011).
3 The term in its modern usage originates with T.H. Green's *Lectures on the Principles of Political Obligation* (1986) delivered in 1879–1880.
4 This, of course, does not mean that there were *no* challengers. The Cathar and Waldensian movements, for instance, were disruptive and visible enough to be deemed heresies, with the Cathars being the targets of the Albigensian Crusade by Pope Innocent III, and the Waldensians being subject to an order of extermination by Pope Innocent VIII. See Lambert (2002).

5   Let every soul be subject unto the higher powers. For there is no power but of God: the powers that be are ordained of God. Whosoever therefore resisteth the power, resisteth the ordinance of God: and they that resist shall receive to themselves damnation.

(Romans 13:1–2).

6 In spite of these historical limitations, modern political obligation theorists have emphasized a cluster of historical concerns that bear a family resemblance to the current framing of this problem, including questions of loyalty, communal belonging and allegiances, freedom, order, and justice.
7 Parekh identifies nine common points of reference in this discourse that have been both durable and influential. While they are not assumptions shared by all obligation theorists, and more recent developments have arguably lessened the unqualified emphasis made on all points, "many of them made most of them" and the remnants of each of these assumptions can still be felt throughout the current state of the discourse (Parekh 1993, 237, n7). First, they have assumed that in order for a community to last, its members must obey its laws out of obligation, not simply habit, fear of punishment, or enlightened self-interest. Second, that this obligation was moral in nature. Third, many assumed that political obligation had to be derived from a single source or principle (consent, fairness, etc.). Fourth, that it was possible to develop a culturally neutral and universal theory of political obligation. Fifth, that this obligation entailed at least a minimal stringent applicability to all citizens. Sixth, that the principle grounding political obligation was the same for every citizen. Seventh, that the primary concern of a citizen's political obligation was to a single state, rather than to supra- or sub-state groups, or to multiple states. Eighth, theorists divided residents of a state into citizen and non-citizens, treated citizens as primary, yet asserted the equal obligation for both to obey the law. Ninth, while some theorists have argued that gross mistreatment could exempt a subject of their political obligations, that exemption was limited to those who were mistreated, and not expanded to everyone (237–239).
8 Direct appeals to divine will are more frequently found in pre-modern conceptions of obligation, but there are important continuities between conceptions of divinity and some modern theories of political obligation.
9 The "we" here refers primarily to scholars of political obligation, but as we will quickly see, it includes all political orders and most people to varying degrees.
10 See David Couzens Hoy's *The Time of Our Lives: A Critical History of Temporality* (2009).
11 For a recent attempt to insert and bridge the political anarchist tradition with modern political obligation discourse (grounded in a political anarchist theoretical framework), see Magda Egoumenides' *Philosophical Anarchism and Political Obligation* (2014).

12 *Introduction*

12 Not all modern obligation theorists engage in flippant or bad faith dealings with the broader anarchist tradition. In their brief appearances, Carole Pateman (1985) gives William Godwin and Peter Kropotkin an admirably fair reading, even while arguably over-estimating the importance and continuity of Godwin's ideas for later and more significant anarchist theorists. John Horton (2010) also presents his criticisms of political anarchism while being relatively even-handed toward its actual positions and theorists. He commits a common mistake, however, by glossing over the importance of the anarchist critique of hierarchy as an active force for encouraging our crueler, sociopathic, and prejudicial characteristics as human beings, very much in the spirit of the Milgram and Zimbardo experiments on obedience and authority. Political anarchists do not simply oppose the state because authority as such is considered evil (although some may hold this position), but may also oppose it because of what it represents and generates as the exemplar of a hierarchic tendency in social organization – one that proceeds by qualitative degrees of intensity, rather than through a simple binary.

13 There are a variety of projects that bear some affinity with the spirit of our current endeavor, even if they differ in their de-emphasis on temporality, or in their use of it to address cousin problems to modern political obligation discourse. While not principally addressing modern political obligation theory as such, Mabel Wong's (2010) dissertation shares many theoretical affinities with the spirit of this project. Drawing substantially and creatively from Bergson, Deleuze, Anderson, and others (including a creative reading of Rousseau as a political temporality theorist), Wong provides a careful analysis of belonging and community, the role that temporality necessarily plays in their constitution, and the simultaneously promising and threatening futures that time poses for their existence. Paulina Ochoa Espejo (2011) uses a temporal lens drawing from by Bergson, Anderson, Habermas, and several others to address the theoretical and practical problem of how "the people" is constituted as a distinct entity for democratic states to ground their operation and legitimacy at all. Eugene Holland (2011) rehabilitates the concept of citizenship within Deleuze and Guattari's framework on "nomadism," which we will address later in this book. Alexandre Lefebvre (2008) uses Deleuze, Bergson, and others to develop a Deleuze-inspired and temporally informed theory of jurisprudence.

References

Arendt, Hannah. 2010. *Eichmann in Jerusalem: A Report On the Banality of Evil*. New York: Penguin.

Bergson, Henri. 1991. *The Two Sources of Morality and Religion*. Notre Dame, IN: University of Notre Dame Press.

Blundell, Mary Whitlock. 1991. *Helping Friends and Harming Enemies: A Study in Sophocles and Greek Ethics*. New York: Cambridge University Press.

Dumézil, Georges. 1988. *Mitra-Varuna: An Essay on Two Indo-European Representations of Sovereignty*. New York: Zone Books.

Egoumenides, Magda. 2014. *Philosophical Anarchism and Political Obligation*. New York: Bloomsbury.

Green, Thomas H. 1986. *Lectures on the Principles of Political Obligation and Other Writings*. New York: Cambridge University Press.

Hobbes, Thomas. 1949. *De Cive: Or, the Citizen*. Edited by Sterling P. Lamprecht. New York: Appleton-Century-Crofts.

Holland, Eugene. 2011. *Nomad Citizenship: Free-Market Communism and the Slow-Motion General Strike*. Minneapolis: University of Minnesota Press.

Horton, John. 2010. *Political Obligation*. Second Edition. New York: Palgrave Macmillan.

Hoy, David Couzens. 2009. *The Time of Our Lives: A Critical History of Temporality.* Cambridge, MA: The MIT Press.

James, William. 1890. *The Principles of Psychology, Volume 1.* New York: Henry Holt and Company.

Lambert, Malcolm. 2002. *Medieval Heresy: Popular Movements from the Gregorian Reform to the Reformation.* Third edition. Malden, MA: Blackwell Publishing.

Lefebvre, Alexandre. 2008. *The Image of Law: Deleuze, Bergson, Spinoza.* Stanford, CA: Stanford University Press.

Lepre, George. 2011. *Fragging: Why U.S. Soldiers Assaulted Their Officers in Vietnam.* Lubbock, TX: Texas Tech University Press.

Maistre, Joseph de. 1993. *St Petersburg Dialogues: Or Conversations on the Temporal Government of Providence*, translated by Richard A. Lebrun. Montreal: McGill-Queen's University Press.

Ochoa Espejo, Paulina. 2011. *The Time of Popular Sovereignty: Process and the Democratic State.* University Park, PA: The Pennsylvania State University Press.

Parekh, Bhikhu. 1993. "A Misconceived Discourse on Political Obligation." *Political Studies* 41 (2): 236–251.

Pateman, Carole. 1985. *The Problem of Political Obligation: A Critical Analysis of Liberal Theory.* New York: John Wiley & Sons.

Patton, Paul. 2000. *Deleuze and the Political.* New York: Routledge.

Pitkin, Hanna. 1966. "Obligation and Consent – II." *American Political Science Review* 60 (1): 39–52.

Plato. 1987. *Gorgias.* Translated by Donald J. Zeyl. Indianapolis: Hackett.

Wong, Mabel. 2010. "Belonging in the Midst of Time: Temporalities of Community from Rousseau to Deleuze." PhD diss., The Johns Hopkins University.

1 Time and Temporality

Time is a curious thing. For the greater part of our waking lives, it is invisible. Certainly, as we go about the routines of the day we are sensitive to the clock. Common habits and patterns of daily life – waking up or going to sleep at a scheduled hour, going to work for a certain duration, eating a certain number of meals at certain intervals – are more familiar and hum-drum intrusions of time into our awareness. Calendrical memorializations and holidays provide periodic markers of collective meaning and significance, invoking a renewed sense of continuity and "mnemonic synchronization" between past and present (Zerubavel 2003, 4). Ceremonies celebrating the achievement of new life stages provide affirmations of individual life direction and the fulfillment of collective future expectations. And, of course, death and its harbingers provide an ever-looming horizon for all of our life plans, adding a bittersweet certainty amidst much fragility; the bodily pains of old age can bear both memories of prior youth, as well as reminders of what is to come, while the corrosion of memory itself can provide an immediate experience of the contingency of our grasp of any sense of unity across time. Each of these formal and informal demarcations and perforations within time organize and give significance to the behavior and lives of individuals and populations.

It is not time that we usually reflect upon when looking at a clock, however, but "the time"; our traversal along the face of a clock measured by the passage of the hands between essentially contrived and conventional markers distributed in space. In this regard, is there any significant difference between the passage of the hands of the clock and the rotations of the Earth journeying around the Sun that inform the Gregorian calendar? Perhaps in the scale of durations covered, or in the fact that one is materially a product of human manufacture. There is not, however, a difference in kind, at least in so far as spatial positioning is used as a representation of time's passage. Markers of life progression – such as birthdays, reaching maturity, marriage, or retirement – are themselves effectively hands on a clock, though the time measured is not quite the same. Instead, these special events mark the achievement of a particular position along an expected trajectory; they are representatives for time, twice removed. Even death can function as a stand-in for time. Rather than just a simple biological fact, death can provide a future horizon in our imaginations – far away in our youth, to the point of effective invisibility, and looming increasingly closer as we age[1] – that directly affects the content and character of our lives.[2] Time itself generally remains in the background of our experiences and perceptions, and is rarely an extended object of our reflections or concerns. It is, for most people most of the time, effectively hidden.

This general invisibility of time is not a wholly mysterious phenomenon, nor is it something that we can absolutely dispense with. Conventional philosophers from Plato, Descartes, and Kant to the present have considered the nature of thought to be fundamentally truth-oriented, and telically driven toward the discovery of reality.[3] On this account, in what Deleuze refers to as thought's "dogmatic image," the purpose and character of the faculty of thought is to know (1994, 131). Ignorance, in turn, is cast as an aberration, a stage of incompletion, or a lesser form of real thought. As a result, these philosophers have quite a bit of trouble explaining this ubiquitous and seemingly crucial character of our experience with time. How should we consider the relationship between thought and truth, if both the basic tasks of living and the most rigorous acts of reflection and conceptualization demand a kind of ignorance? As active, conscious, living beings, even simple tasks require some degree of planning, directing, categorizing, contextualizing, organizing, and purposing for survival; bringing fragments of the past to bear on an imagined present, in order to project possibilities for alternative futures.

Complex social organization entails its own temporal demands alongside these. The clock may facilitate coordination among disparate persons, yet may also become a "tyrant," homogenizing and regimenting our activities to fit a schedule, rather than allowing for variation, shifting tempos, or alternative desires.

> The date book becomes the master of the master, and the punch clock the master of the servant. We rise not when we are refreshed and ready for the day, but when the alarm sounds. We eat not when we are hungry but when the timetable dictates. We may feel like prolonging an activity we are pursuing with enjoyment, but must turn to another because it is next on the schedule. We may want to take more time for reflection on a troublesome problem, but the calendar calls for a decision.
>
> (MacIver 1962, 119–120)

"Time as measured" is the mechanism by which active life is recorded and ordered, and the means by which a life can be lived, but it contains both instrumental value and dangers alike (ibid.). Rather than being oriented toward truth (a notion that itself takes as given a certain image of time imbued with purpose), the activity of thought is a fundamentally practical endeavor. It obscures our immediate perception of time in order to produce the categories, symbols, and other diagrams of "solidification" and "division" that we apply to the world, and through which we are able to generate a "fulcrum for our action" (Bergson 2004, 280).

It is precisely this obscurity involved in our conventional conceptions of time that makes a serious analysis of the dimension of temporality and its processes

16 *Time and Temporality*

so important for understanding social and political life. Conventions, traditions, and routines, collective and individual memories, perceptions of purpose and place, and the imagination of possible futures are all key elements of the constitution of social life, and all depend utterly on temporal processes, including the process of ignoring and forgetting their temporality. As Henri Bergson rightfully observed, however, forgetting the temporal dimension undergirding social life leads to "difficulty after difficulty" when attempting to understand social and political phenomena (Bergson 2001, 139). Practical life demands a degree of amnesia in the face of time, but explanation requires its recovery.

By focusing on time as a dimension to be analyzed and something to be explained in relation to political obligation, we will be able to see "the problem of political obligation" anew. In peering behind the veil of practical life and its (necessary, if stultifying) demands of compliant habituation and affirmation of things as they seem, we can attempt to assess time more directly. Moving out beyond the reach of the flooding lights of everyday convention that effuse the central hub of what Josiah Royce refers to as "the city," we can make out the faint glimmer of newly visible constellations of problems traveling above the horizon.[4] Of special concern in doing so are bringing to the fore the different ways in which time is experienced, the different means by which it is segmented, channeled, and suspended, and the processes by which it is sublimated and transformed into forms of stasis and homogeneity in our individual and shared perceptions. These processes are central to understanding how theories of political obligation have been constituted, how they maintain internal coherence as distinct and rival discourses, and how they sustain any effective moral force for those who have internalized them.

In this chapter we will provide an overview of the philosophy of time, focusing on those elements that will be most pertinent for developing the theoretical framework guiding this work as a whole. First, we will dwell on the concept of temporality, clarifying its relationship to time, and outlining some ways it has been conceptualized historically. We will then sketch out the major theoretical contributions of two theorists who will see the most use throughout this project – Henri Bergson and Gilles Deleuze. Finally, we will elaborate on the implications and value of their work for theorizing political obligation.

Time and Temporality

Time is unique, and holds a place of special importance in philosophical inquiry. As David Wood argues, even when not directly addressed, the peculiar "hydra-headed" quandaries and challenges that time poses for human understanding and life leave it always lurking at the edge of our perceptions. Behind the most fundamental concepts and problems of philosophy dwells this "shadowy form" whose influence is felt even when unseen. Change and finitude are problems of time, certainly, but just as certainly are meaning, truth, the self, freedom, and society. Time both frames and instigates these (and other) core ideas as problems of significance, and threatens their dissolution and insignificance. Consequently,

Time and Temporality   17

much philosophy reads like the construction of sea-walls against it. For time is the destroyer of all we are proud of, including pride itself, and it even threatens the realization of philosophy's highest ideals. Time is the possibility of corruption at the deepest level. And yet, without time's synthetic powers, without organized temporal extension, there would be nothing to be corrupted. Time makes as well as breaks. Time giveth and it taketh away.

(Wood 2007, 24)

Time has a pervasive power over us and our endeavors of which we cannot help but experience the consequences. It is a basic structuring dimension of our lives. Like water to fish, it is a ubiquitous and saturating element of the world we inhabit and live through. It is this very saturation, however, that has posed some of the thorniest problems and helped generate enduring theoretical divisions in efforts to make sense of time. Philosophers of time and cognate theorists have often found themselves faced with two primary facets of time that, while distinguishable, are also inextricable from each other (at least insofar as human inquiry is concerned).[5] David Couzens Hoy provides a useful preliminary distinction between these two facets of time, and this distinction will be useful for framing the general scope of our analysis: the "time of the universe" and the "time of our lives" (2009, xii).

The "time of the universe," or what Hoy also refers to as "universal time" or "objective time," is the first facet of time to consider. It is the aspect which has traditionally been the concern of scientists, as well as many metaphysicians, naturalistic and otherwise. This is time considered as a dimension of the fabric of the universe itself. Some of the major questions posed by the theoretical physicist Stephen Hawking in *A Brief History of Time* (1998) are representative of this manner of framing and problematizing time. Does time have a beginning or an end? How are speed and the passage of time related according to Einstein's theory of relativity? Does the apparent speed-of-light barrier in this universe render time travel impossible? Are there multiple or infinite coexistent threads of time corresponding to multiple or infinite possible realities? Manifesting as a set of certain kinds of problems with a correspondingly limited range of admissible types of answers, this approach to conceptualizing time corresponds to the mode of practical reasoning that has defined modern science. This way of thinking about time is not the manner in which we will be primarily dealing with time in this project.

The second facet of time, and the one which is the principal concern for this project, is that of "lived time" or the "time of our lives." It concerns time at its intersection with lived existence, experience, and perception.[6] Hoy usefully refers to this facet of time as "temporality" in order to distinguish it from the common conflation of universal time with "time as such," and we will generally continue using that distinction here (Hoy 2009, xiii). As implied at the beginning of this chapter, temporality raises questions that cut to the heart of human experience and understanding, and poses some rather significant problems for both the maintenance and understanding of individuality and social life. It concerns, at bottom, our attempts to engage (or disengage) with the inevitable, yet often

18 *Time and Temporality*

unpredictable quality of change itself, and all of the thrill, anxieties, and possibilities this encounter can engender. Is there a unity to the self across time, and if so, of what sort? What is the role of memory in constituting personal and shared experience? How are perceptions of collectively shared pasts, presents, and futures generated, and what are the consequences? What does it mean to perceive time as "flowing" in a particular direction, doing so at different speeds, or as having a particular shape? How do norms or traditions endure across time? What are the political consequences of nostalgia for the past, or hope for the future? If universal time raises questions about the materiality of time, and what (or whether) it is independently as an operative mechanism of the universe, temporality asks us to interpret our experience of time. The manifestation of that experience is a given (the "reality" or "ideality" of that experience is a separate issue). When thought of in terms of temporality, time becomes a key category through which we can problematize our certainties and touchstones, and reassess some of the more enduring questions of human experience.

It is especially important to distinguish this approach to conceiving of time from that of Immanuel Kant, whose influence on modern philosophies of time (and modern philosophy in general) would be difficult to overestimate. Kant's analysis of time was both revolutionary and profoundly unfortunate. His overarching concern with regards to time was its source; whether time came from our minds, or from "the starry heavens above."[7] In order to answer this question, he developed a more comprehensive account of the nature of experience, aimed at the prevailing philosophical traditions of his day. Against the empiricists who argued that the mind experiences data immediately and directly, and the idealists who denied or highly doubted that we experience the existence of objects in the world at all, Kant posited a nuanced synthesis of the two positions that aimed to overturn them both, called transcendental idealism. The complex details of Kant's transcendental idealism are beyond our present scope. What is significant to note here is that Kant concludes that the mind does indeed have a role to play in structuring our experience of the outside world, through a synthesizing process of the faculties of the mind. Even so, the operation of those faculties presupposes the independent existence of "objects that exist in space, and time outside me" as a priori and universal conditions of possible experience (Kant 1996, B274). Kant thus conceives of time (along with space) as an unchanging, universal, and homogeneous a priori condition for the possibility of experience *in general* (A34).

Time, for Kant, is vital for understanding the possibility of human experience and cognition, yet simultaneously it appears in his account to be oddly removed from the determination of any particular experience. Ultimately, he does not distinguish between time and temporality as we have parsed them here, largely it seems as a result of his focus throughout his philosophical projects on the identification of ordered, universal, and generally applicable rules and conditions of possibility at work in the world, as well as his pre-phenomenological acceptance of the intelligibility of a mind-world dichotomy. His efforts were revolutionary in that they interpreted time as partially a function of human cognition, and recognized the manner in which human experience is enmeshed in time. They were

Time and Temporality 19

unfortunate, however, in that they prematurely foreclosed the possibility of understanding the contingencies, particularities, and mutability of the lived experience of time by universalizing and homogenizing time up front, and subsequently attempting to fold the relationship between mind and time under the "baggy" constructs of the "transcendental ego" and "unity of apperception" (Moulard-Leonard 2008, 7). As Hoy sums this up, Kant's philosophy portrays "time [as] an a priori condition of every experience, even if it is not thematized in the experience" (2009, 7). The practical effect of the Kantian position has been to recognize the significance of time as a problem for understanding the production of human experience, while also (in failing to develop a theory of temporality) relegating it to the periphery of practical analytical importance. This relegation will be contested throughout the remainder of this work.

We should be cautious about interpreting the distinction between universal time and human temporality in a rigid way, or as a strict metaphysical separation. The endless permutations of the human perception, experience, and construction of time are, in practice, inseparable from, embedded in, and indeed predicated upon a material universe in which things change, and change in particular ways. The existential perception of a looming, terminal future horizon growing ever closer only makes sense by virtue of the reality of biological death. The concept of the Gregorian calendrical year is a major, taken for granted, cultural artifact, and yet is only comprehensible by virtue of the Earth's journey around the Sun. That we can empirically measure and predict aspects of biological death and planetary motion, and do so by referring to details and theories of universal time, does not supersede or negate the significance of temporality.[8] The materiality of the world affects our perceptions of time, and vice versa.[9] Attempts to collapse one into the other – say, by asking whether time is real or "just" something imposed on the world by our minds – reproduce the same unhelpful dichotomous stalemates between ideality and reality, or subjectivity and objectivity that dominated Western philosophy prior to Kant's Copernican revolution. For our purposes here, such a rigid distinction or opposition would not be simply unhelpful, but also downright nonsensical; a violent cleavage in our understanding of the complexity of time and our relationship to it.

As Levi Bryant also notes, Hoy's own arguments regarding the nature of time and human experience can cast doubt on the defensibility of automatically privileging human subjectivity as a focal point for understanding lived time (if these arguments are followed to their broader, logical conclusion, which Hoy does not fully do). For Hoy, temporality precedes and produces subjectivity (rather than the inverse, as posited by Kant). Subjects are not stable wholes, or transcendental kernels simply moving through time – they are emergent. Consequently, human subjects (as well as the rest of the universe) become products of processual, dysteleological change. If processes of change produce both subjects and universal being itself, then both the urge to draw a line between human time and universal time, and the "Ptolemaic gesture" of placing humans at the center of existence and one's analytical frame become problematic (Bryant 2009). Furthermore, the possibility of even conceiving of a universal time that is radically separate from lived time is a product of historical context. It is only with the

20   *Time and Temporality*

death of God and the snapping of the Great Chain of Being brought on by modernity that a sharp demarcation between Subject and Object, Mankind and Universe, became widely thinkable.

In spite of some of these potential ambiguities, it is still useful for us to make this conceptual distinction between universal time and temporality here for several reasons. Practically, it is useful so that we may more clearly delineate the scope of the problems that we are examining in this project. As interesting as they are, and as peripherally and incidentally useful as they may end up being for situating our analysis of political obligations, theoretical discussions regarding how time and space relate in the broader processes of the cosmos are generally beyond the scope of this work. While M-theory and physicists' divergent interpretations of its implications brush against questions relevant to our inquiries, they are generally tangential. Most importantly, we are primarily concerned here with making sense of a few peculiarly human concepts and problems and the manner in which they have been previously treated. Consequently, we will restrict our use of the literature on time to that which most helps us analyze these issues. While Bryant's suggestion that we may wish to move beyond the Ptolemaic gesture into a more robust and creative metaphysics is one I consider valuable, in this case I am not trying to subtly reconstitute humanity's position at the hub of a universal pinwheel. Rather simply, I am taking a leaf from Deleuze's functionalist pragmatics and asking what, how, and whether a concept or theoretical tool works, and what it enables us to see that we could not see as clearly before (Deleuze 1995, 8). While some of the analytical and conceptual concerns of universal time and temporality will overlap (since we will take it as granted that our lived time takes place within a physical universe), making this distinction between the two allows us to perceive a cluster of interrelated problems and experiences that broadly pertain to similar temporal phenomena. Framing our inquiries through temporality as we have defined it (and will continue to refine it) will make our analysis of political obligation more cogent and manageable, and let us engage in some much needed critical reappraisal of obligations.

Theorizing Temporality

There has been tremendous diversity in attempts to theorize the nature of our relationship to time, even when there is no explicit distinction made between time and temporality. This should come as no surprise, since the questions raised by temporality touch upon so many different facets of our lives, both practical and theoretical. As a result of their wide reach in the human condition, these questions have been faced by both pre-modern and modern societies, and the results have been creative and insightful means of interpreting and shaping experience and behavior.

There is still a common tendency to attribute a simplicity and homogeneity to the ideas and efforts of pre-modern societies and individuals.[10] Such views are in large part the inheritance of earlier efforts to establish a stark rupture between the pre-modern and the modern, staging the moderns as the bearers of rationality

Time and Temporality   21

and progress, and casting their predecessors into the role of backwards and superstitious preludes to the maturity of the species. Portraying pre-modern thought in this way is a profound disservice to the depth of ingenuity and intelligence that pre-moderns have brought to bear in attempting to make sense of the world as well as inaccurate, ignoring their contextual diversity and real differences in their substantive theoretical positions. It also masks the continuities between pre-modern and modern thought, especially regarding attempts to come to terms with time.

The most common pre-modern images of time portray it as circular, linear, or some combination of the two (Rosen 2004, 3). Circular or cyclical accounts of time treat time as a closed loop, and are often aligned with the patterns of seasons, lunar cycles, narratives of birth-death-renewal, or a larger cosmic calendar. In Tibetan Buddhist traditions, the concept of _Kālachakra_, or "time-wheel," provides an account of cyclical temporality spanning from the scope of universal birth and death, to its counterpart in individual bodily and spiritual practice.[11] In what can be understood as a variant on circular time, some pre-modern cultures have maintained a marked sense of atemporality, lacking a distinction between past, present, and future as successive tenses of time, or of phenomena as being connected through a linear conception of causality. A member of the Trobriand Islanders, for instance, traditionally perceived

> no boundary between past Trobriand experience and the present; he can indicate that an action is completed, but this does not mean that the action is past; it may be completed and present or timeless … he places the event situationally, not temporally.… What we consider a causal relationship in a sequence of connected events, is to the Trobriander an ingredient of a patterned whole.
>
> (Lee 1950)

Through organizing social life into repeated patterned activities that are integrated into a necessary tapestry of acts, they could maintain a strictly nonlinear temporality. Periods of ancient Chinese temporality demonstrate very similar characteristics, with cyclical thinking about nature and humanity being a dominant force (Bodde 1991, 133). Past, present, and future could be simultaneously brought to bear to explain "why," for instance, a lord was unable to rise to dominance, without requiring a sequentially ordered account of causation.[12]

Linear time is more familiar to modern senses of temporality. In it, time is flowing in a particular direction, and potentially following a teleological or eschatological path. Hesiod, the ancient Greek poet, provides a declensionist narrative of humanity's trajectory in his _Works and Days_ (2006). In his account, the Ages of Man have been made of successively inferior materials, both in terms of conditions and quality of people; a past idyllic Golden Age gives way to Silver, then Bronze, then Heroic,[13] and Iron.[14] In Medieval Europe, the Church made thorough use of the widely held belief in an always imminent, yet always deferred End of Days to ground its theological and sociopolitical legitimacy and power. Its claim to authority over decisions regarding the validity of visions of

22 Time and Temporality

the future and prophecy was so integral to the maintenance of temporal and institutional unity, Reinhart Koselleck notes, that it was quite willing to execute those who attempted to circumvent this purview; Joan of Arc and Savonarola stand as testaments to this (Koselleck 2004, 13).

What pre-modern temporalities share, then, is not so much a unified sense of the shape or direction of time, as the distinction of not being modern. If modern temporalities, as we will explore later, became defined by a particular sense of separation of people from an overarching temporality and place within a wider cosmic order, as well as a sense of separation from the past, pre-modern temporalities are those which lack these dislocations. They retain a sense of unselfconscious unity with an overarching and unifying account of the world and the tenses of time; modern temporality is thus defined through a self-conscious disunity with the past. In the pre-modern medieval European context, for instance, the Great Chain of Being is still intact, the past, present, and future have a greater degree of both simultaneity and continuity, and, in spite of strife and misfortunes, a deeper sense of unity between individual, community, Christendom, and cosmic order remains. We will address distinctions between pre-modern and modern temporalities more thoroughly in Chapters 2 and 3.

Much of modern and contemporary philosophy of temporality has been a reaction to both the temporalities of pre-modernity and the theoretical openings enabled by Kant. For these thinkers, time is not something distant from human experience, nor is it usually static. It is something that we can relate to and perceive in very different ways, and even potentially transform. To try to cover all of modern philosophy of temporality would take us far afield, but we can look at a few influential examples.

Martin Heidegger, for instance, takes Kant's arguments regarding the necessity of a universal time as a condition of experience and inverts their ontological priority. Rather than a given universal time enabling experience, it is qualitative temporality that makes any objective time intelligible. This does not mean that a given individual conscious subject can simply create a universal time arbitrarily. Instead, it is through the encounter with time that a discrete subjectivity emerges. As we emerge in the world, we encounter a deep boredom at the heart of existence. In the face of the anxiety and indifference that existence entails, the possibility of creating significance for one's life lies in the possibility of living "authentically," of having a "moment of vision" that generates a sense of unity in one's life between past, present, and future, and living in accordance with that unity so as to meet the future in an intentional and determined way (Heidegger 2010).[15]

Walter Benjamin challenges Heidegger's focus on the future through an interpretation of Paul Klee's painting, *Angelus Novus*. Benjamin accepts Heidegger's narrative of time coming at the present from the future, but (referring to the painting) the angel moving into this future is looking backwards. A forward-looking angel would see the connections between events coming at them, and be able to fashion the unity and purpose that Heidegger deems necessary. By being propelled into the future, yet only being able to look backwards, the angel sees nothing but "one single catastrophe which keeps piling wreckage upon wreckage

Time and Temporality 23

and hurls it in front of his feet" (Benjamin 1969, 257). Our lives are confusing, precarious, and filled with contingency, and if there is a *telos* to them, we are unable to grasp it from our vantage point towards time. While we are moving into the future, the wreckage of the past is always borne along with us. The future may be blind, then, but the present is at the very least a repository of the past. We can take no teleological certainty from this, but we can draw a "weak Messianic power" from it, and use the force of accumulated memory and history (written "against the grain") as a means of instigating revolutionary class struggle and political transformation (ibid., 254–262).

Pierre Bourdieu eschews Heidegger's focus on the future and his sense of the future coming at the present, and instead emphasizes the importance of the past as something continually reproducing itself in the present. Our behavioral habits, social structures, traditions, and common sense understanding of the world – in sum, our *habitus* – are largely inherited from a past that continues to act. We may certainly act with anticipation for the future, but even in so doing, he argues, we are continuously (if implicitly) still looking back into the past in order to make that future (Bourdieu 1992). Time is an "act of construction" for Bourdieu, but it is constructed by "dispositions and practices" of the past reproduced in the present rather than "the thinking consciousness" (2000, 206).

Jacques Derrida, like Benjamin, appeals to a kind of "Messianicity" in framing his interpretation of temporality. This Messianicity is not religious in character (there is no "Messiah"), but is instead intended to invoke a particular relationship toward the future. Derrida makes a distinction between two kinds of future: the predictable, and the unpredictable. While we have normal expectations toward what will happen in the future based on our past experiences and the weight of norms and tradition, the unpredictable can intervene at any time. More than that, Derrida insists that the unpredictable *will* happen, even though we cannot say how. Thus, he distinguishes between the teleological, determinate progress narrative of Kant and Hegel, and the (Messianic) eschatology of the inevitability of disruption, "otherness," and possibilities for transformation. This anti-teleological eschatology links the inevitable possibilities (yet uncertain outcomes) of change in the future to the immediate present as a kind of call to political intervention. Rather than simply waiting for progress to fulfill itself, or invoking a Utopian hope, Derrida argues that messianicity is "anything but Utopian," and instead "mandates that we interrupt the ordinary course of things, time and history here-now; it is inseparable from affirmation of otherness and justice" (Derrida 1999).

While many of these temporality theorists offer useful insights into the nature and lived experience of time (and will be tapped on occasion as needed), the theorists most useful for developing the theoretical framework of this study are Henri Bergson and one of his major channels of contemporary reception, Gilles Deleuze. Both Bergson and Deleuze take the problem of time for philosophy and life very seriously, and it plays a central role in each of their larger philosophical projects. Most importantly, they provide tools for understanding the role that time and its permutations play in social and political life. Bergson's method of intuition and Deleuze's three syntheses of time, for instance, each attempt to drill beneath the ice of social conventions and representations, and map out the

24 *Time and Temporality*

movements and channelings of time occurring just beneath the glossy surface. Why, you might ask, will we be using both Bergson and Deleuze in conjunction with each other? After all, they had no direct interaction or collaboration with each other, and, owing to age and time, their direct scholarly interactions were distinctly one-directional. While a fair question, this will need to be addressed more fully after their ideas and backgrounds have been explained in greater detail. It should be sufficient here to note that the unique character of Bergson's and Deleuze's thought, their similar concerns, and the contexts in which each wrote (and what they wrote against) make valuable combinations and hybridizations of their projects and theoretical innovations possible, especially with regard to the problems of time and political obligation.

Henri Bergson

Henri Bergson established his early philosophical bearings within an intellectual climate that was replete with concerns for unity, space, order, and homogeneity. Neo-Kantian sensibilities dominated the French university and philosophical culture of the late nineteenth and early twentieth century. In Western cultures generally, there was (at least early in his life) the profound optimism surrounding scientific progress and mechanical achievement known as the Second Scientific Revolution. This optimism sustained the mechanistic image of physics and the world that had its roots in Descartes, receiving new life through a variety of positivisms which drew inspiration from the work of Auguste Comte. Hippolyte Taine and Gustav Fechner developed a mechanistic conception of cognition and mind, while Herbert Spencer applied a conjoined mechanistic positivism and teleological progress narrative to his analysis of biological evolution (Guerlac 2006, 14–28). Reacting through and against each of these, Bergson advocated a concern for time over space, heterogeneity over homogeneity, change over order, and a form of intuition over abstract or mechanistic reasoning.[16]

For Bergson, considering time and our relationship to it is crucial for understanding the character of human perception and experience. Like Kant, Bergson sees time as providing the conditions for the possibility of experience. Unlike Kant, however, Bergson does not consider time to be a homogenous and universal constant providing the conditions for the possibility of all experience *in general*. Rather, it is "immanent or tightly fitted to what [it conditions]," providing "the conditions of experience in all its peculiarities, in its uniqueness or singularity" (Moulard-Leonard 2008, 7). In order to think about time in this way, we can't only consider it in terms of the calendar, the clock, or even the more nebulous future plan. These are spatial representations of time that have their practical uses, but they presuppose certain things that Bergson wants to challenge. We instead need to interpret time as something more immediate and constitutive of our existence as particular beings, and that both provides conditions for our situated experience of the world, and poses a practical challenge for our existence as active, living beings. Bergson labels this aspect of time *la durée*, or "duration." One aspect of the challenge posed by duration is the difficulty of actually accessing it experientially, not because it is impossible, but because we have learned to both actively and

Time and Temporality   25

habitually suppress and mask it, converting it into a ample array of spatial proxies. In order to theorize time as duration we need a tool. Bergson provides one for us in the form of what he calls "intuition."[17]

Bergson's Intuition and Duration

Bergsonian intuition is not simply a gut feeling, a hunch, a sudden insight, or a moment of Zen-like *satori* (let alone a flash of divine inspiration) as with the colloquial uses of the term. It is also quite different from the kind of intuition appealed to by many political obligation apologists, which has much more in common with colloquial uses.[18] Bergson did not, however, choose this term arbitrarily. These colloquial meanings do suggest part of what Bergsonian intuition embraces and attempts to uncover, namely a better glimpse into the real nature of things. They are limited, however, in the accidental and passive character through which such insight is supposedly achieved. Conventionally, one is set upon by an intuition. It is an unexpected and unwilled glimpse. Bergson's form of intuition, on the other hand, is far more deliberate and directed than these conventional intuitions. Not only is it more intentional, it requires a "vigorous effort" to use effectively (Bergson 2001, 129). This higher requisite effort is not a product of philosophical complexity as much as it is a consequence of the resistance we naturally provide against what Bergsonian intuition is designed to expose, prod, and render vulnerable. Bergsonian intuition encounters resistance, because it entails abandoning and inverting (at least temporarily) the consistencies, order, and solidity of the conventional, practical viewpoints under which we all normally operate.

One of the major claims in Bergson's philosophy is that time and space are constantly being conflated and confused, not simply in terms of our understanding of the ontological character of the universe, but throughout our everyday experiences. Space is generally regarded as a homogeneous medium. For Kant it is an a priori form of sensibility that makes experience and qualitatively different sensations possible. As a homogeneous medium, it provides a standard of comparison upon which such differences can be identified and arranged in relation to each other. When Kant performs the same maneuver for time, however, it is also treated as if it were an unchanging, overarching, homogeneous medium. Bergson considers this extremely problematic. In conceiving of both space and time as constant, a priori, homogeneous background conditions, Kant wants to make homogeneity and unity the epistemic ground that makes experience possible. In doing so, he ends up homogenizing time, and treating it as little more than a "ghost of space haunting the reflective consciousness" (Bergson 2001, 99). Bergson finds this inadequate, arguing that

> if space is to be defined as the homogeneous, it seems that inversely every homogenous and unbounded medium will be space. For homogeneity here consisting in the absence of every quality, it is hard to see how two forms of the homogeneous could be distinguished from one another.

(98)

26   *Time and Temporality*

Aside from generating a conceptually muddled redundancy, collapsing time into space and treating both as homogeneous dimensions gives us no dimension to account for change and qualitative distinctions.[19] Time conceived of as a homogeneous medium is thus a "spurious concept, due to the trespassing of the idea of space upon the field of pure consciousness" (ibid.). Bergson argues instead that time and space are in fact radically different, the first pertaining to qualitative difference and change, with the second pertaining to homogeneity and quantitative distinction. Even though they are radically different, we constantly convert time into space – and we must. It is a necessary illusion we produce in order for us to live and act in the world. This being a necessary process does not, however, make it an unproblematic one.

As a form of qualitative multiplicity, time, for Bergson, is the force of change and newness in the world itself. It is heterogeneity and, against Kant, the "ground" of immediate lived experience. This does not mean that the experience of time is the only "true" experience,[20] but it does imply that it is ontologically primary in the nature of experience. The perception of homogeneity in the world, then, should not be taken as a given, but rather instead to be explained. If we were to experience only time, we would find ourselves in a kaleidoscopic stream of sensations, experiencing each moment flowing into the next without perceiving the passage of clock time, distinctions of objects, or of categories of sensation. Suggesting that we would "find ourselves" doing these things is itself somewhat misleading. Active reflective consideration of one's position as a particular person in relation to other things already suggests a distancing of oneself from the immediate experience of time. We would be, as in successful Buddhist *zazen* meditation, absorbed within in a continuously renewed, purely present moment. This interpenetrating flow of immediate experience and sensation is our encounter with duration.

Space, on the other hand, is homogeneity. It is not simply a given dimension of the world (and should not be conflated with "matter" or "extensity").[21] Rather, in our lived experience, the perception of space involves an "act of the mind" (Bergson 2001, 94) in "reaction against the heterogeneity that is the very ground of our experience" (97). Space is thus a cognitive construction that places and juxtaposes some objects within an imagined homogeneous medium.[22] Imposing this homogeneous medium onto the world entails a conversion, then, of time into space, of difference into sameness, and change into stability. Language, identity, and much of thought itself depend on the spatialization of time – our imposition of a simplified, ordered homogeneity over and in the place of the radical difference and flux inherent to the processes of time and the world itself. We invest a lot of personal psychological energy in the maintenance of these "symbolic substitutes" for the complexity and "confusion" of reality (139). They give us a sense of security, direction, and value for our lives, and are necessary for us to actively live at all.[23]

Social life, Bergson admits, can only exist through the generation of some shared perception of homogeneous space. It requires the construction of a "practical viewpoint" – especially a sense of being a part of something held in common, shared expectations for behavior, and the upholding of conventional

Time and Temporality 27

myths that consolidate these homogenizing procedures – in lieu of the radical mutability, particularity, and heterogeneity comprising real individuals and their complex relations with each other. Although filtered through Walter Benjamin, it is Bergson's conception of the social role of time and space that undergirds Benedict Anderson's analysis of the emergence of nationalism in his *Imagined Communities* (1991). Imagining the nation requires a means by which a large, semi-anonymous group of people can nevertheless perceive themselves as part of a contiguous set moving together and cohesively as a "We" through time, with a shared past, present, and future (and for the modern nation, without the aid of the unifying temporalities provided by the pre-modern conception of Being in relation to the cosmos). Anderson's famous use of the concept of "homogenous, empty time" that facilitates this is simply a social form of Bergson's conception of spatialization (24). In spite of its utility, always remaining comfortably within the practical viewpoint leads to "difficulty after difficulty" when attempting to actually understand our lives, since its very existence depends upon this "absurd" process of organized blindness and ignorance (Bergson 2001, 139). It also entails potentially problematic consequences for our attempts to live them.

Consequently, Bergson offers intuition as a method which attempts to look behind the "thinly woven veil" of conventions that we depend on to sustain our day to day routines and that structure social and political life (133). Intuition entails a rigorous inversion of the practical viewpoint. It attempts to momentarily re-establish perceptions of duration, time, and processes of change in lieu of our impositions of stability, sameness, and space in order to better understand our experiences, and perhaps more importantly, help us orient the direction of our lives.[24] In his *Bergsonism* (1991), Deleuze argues that Bergson's intuition has three kinds of acts that comprise its rules as a method.

The first rule tells us to "apply the test of true and false to problems themselves" and to "condemn false problems and reconcile truth and creation at the level of problems" (Deleuze 1991, 15). Truth value isn't simply a property of solutions or answers, but can be asked of questions themselves. Posing questions is an act of creation, invention, and a determination of pertinent values, and thus the nature of a question posed can delimit the kinds of answers that become admissible and imaginable. Finding the right solutions (which do matter, for Bergson) depends also on questioning the way problems are posed. Consequently, there are two kinds of "false problems" for Bergson. The first is the "nonexistent problem," which "contains a confusion of the 'more' and the 'less'"[25] and the second is the "badly stated problem" which contains "badly analyzed composites that arbitrarily group things that *differ in kind*" (17–18).[26]

The second rule tells us to "struggle against illusion, [and] rediscover the true differences in kind or articulations of the real" (21). Bergson knows that "things are mixed together in reality" and that "experience itself offers us nothing but composites" (22). We compensate for the messiness of reality by imposing distinctions, divisions, and concepts that group elements of our world together. The problem arises when we forget ourselves in our spatializations, and forget both how to distinguish between time and space, heterogeneity and homogeneity, and

28   *Time and Temporality*

that we have made composites out of them in the first place. Failing to act against this condemns us to "live among badly analyzed composites, and to be badly analyzed composites ourselves" (28).

The third rule tells us to "state problems and solve them in terms of time rather than of space" (31). The method of intuition "presupposes duration" and thus the division between duration and space, but it is not enough to simply accept that they are distinct (ibid.). Instead, we must understand the processes behind the distinctions. The nature of those processes uncovered by intuition is the distinction between duration (time) and space which we have already made, with duration tending[27] to "bear all the differences in kind (because it is endowed with the power of qualitatively varying with itself," while space "never presents anything but differences in degree (since it is quantitative homogeneity)" (31).

One of the key observations that Bergson derives from his use of intuition is that, within the context of a given cultural time perspective, we as concrete, particular beings find ourselves doubled. We find that we have a "second self" that "obscures the first," yet without which we could not live (Bergson 2001, 138). On the one hand, we experience ourselves and the world through our concrete yet finite and mutable bodies of flesh and bone. It is this discrete, embodied self – what Bergson refers to variously as our "concrete self" and our "fundamental self" – that experiences the continuous and unbroken flow of change and newness (duration) in the world in each immediate and passing moment of the present, melting into the next. It is our self at each moment, prior to the (almost immediate) incursion of symbolic representations, distinctions, categorization of sensations, and the integration of these into an imagined continuity that generate a "sense of self" in relation to the world.

On the other hand, we cannot live as beings experiencing pure duration for all time. Our constitutive psychological reactions against this possibility aside, to do so would entail an utterly paralyzing confusion in the purest sense. Maintaining a sense of self and providing meaning and purpose for the life projects that make directed action (and thus conscious life) possible are achieved only through processes of structuring, projecting, and spatializing time. Rather than the conventionally diachronic image of the movement of time, with discrete (if infinitely divisible) moments following each other like pearls on a string, or as if linked in a chain, time for Bergson is largely *synchronic*. The past, present, and future are not simply given tracks of time that we move discretely along, with the future falling (somehow) into the past, and imperceptibly slipping by an infinitesimal present into oblivion. They co-exist simultaneously.[28]

Why does the present feel more solid and real than the past or the future?[29] The present is where I imagine events unfolding, where I feel myself living, where I think of myself as acting, deciding, and thinking. When I stub my toe, I feel the pain in each present moment as long as it lingers. Yet what defines this present moment, or its boundaries? In portraying what he takes to be a conventional account, Bergson says that "the essence of time is that it goes by; time already gone by is the past, and we call the present the instant in which it goes by" (2004, 176). While this common sense view captures part of our experience, it isn't wholly adequate. While there may certainly be an "ideal present" as a kind of "pure conception [of] the indivisible limit which separates past from future" this is not the present that we actually experience in our lives (ibid.). Instead, the "real, concrete, live present – that of which I speak when I speak of my present perception – that present necessarily occupies a duration" (ibid.). It does not exist within the idealized "mathematical point" of the present instant, but rather extends both before and after us, so that "what I call 'my present' has one foot in my past and another in my future" (176–177).

Bergson insists on this conception of the lived present, and does not simply present it as an alternative to the notion of the present as an infinitely small point in time. How is it, though, that the present can be defined in a way that contains part of the past and the future? As a skeptic might ask, hasn't the past ceased to be by definition? Bergson argues that the proper question is not whether the past has ceased to exist once something has slipped by the idealized present moment, but rather

> whether it has simply ceased to be useful. You define the present in an arbitrary manner as *that which is*, whereas the present is simply *what is being made*. Nothing *is* less than the present moment, if you understand by that the indivisible limit which divides the past from the future. When we think this present as going to be, it exists not yet; and when we think it as existing, it is already past. If, on the other hand, what you are considering is the concrete present such as it is actually lived by consciousness, we may say that this present consists, in large measure, in the immediate past.
>
> (2004, 193–194)

The present is distinct in being the source or site of the production of activity and change, but this does not mean that the past (or future) does not *exist*. Our experience of the lived present includes our "perception of the immediate past," since even in the moment of describing our experience that moment slips into the past, and yet is still perceived to be part of an active present (until we reflect on it having passed) (177). It is not only the most recent immediate past that survives as part of the present, but, Bergson says, all of the preceding immediate pasts, wherein "the whole of our past psychical life conditions our present state, without being its necessary determinant" (191). We accumulate memories as we go through life, and bring that constantly evolving stock of memories to bear in our experience of each new moment. Indeed, we could not perceive a (lived) present without already having a store of past memories to make that present comprehensible (or an "experience" at all).[30]

The lived present also includes our anticipation and "determination of the immediate future" (177). In our lived present we are persisting and moving through the world. We have an attitude and disposition toward the world in which we find ourselves and the future as it appears before us, and as active, living beings, that disposition constitutes part of the boundary of the lived present in which we experience ourselves living.[31] Our cumulative past experiences shape our disposition toward and expectations of the future, and as those

30　*Time and Temporality*

futures are incorporated into our past via our activity of the present, the process repeats and each is transformed. We unconsciously hold all of these together in a continuous and flexible circuit that functions to sustain the temporal bubble of the lived present in order to make our world amenable to being comprehensibly experienced, as well as acted within and upon.

This picture, though, is itself incomplete. We are not running on a predictable autopilot, simply functioning as one-dimensional sensory calculators – at least not always. The demands of practical life and "the necessities of present action" can certainly keep us focused on the present moment and the task at hand, whatever that might be (199). Bergson does not want to say that we simply accumulate memories and experiences that then play only a passive, impressionistic, structuring role. When we are able to break free of the demands of present action, we are able to actively recall memories, bringing them rushing into the lived present, or alternatively, taking a leap into the past. Through a similar action, we are able to imagine new future possibilities or plans.[32] In each of our lives, we fluctuate (sometimes unexpectedly) between the extremes of a focused, pointed existence ruled by necessity, activity, accumulated habit, and passive memory, and the realm of pure memory, imagination, vision, and the contemplation of universals – the realm of the dreamer (201, 211).[33] It is in the moments where we distance ourselves from the immediate present that we are able to engage in substantial reconfigurations of our living present: bring our past memories to bear on recent events, re-examine our expectations and life direction in response to new memories, and consider our imagined present place in the world.

In Bergson's synchronic temporality, we thus engage in temporal *projection*. Time isn't something we only diachronically travel along, but rather our experiences of it (and its contours) are created in each moment. We actively (though not always consciously) try to produce and reproduce an imagined past, present, and future, and attempt to unify these projections as a means of maintaining a cohesive sense of place, life direction, and purpose. It is also through them that, in the face of the confusion and flux of duration, we are able to orient ourselves in the world and make intentional action possible. For Bergson, temporal projection is a necessity for sanity, comfort, and survival.

Not only have the practical demands of survival and psychological security made a life of continuously experiencing pure duration impossible, we are also always already beings that have developed within a social context. We have developed corresponding practical viewpoints with attending norms, habits, rituals, memories, expectations, personal identities, social roles, legal personae, and life projects to navigate the complexity of this context alongside others. This amalgam of socially inherited distinctions, categories, symbolic representations, and narratives through which we define ourselves as integrated and integral beings in relation to the world is what constitutes our second self. While Bergson refers to this second self as our "superficial" self, it may be more useful to follow his occasional labeling of this as the "conventional" ego or self (133). For Bergson, we are driven to "solidify" our immediate experiences and sensations, and thus:

Time and Temporality   31

Consciousness, goaded by an insatiable desire to separate, substitutes the symbol for the reality, or perceives the reality only through the symbol. As the self thus refracted, and thereby broken to pieces, is much better adapted to the requirements of social life in general and language in particular, consciousness prefers it, and gradually loses sight of the fundamental self.

(2004, 128)

I am not simply this contingent configuration of flitting particles that has already become something utterly new with each passing moment (although I *am* that). Neither am I, correspondingly, only experiencing each moment of that contingent existence in fluid succession (although I *am* doing that). I am *also* a being that makes distinctions and divisions among those sensations, including divisions between internal states and external objects (and between the "internal" and "external" at all). I sustain a sense of self and the past through memory, project various plans and goals for myself into the future, and act in the present by synthesizing these projections and bringing them to bear in relation to other constructed categories and divisions of the world. I consciously and unconsciously unify them into a sense and representation of myself for the practical demands of living.

We have, in other words, spatialized this complex heterogeneity of our world, ourselves, and our social context into usable representations. But, in so doing, we have had to selectively banish time and superficially refract ourselves into discrete categories, personae, and functions that can operate within this setting. Most importantly for us here, we have had to forget the spatializing processes at the origin and heart of these conventions and representations and instead treat them as given, solid objects in our experience. We forget the intercession of the mind in the imposition of stability in perception, and collapse the two moments of experience – from duration to spatialization, concrete to conventional self – into one badly analyzed composite.

The split between the concrete and the conventional self rests ultimately upon irreducible and often conflictual poles of our experience and the divergent needs of our psyche. It is no simple or effortless task to unsettle things that have been taken for granted, and upon which we have erected the architecture of our personalities and perceived world. As we will discuss in the next chapter, the emergency of modernity and the shockwaves of social, cultural, and personal crises this generated were made possible through such a mass dislocation of identity, temporal projections, place, and sensibility, alongside other material and institutional upheavals. The doubting of René Descartes that has conventionally inaugurated European modernity was driven by a persistent anxiety and unease, particular over his inability to walk confidently in his life path after the collapse of the cultural time perspective of Europe's Middle Ages. Miguel de Unamuno is a striking exemplar of the consequences of being unable to maintain an effective conventional self. In *Tragic Sense of Life* (1954), he recounts his anguished experience of agonized doubting that accompanied the destabilization of his conventional self amidst modern conditions. This doubting, like that of Descartes', was brought against the external world he perceived around him.

32   Time and Temporality

It reached further, though, down to fundamental questions about his ability to know himself, including (going beyond Descartes) doubting his own doubting and the motivations behind it, and doubting if he is what he thinks he is – or even *is* at all – at any particular moment.[34] While Descartes' doubting was "methodic," Unamuno's was desperate and agonized, his work seeping tragedy throughout. Differences aside, both are examples of the struggles and compulsion at the level of the conscious and unconscious to maintain an effective structuring temporality, and a stable and convincingly unified conventional self.

This Bergsonian tendential urge toward the consolidation of experience in the conventional self is, in effect, the struggle to exercise what Michael Weinstein refers to in his interpretation of Bergson as "control" (Weinstein 1979, 8). Control is not simply brute, physical coercion, but "our active and practical response to our radical dependency upon what lies beyond our life" (45). It is a means of securing against bodily and psychological threats and dangers, of warding off the dissolutions and precarities posed by time, of taming the unexpected through the making of plans, and of identifying one's place in the world through an account of "the way things are." In one's mind control manifests through attempts to consolidate and unify the conventional self through categorizations and personal past-present-future projections, and within a complex social situation control is exercised through the navigation of our standing and esteem among a complex network of social relations. Control "exacts the sacrifice of personality to assure the maintenance of individual identity" (9). The urge for Bergsonian control thus rests upon the gnawing persistence of fear, a fear that reveals itself in moments when our efforts at control falter; fear of harm, loss, betrayal, survival, death, worthlessness, oblivion (50–55). Recognition of and empathy with such fears are vital for understanding the intransigence of the conventional self, and the various palliatives constructed to maintain its efficacy (of which, I will argue, political obligation theories can function as one).

Weinstein refers to control's opposite pole as variously "expression" and "appreciation." In the moments wherein we are able to relax our securitization efforts, reflect on our relationship to and place in the world without anxiety, and open ourselves to what is new, we can exercise an expressive appreciation – even though the resulting experiences of this appreciation will subsequently be submitted to control, and reintegrated into the (perhaps newly configured) conventional self. What is significant for us to take away here is that this pull between expression and control, between our openness to the contingencies highlighted by the concrete self's engagement with duration and the securitization demanded by the conventional self, is not something we can simply overcome. Some may attempt to seize upon one side or the other in this dichotomy in order to resolve the tension,[35] but to successfully do so would demand that one be either a "prisoner of fear" who denies the messy and mortal concrete self entirely, or if one sought to deny the conventional self, "a suicide with no care for self-preservation or a saint with no destructive impulses" (Weinstein 1979, 8).

Bergson warns that he is not actually intending to "split up the personality" in making this distinction (Bergson 2001, 138). He is not claiming that we have an

Time and Temporality 33

original true and autonomous self that is only corrupted by its entrance into society. Nor should his division be read as either a close parallel to the Freudian model of the ego, or a statement regarding what we "ultimately" and "truly" are, with the concrete self playing the role of some intrinsic essence. Rather, Bergson's image of the doubled self captures the irreducibly divergent and conflicting processes that make up our experience of ourselves and the world. There is no harmonious ground from which we can escape the absurd pull in our lives between radically heterogeneous and interpenetrating (yet paralyzing and psychologically unsettling) streams of new sensation and our openness to them, and the homogenizing, constructed illusions and ordered ignorance of raw heterogeneity which allow us to act in the world, maintain social expectations, and provide our personal lives with "well distinguished moments," identity, and a sense of direction and purpose. We cannot practically escape these vicissitudes, or collapse our experience purely into one or another side of this tension, but we can try to understand these processes, and in so doing perhaps keep ourselves from confusing "the real" for its "symbolical substitute" (139).

It is worth noting that Bergson's emphases in and reaction to his own intuitional inquiries changed over time. In spite of Deleuze's poststructural stamp on contemporary interpretations of his work, Bergson is ultimately a modern, and his works are driven by modern concerns. It is in his early work, especially *Time and Free Will*, that Bergson first develops the method of intuition, and the concept of duration. In *Matter and Memory*, he develops both further, incorporating, among other things, the role of memory in the constitution of our experience of time and sense of self. In these, he identifies many of the constitutive tensions of our existence, and is often ambivalent about their overcoming. His later works (although, even by *Matter and Memory* we can see a shift of emphasis), however, including his work on obligation in *The Two Sources of Morality and Religion* increasingly concern themselves with a quintessentially modern problem: how to harmonize our social and individual being, and how to establish a system of transpersonal meaning as a way of facilitating this. It is the earlier Bergson who will be of most use to us here. His earlier conceptual tools will be of the most use for developing our temporal analysis, while his later focus on the *élan vital* or "vital impetus" of life itself offers a "solution" to a problem that I considerable ultimately irresolvable, except through a tremendous effort of Procrustean metaphysical speculation and spatialization (which his later projects ultimately amount to, in spite of Deleuze's retroactive attempts to salvage them).

Gilles Deleuze

Gilles Deleuze emerged from a philosophical context that was not altogether unlike Bergson's. For both Bergson and Deleuze, their targets and opponents were theorists who prioritized unity and identity over newness and difference. While Bergson found himself arrayed against Kantians and mechanistic positivists, Deleuze found himself surrounded by a trenchant and ubiquitous Hegelianism. Philosophers such as Jean Wahl, Jean Hyppolite, and Alexandre Kojève played a pivotal role in translating and integrating Hegelian concepts into the

34 *Time and Temporality*

French Continental tradition, influencing Surrealists, Marxists, and Existentialists alike. Their efforts led to a predominant Hegelian stamp being left upon French philosophy from the 1930s until the deconstructive efforts of the 1960s (incidentally, displacing the Bergsonian influence that had been strong through the 1920s). Reacting against this and other restrictions[36] within the French university system and intellectual culture, Deleuze's early work is often implicitly polemical, and provides creative transformations of traditional philosophers through highly unconventional readings.[37] His subsequent work carries on this reaction through the creation of concepts and conceptual systems designed to attract our gaze away from representations and ideal Forms, destabilize them, and encourage us to, following Nietzsche, think in an "untimely" fashion.[38]

Key to Deleuze's reaction against the philosophical traditions that emphasize unity is his desire to develop a way to theorize that which is truly new. While this may not seem to be a terribly controversial or challenging endeavor at first glance, Deleuze wants to be able to conceptualize the new without having that newness immediately subsumed under the long reach of the Hegelian dialectic and defined as an ancillary, negative extension of a given unity, or as an illusory shadow of a timeless, ideal form that posits itself as what is truly Real. Deleuze argues that the dominant traditions of Western philosophy, including the whole of the Platonic tradition, which, by way of Christian theology, extends through Kant and Hegel, have emphasized the priority of unity and continuity. They have rested upon two crucial sets of assumptions in doing so: the priority granted to Being, and the centrality of representation in their account of the nature of thought (Deleuze 1994, 262–265). Consequently, in emphasizing the priority of newness and difference and challenging the primacy of Being and representational images of thought, Deleuze finds himself at odds with much of Western philosophy and its prevailing assumptions.

Deleuze's early original work develops this position through extended reflections on the concept of "difference," especially in his *Difference and Repetition* (1994).[39] In its colloquial form, difference suggests a difference *between* two or more given opposed things, or the difference *within* one thing across time. In both cases, difference is treated as secondary to an already assumed commonality and underlying sameness that allows comparison, and an already given opposition between the things being compared. It becomes a "reflexive concept" that functions as an instrument of comparing objects or states with taken-for-granted comparability (34). It has no content in and of itself, but is instead always a mediator between a set of givens. The consequence of this, Deleuze argues, is the burial of that which is concretely unique and particular in each new moment. As with Bergson's spatialization, this burial can provide some practical utility for navigating within a given system. It can also, however, lead to similar kinds of symbolic violence; the absorption of the radically unique into an all-encompassing account of Being (a la Hegel), or the reduction and disposal of a subject's particularities for the sake of "[forcing them] into a previously established identity" and fitting them into given categories or concepts of representation (51).[40] The political consequences at their most extreme scale and intensity are totalitarian and fascistic. Rather than uncritically presuming the primacy of

Time and Temporality 35

unity and identity, Deleuze gives ontological and strategic priority to difference, but difference of a particular kind. Rather than theorizing difference as a negative form of a given unity, Deleuze wants to create an account of "difference in itself."[41] By privileging difference in itself, Deleuze gives us an account of the world as being comprised of "a swarm of differences, a pluralism of free, wild, untamed differences" (50). Particularity, change, and newness are the default, and unities, representations, and identity either presuppose or are imposed upon this ontological ground. Philosophical traditions that begin from the assumption of given identities, unities, and representations are a site of "transcendental illusion," always attempting to capture the particularities of the world and force them under a stable or even universal image.[42] There is always an "unrepresented singularity" that neither fits nor recognizes itself in the representation precisely because these representations and unities are imposed reductions of the particularities and difference which ontologically constitute the world (52).

With the concept of difference, Deleuze draws significant inspiration from Bergson,[43] especially from the concepts of duration and intuition. It is by adapting Bergsonian intuition that Deleuze is able to problematize the conventional conception of repetition as the repetition of the same by identifying and drawing out the ways in which we create unities and continuities between irreducibly multiplicitous objects and moments, often without even recognizing that we are doing so. The multiplicity entailed in difference is inspired by the qualitative multiplicity of duration described by Bergson. If duration is the molten flow of change in the world uncovered by the intuition of time, difference can be seen as the radically unique particularity instantiated through the flow of time at any given moment. The apparent-yet-illusory unities established out of difference are not simply cast away by Deleuze as false "ideology," although there can be plenty of misperception entailed with them. They are instead treated as products or artifacts generated out of continually emerging conjunctions of difference.[44] They are outcomes whose production demands explanation, rather than a foundation upon which one should repose.

Bergson's philosophy, especially his identification of the importance of duration and his development of the method of intuition, was a significant influence for Deleuze. This does not, however, obviate the value of Deleuze's subsequent work. By drawing from Nietzsche, Spinoza, Proust, and others, and incorporating them into his early Bergsonian formulations, Deleuze eventually goes beyond Bergson in several key respects. One of the most striking differences between Bergson and Deleuze pertains to their comparative emphases on continuity versus discontinuity and life versus death. Even while recognizing the tensions between our poles of experience, Bergson is still committed to a conception of the ego as something enduring, even if he does not do so in a manner as explicit or straightforward as that of the Cartesian Cogito. His conception of time and duration are also marked by an implicit sense of "melting" continuity that fits awkwardly at times with his emphasis on the association of time with heterogeneity (we will return to this issue of Bergson's continuities soon). Deleuze, on the other hand, seizes upon discontinuity, fragmentation, and

36   *Time and Temporality*

dissolution in his account of time, thought, subjectivity, and political change. Aside from the historical division of Bergson living and writing most of his work in a more intellectually optimistic pre-World War II period and Deleuze doing so in its aftermath, Deleuze was deeply affected by his encounter with the works of Marcel Proust[45] and Friedrich Nietzsche.

It is in Nietzsche, though, that Deleuze finds the critical concept of the "eternal return."[46] Through a unique and highly influential reading of Nietzsche's philosophy, Deleuze uses and transforms the eternal return into a machine that puts the concept of difference in motion, and alters the way we think about repetition. Arguably the most important point in his reading is the observation that rather than the eternal return implying an endless return of the *same* in a kind of infinite time loop, it actually entails the return of that which is *different*.[47]

> We misinterpret the expression "eternal return" if we understand it as "return of the same". It is not being that returns but rather *the returning itself that constitutes being* insofar as it is affirmed of becoming and of that which passes. *It is not some one thing which returns but rather returning itself is the one thing* which is affirmed of diversity or multiplicity.
>
> (Deleuze 1983, 48, emphasis added)

This interpretation of the eternal return serves two major functions for Deleuze. The first function is that of a frame for developing an affirmative life philosophy and ethic. This affirmative life philosophy is one that emphasizes difference, change, chance, multiplicity, and the expansion of one's powers and abilities (190). The second function is ontological. Cyclical interpretations of the eternal return assume the identity of the person who and the world that will be undergoing the return. They make the same mistake as Plato and Hegel, starting from being and ending at being, with change and difference serving only an interstitial and derivative function. Deleuze instead takes the process of change itself as being primary, with the eternal return then suggesting the infinite production of (initially) unbound difference as the ontological ground for understanding unity and change in the world.[48]

Through this reading of the eternal return, Deleuze uses Nietzsche's concept of "becoming"[49] in order to characterize the relationship between difference and repetition. In Deleuze's hands, becoming is the continual production of difference operative in the world. It is a kind of process offered by Deleuze in order to conceive of change without having to resort to the prior unities and continuities deployed by the Platonic tradition of representation and so often implicated in the static concept of "Being." In this sense, it is very similar to Bergson's concept of duration. As Cliff Stagoll describes it, "becoming is the pure movement evidenced in changes *between* particular events" (2010). This "pure movement" is not simply the traversal between two points or states of being. Becoming is usually thought of in these terms, as a kind of representation of the distance traveled between a set or series of points. Since this conceptualization would leave those points and their relationship as unexplained givens, and reduce becoming to an empty exercise in rehearsing the connections and

Time and Temporality 37

continuities that one has already drawn between them, Deleuze is not content with this. Instead, becoming is the operative, dynamic principle of change evinced in the world itself. It is not simply the imagined path of change that has occurred or must occur in order for a difference between states or places to be traveled – not the fulfillment of a teleology or distance to a goal. Rather, becoming is itself dysteleological (even though it may become channeled towards the teleologies of particular representation, ideas, and social systems). It is the singular production of changes in particular circumstances that makes particular perceptions of difference between one point in time and another possible.[50]

Although they appear similar, becoming is not identical to duration. While duration ostensibly operates as the force of change and heterogeneity, in Bergson's hands it retains a degree of implicit unity and continuity. This is especially the case, as we have mentioned, with his later increasing reliance upon the *élan vital* as a device for explaining duration's creativity. It is also evident in the examples and language through which Bergson expresses his understanding of duration in action. As Gaston Bachelard argues, "Bergson often tones down [the language of] heterogeneity so that, as a result, succession seems like a change where things fade and merge into one another" and even when he reaffirms the presence of heterogeneity in this, the sense of continuity is maintained by "a whole family, an entire closed cycle of metaphors that constitute the language of continuity, the song and indeed the lullaby of continuity" (2000, 121). Bergson's account of memory and the existence of the whole accumulated past in a contracted form in the present can also introduce a degree of implicit continuity that fits uncomfortably with his own account of duration as heterogeneity. It serves well for giving an account of how habit and memory can ensure ego continuity, but Deleuze does not find it adequate for explaining how we can think of the new emerging.[51] As Nathan Widder argues, Bergson's conception of the pure past (the past considered "as such" and independent of any particular content) reproduces a kind of "Platonic gesture," turning the past into a "transcendent" abstract principle for maintaining a sustained connection through time (2012, 140). Bergson rejects the reality of Platonic forms, but the pure past at times appears to exercise a comparable function in sustaining temporal unity. Consequently, "this transcendence of the past suggests that Bergson does not so much overturn a linear, chronological order of time as simply complicate it" (141). Although Bergson formally posits the centrality of heterogeneity for duration, his desire for continuity (especially of time, "life," the ego, and memory) increasingly leads him to quietly resist disruption, discontinuity, and heterogeneity having any substantial effect on his portrayal of duration.

By comparison, Deleuze's conception of becoming is more amenable to a vision of processual change with discontinuity and fragmentation, sudden emergence and disappearance. The philosophy of time that Deleuze draws from it, as we will see shortly, does not depend upon pure memory as a principle of continuity, but rather only incorporates it as one "synthesis" of time among three.[52] It is useful to think of becoming as an extension of Bergson's insights beyond where Bergson himself was willing to fully go. Ultimately, while Deleuze begins from a more closely Bergson-inspired conception of difference, this evolves

38 Time and Temporality

(even by the middle of *Difference and Repetition*) and elaborates into becoming, something that is more clearly Deleuze's own and which bears the stamp of both Nietzsche's and Proust's influence.

While he owes much to Bergson's philosophy of time, Deleuze ultimately develops a more comprehensive and nuanced one of his own. We can see a similar rift emerge between Bergson's and Deleuze's conceptions of time to that which emerges between their conceptions of the ego and of duration. Bergson's reflections on time heavily emphasize the importance of memory in the formation of temporality. While incorporating part of Bergson's account, Deleuze gives us three syntheses of time in order to conceptualize the ways in which temporality operates.[53] These three syntheses are not commensurable with the past, present, and future. Each synthesis is instead a kind of cluster of interactive transformations, or what James Williams refers to as a "network of asymmetrical formal and singular processes" (2011, 3). The past, present, and future appear in each synthesis, but are not absolutely independent from each other. Unlike futurity in Heidegger's philosophy, or the accumulated "wreckage" of the past in Benjamin's, no one part of time receives overall ontological priority.[54] Instead, they simultaneously and synchronically manifest in different ways, differing in appearance depending on which synthesis you are addressing. Deleuze wants to explain how we can think about our experience of time, especially its passage, without resorting to the conventional linear diachronic image. He appeals to these three syntheses to provide this explanation. Perhaps the most difficult, yet important implication of Deleuze's syntheses is that they are not simply different vantage points on time *in general*. Even thinking of time as Bergsonian duration suggests a degree of temporal unity and continuity that Deleuze finds problematic. The processes of becoming that are operative in each synthesis instead make *multiple times*. We can clarify this point and draw out its implications after we have elaborated on each of the syntheses.

In the first synthesis of time, the past and future are conceived of as dimensions of the present. It may be useful here to recall Bergson's critique of how conventional diachronic images of time tend to define the present (understood as a singular moment) as being more "real" than the past or future. Deleuze also rejects this privileging of the reality of the idealized present moment over the past and future, and instead understands the present (at this synthesis) as a larger "living present," which (like Bergson) contains the past and future. As Williams characterizes this conception: "We do not travel through time as an unchanging body and mind. Instead, all present processes resonate in waves through the past and future as dimensions of events determining a living present" (2011, 11). Processes in the living present determine processes in the past and future by "synthesizing" them through a mechanism known as "contraction." Contraction is the bringing together of different moments and processes of the past and future, while synthesis is the convergence of different moments and processes produced through contraction; to synthesize involves contraction, while contraction produces synthesis (Deleuze 1994, 70–71). When I say bringing together, we should not think of this as a conscious act. Rather it is explicitly *not* a conscious activity at this synthesis, but instead pertains to the pre-reflective and unconscious processes by which the past and future transform each other in our living present.

Deleuze argues that the first synthesis of time should be understood as a "passive" synthesis. This is not because this synthesis does nothing, or is only acted upon, but rather because the processes at work here are not carried out consciously by the mind, and thus are not "active" (71). Passive synthesis "occurs in the mind which contemplates," but does so "prior to all memory and all reflection" (ibid.). It produces the complex of internalized expectations, impressions, and one's comportment toward the world that serves as the "foundation" upon which the active syntheses of reflection, memory, and intellect can operate, and that constrains and directs those operations. It is not limited to the habits of the mind or sensory-motor habits, then, but also those habits which constitute us (indeed are us) at a very basic level, those "thousands of passive syntheses of which we are organically composed" (74).[55] We are not some singular soul, but are rather a convergence (a contraction) of an infinitely small number of ephemeral systems and processes (which are themselves contractions), and as we live in this world it transforms us deeply at a bodily, subconscious, and pre-reflective level. The events of this past aren't just filed away, but actively transform the ways in which we carry ourselves toward the future.

A child who is repeatedly beaten by a parent in their youth may repress and forget the conscious memory of each blow by the time they reach adulthood, but they will nevertheless be transformed in their constitutive willingness to trust, their feelings toward themselves, and their disposition toward the world. It is in this sense that the past and future are contained in the living present, and are themselves transformed as time passes. The past is literally changed, because it has no existence independent of its contraction in the living present. The abused child's past accumulates and changes as they continue living, but cannot be said to be inert in relation to the present or the future. The future is also changed, but not by present processes setting off a linear causal chain of events that are simply waiting to actualize. This kind of linear, Newtonian conception of time is precisely the kind of diachronic conceptual overlay that Deleuze wants us to recognize as a convention possessing significant limitations, and move beyond.[56] Instead, the future is changed by processes in the living present contracting and constraining all of the possible outcomes of the future in a different way. The future is not chiseled in stone, but neither is it pure chance. Having been abused, the child's past will actively transform their possible future life course, especially in terms of how they emotionally and constitutively bear themselves toward others and the world in the future, but it does not create a simple linear teleology that they can then be expected to travel along. This process of pre-reflective contraction of the past and future in our ever-changing living present creates the first synthesis of time (97).

The second synthesis of time treats the past as central. It is not only a synthesis of the past, but also a synthesis of memory. While the first synthesis draws from Hume's account of habit, the second synthesis draws largely from Bergson's discussions of memory. When we focus on the present in the first

40   *Time and Temporality*

synthesis, the past and future are seen as processes that contract in and function as dimensions of that present. They present "repetitions of instants," bleeding into each other (70). In "contrast, from the point of view of the reproduction involved in memory" it is the past that we see as central, and the present and future that become dimensions of it (80). Habit is the "foundation" of time that "constitutes the life of the living present," says Deleuze, and "everything depends upon a foundation" (79–80). If habit is time's foundation then memory "grounds" it and lets us conceive of time's passage (79). Memory depends on habit, but it is memory that "constitutes the being of the past" (80). We don't need to go over Bergson's understanding of duration again here. What we can say is that it is at this second passive synthesis that the endurance of memory in the present and future interjects itself. In treating memory as primary, Bergson gives us an account of time wherein both the passing present and the expected future are functions of memory and the influence of the whole past (the "pure past" – the past as such). Our past memories create the conditions and experiential framework for us that allow any particular passing present to be incorporated into our experience. Adding on to this, Deleuze appeals to Proust (who "picks up the baton from Bergson") who reminds us of the further importance of "reminiscence." Reminiscence is the ability of memory to not only provide the possibility of experiencing the present or projecting into the future, but to actively intrude upon and fill up our awareness in the present (84–85).

It is with the third synthesis of time that Deleuze goes beyond the idea of passive synthesis.[57] Rather than identifying a domain of active synthesis as Kant did with his attempt to preserve our moral autonomy by appealing to an atemporal transcendental dimension that could unify individual subjects, Deleuze breaks the subject down entirely. Based largely on Kant and on Nietzsche's eternal return, the third synthesis stands in clearer contrast with Bergsonian duration and as Widder argues, "fractures both time and the self that exists within it" (2012, 141). The third synthesis treats the future as central, and the past and present as dimensions of it, but this is not a teleological end point in an arc of progress. It is the future as a terminal end point of all things, and the power of the principle of the eternal return (and the idea of difference) as a force for dissolution lying underneath all unities and certainties.

Deleuze opens his discussion of the dissolution of the subject by addressing Kant's critique of Descartes' Cogito. The Cartesian Cogito depends upon the existence of an "undetermined" element of the self, which ultimately rests on the assumption that the continuous creative force of God will sustain our individual unity over time (Deleuze 1994, 86). In order for there to be an "I think" that is indicative of a foundational self that one can believe in, there must be an "I am" that is undetermined by alien causal forces. It is by introducing time as a condition for the possibility of experience that Kant undermines the spontaneous will of the Cartesian Cogito (85). In doing so,

> The consequences of this are extreme: my undetermined existence can be determined only within time as the existence of a phenomenon, of a passive, receptive phenomenal subject appearing within time. As a result, the

Time and Temporality   41

spontaneity of which I am conscious in the "I think" cannot be understood as the attribute of a substantial and spontaneous being, but only as the affection of a passive self which experiences its own thought – its own intelligence, that by virtue of which it can say I – being exercised in it and upon it, but not by it.

(86)

In doing so, Kant "fractures" the self entirely, "from one end to the other" (ibid.). We are left as a creature that thinks about itself, imagines itself, but the "I" is fractured by being a product of forces beyond us. Even when we think we are exercising will, that we are a single, autonomous, free self, we know this to be false by virtue of our relationship to time itself. Kant attempts to unify the self in response to this (as we discussed earlier), but the initial damage is done. From here, Deleuze takes us on a wide arc through Nietzsche, Freud, Proust, Borges, and Kierkegaard, among others. It is Nietzsche's eternal return, though, that best reinforces what Deleuze identifies as significant in Kant's fracturing of the self. The eternal return entails the production of difference and newness, not sporadically, but constantly. It is the concept Deleuze uses to understand the force of time as change in itself. Out of this difference, we produce tenuous unities, convergences, and representations, and posit the existence of homogeneities and endurance. On these we build systems, societies, and our very sense of a unified self, but "the same and the similar are only an effect of the operation of systems subject to eternal return. By this means, an identity would be found to be necessarily projected, or rather retrojected, on to the originary difference" (126). These solidities and continuities are "fictions engendered by the eternal return" in the sense of their being constructs built upon the shifting sands of time's force of change (ibid.). The eternal return is our future, then, but it is the future as the haunting inevitability of difference that threatens and guarantees the end of continuities. This third synthesis treats the "present [as] no more than an actor, an author, an agent destined to be effaced; while the past is no more than a condition operating by default," and the future itself represents the always-lurking "final end of time," referring to the time projections, shelters, and continuities we try to build out of this world (94).

Contrary to attempts by critics[58] to reduce these syntheses to a singular or overarching concept or logic of time under which they can all be contained, Deleuze's three syntheses should be understood as irreducible. As Williams argues, this gives us an account of time that is inherently multiple, and any attempt to reduce that multiplicity will transform the meaning of each of time's syntheses (2011, 3–4). For Deleuze

Time is radically fragmentary; as are those processes making and made by time. Much as things exist as time-makers, they also exist as made by fractured and dislocated times, themselves made by other processes. Time and process coexist like reflections in a hall of broken mirrors, offering multiple perspectives to follow and recreate, but never a full image.

(Williams 2011, 51)

42   *Time and Temporality*

Deleuze argues that each synthesis of time depends upon and presupposes the others. If we wish to provide a more comprehensive understanding of the relationship between the production of times and the very different processes which fuel that production, it is insufficient to only look at one of time's syntheses. Even if we look at all of the syntheses, the disjointed, messy, and fractured nature of time prevents any possible overarching and total account. We can map habituating processes for individuals and groups, and trace the temporal projections they develop through accumulated memory, but disruption and discontinuities are themselves a part of this picture. Each depends upon the others, but it is a result of the intrinsically disjointed nature of time (epitomized by the third synthesis) that they cannot give us a unitary account. This is not to say that people do not try to provide this account. Our practical capacity to maintain a sense of temporal unity and project temporalities depends upon masking, forgetting, and ignoring these disjointed elements of our experience of time. As we will see later, modern theorists of political obligation also depend upon the creation of relatively cohesive, temporally unified, and stable representations of political subjects and their corresponding political orders in order to develop the temporal projections required to ground their conceptualizations of political obligation.

Finally, we will also use Deleuze with Bergson, because Deleuze develops a more substantial theory of power and politics. While Bergson claims that we engage in processes of spatialization and adopt a practical viewpoint in order to meet the demands and "requirements of social life," he does not dwell for long on the foundations or formation of those requirements, nor the means by which people become bound up within such webs of necessity. Bergson demonstrates an understanding that power can operate at the level of perception, and that spatialization can function as a form of habituation and discipline. He does not, however, thoroughly develop these more implicit insights in his work, and ultimately leans more heavily upon the metaphysical device of his *élan vital* for his mature political writings. Rather than to Bergson, then, Deleuze's theory of power is principally indebted to Nietzsche, with inspiration also drawn from Spinoza. It is his incorporation of Nietzsche that allows him to develop a more complex theory of power as operating across a social field, and go beyond more conventional conceptualizations which portray power as projected solely from a center-outward, or as a juridically-bound product of sanctioned institutions, or of moral authority.

For Nietzsche, the entire world is comprised of "dynamic quanta, in a relation of tension to all other quanta" rather than simple, discrete atomic units (Nietzsche 1968, par. 635). With each quantum acting and reacting on others through both opposition and collaboration, a field of dynamic force relations is generated, with multiple dispersed clusters and sources. This understanding of force carries into his understanding of the relations between living beings as well. Force relations are thus a ubiquitous dimension of all relations, driven by an entity's "will to power" alongside the will to power of other entities.[59] One significant implication of this account of force relations is that power – understood as the ability to do, be, and create – is fundamentally relational, rather than something that is simply intrinsic, aggregated, or possessed (Deleuze 1983, 40).

It is always composed of irreducible "active" and "reactive" forces of domination and subordination that nevertheless produce certain kinds of unities and forms – "bodies" (ibid.). As Paul Patton notes, Deleuze's appropriation of Nietzsche's concept of force does not entail any particular relationship to violence, simply construed. Rather,

> "force" should be understood, in abstraction from any determinate kind of action or interaction, to encompass all of the means by which bodies interact with one another.... Forces are the potentials for acting and being acted upon which constitute bodies as bodies of a particular kind.
>
> (Patton 2000, 52)

The bodies that are constituted are not simply individual human bodies.[60] Rather, they are "assemblages of particular kinds of force or capacity" (53), since "every relationship of force constitutes a body – whether it is chemical, biological, social or political. Any two forces, being unequal, constitute a body as soon as they enter into a relationship" (Deleuze 1983, 40, cited in Patton 2000, 53). The dominance of some interlocking combinations of forces over others (at both large and small scales) constitutes the bodies that populate our world, while larger and more durable patterns of domination and convergence for a particular array of forces undergird the major institutions and patterns of social relations that define conventional social and political life. As dynamic relationships, these generated combinations can be periodically disrupted and dislocated by subverting extant relations of dominance, disrupting their processes of reproduction, and generating new bodies through the creation of different patterns of force relations. From this understanding of power as dynamic force relations constituting bodies, combined with his conception of becoming, Deleuze develops a complex theory of "assemblages" and "machines" to account for the operations of power in both the social and wider world, and a method of "social cartography" to trace and map out those operations in practice.[61] We will elaborate on these concepts more fully in Chapter 2 when discussing the state, and Chapter 3 when discussing vertical time-binding.

Each of these developments helps provide a more supple view of the nature of temporality, especially as it intersects with questions and problems of political life. While Bergson does not negate the relevance of Deleuze, neither, however, does Deleuze's subsequent work render Bergson's obsolete. For our purposes here, they each provide useful contrasts and counterpoints with each other that should not be collapsed or reduced. Deleuze provides a poststructuralist-inspired restoration of Bergson that, quite simply, aligns with my own theoretical sympathies. Bergson, on the other hand, not only provided core theoretical tools that inspired Deleuze, but can also continue to provide a reminder of the significance of time as a dimension of analysis in attempts to theorize power and political life. While Deleuze arguably develops a far more sophisticated analysis of time and power, in his later works he undergoes a shift in emphasis towards theorizing in terms of space and territory, lines of flight, territorialization, nomadic war machines, striation, and social cartography. While the influence of his earlier

44 *Time and Temporality*

investigations into time are certainly evinced in these later spatial concepts, time as a distinct dimension through which power operates is clearly diminished in priority. It is when he develops his most explicitly political concepts that temporality moves to the relative theoretical background, producing what I consider to be an unfortunately underdeveloped connection between his earliest analyses of temporality and his later spatial analyses. This may have been a worthwhile shift on Deleuze's part, as he and Guattari used these concepts to clarify and articulate phenomena like the distribution and capture of populations and objects in state assemblages, or the means by which these processes of capture are destabilized along lines of flight, but it is by no means a shift that we must limit ourselves to. By keeping Bergson's earlier work present and in productive tension with Deleuze, I affirm the value and wish to restore the relative conceptual priority of temporality in our efforts to understand political obligation.

Bergson–Deleuze Exchanges

Appropriately enough, the relationship between Bergson's and Deleuze's thought is unique and multifaceted, as are recent attempts to make use of this relationship in new hybridized forms. There are several reasons for these attempts. Deleuze's key role in the re-popularization of Bergson in the second half of the twentieth century has strongly influenced Bergson's reception, and left its mark on the elements of Bergson's thought which were subsequently emphasized. Rather than the archetypal phenomenologist found in Merleau-Ponty's reading of Bergson, Deleuze's Bergson served as a proto-poststructuralist philosopher of difference. The Bergsonian revival that followed developed its own momentum, inspired both directly through Bergson and indirectly via Deleuze's reading and applications of Bergson's thought. The rhizomatic[62] nature of Deleuze's philosophical project and style of thinking coupled with his "buggering"[63] method of reading other philosophers has both facilitated and encouraged such re-examinations on a variety of topics.

The most explicit recent hybridization of Bergson and Deleuze is from Valentine Moulard-Leonard. In *Bergson–Deleuze Encounters* (2008), Moulard-Leonard traces the intellectual development of both Bergson's and Deleuze's thought in their respective contexts, while elaborating on both their unique and overlapping ideas. Throughout Moulard-Leonard weaves commentary on one into discussions of the other, teasing out what happens when they are held together at different points without reducing Bergson to a proto-Deleuze. Ultimately, she interprets both Bergson's metaphysical pragmatism and Deleuze's transcendental empiricism as instances (though not identical ones) of a shared "virtual empiricism," the purpose of which is to look past taken-for-granted appearances in the world, identify hidden processes, and give us a better understanding of reality and our encounter with it.

Alia Al-Saji (2004) also brings Deleuze and Bergson together in order to articulate a "Bergsonian-Deleuzian" theory of time that focuses especially on the role of memory in the constitution of our experience of time. While conventional representations of the past and present treat them as diachronic in relation to each other, Bergson and Deleuze adopt a synchronic view, wherein the past and present are coexistent and continuously co-created. By exploring the role of the "virtual image" in Bergson's philosophy, Al-Saji draws out the significance of this understanding of memory and time for the ways in which we understand the constitution of individual subjects, as well as the role an "intersubjective field of memory" plays in mediating and facilitating our relationship with others.

Hybrid readings and non-reductive convergences of Bergson and Deleuze have increasingly appeared in the last decade, and we need not go through them all here.[64] In effect, these hybridized creations developed through reverse readings, combinations, and reconsiderations – truly their own forms of buggering, as Deleuze would have it – have given shape to their own "monstrous offspring." They have created a non-reductive Deleuze-Bergson or Bergson-Deleuze for their own needs and questions, and provided openings for future experimental re-combinations. In the spirit of these recent efforts, this project will freely make use of the tools and methods offered by both Bergson and Deleuze without ignoring their pertinent differences or collapsing one into the other. It will also occasionally draw from those who owe one or both of them an inspirational debt in their own attempts to come to terms with time in relation to lived experience and political life.

How To Use These Ideas Here?

The theoretical trove offered by Bergson and Deleuze contains profound and critical insights into the nature of time and temporality, much of which goes beyond the purview of this work.[65] Of the pertinent elements of their work already discussed, how are we supposed to put them to productive use for an analysis of political obligation? What, in broad strokes, does incorporating this understanding of the temporal allow us to do that would otherwise remain hidden, or at least obscured?

The most important thing this approach provides is a method for what Suzanne Guerlac refers to as "thinking in time" (2006, 2). By cultivating time-consciousness, we can be sensitive to the "obsession with space" that has historically dominated Western philosophy (3). We cannot dispense with spatialization as such, but neither do we have to take any given spatial construct for granted. Thinking in time lets us lay bare the changes, discontinuities, and heterogeneity that are at work behind all claims to stability, continuity, and sameness. It lets us recognize the various and mutable forms of temporal projection that direct and define our lives, such as the creation of shared memories, a common present, a particular arc of future goals or progress, and one's purpose and place within this. It can also help us reconsider the ways in which and the reasons why these perceptions of stability, division, and temporal direction are created, and consequently how new or alternative creations could be pursued.

By thinking in time, Bergson and Deleuze also give us a vitally important corresponding view of subjectivity that accommodates a recognition of temporality, change, and heterogeneity. This will be especially important as a backdrop for thinking about the limits and problems associated with the image of

46   *Time and Temporality*

humanity and individual subjects provided by most contemporary discussants in modern political obligation literature. In both Bergson and Deleuze, we find an ontology of the subject that is distinctly inspired by process philosophy. Rather than an image of a static or given self with more or less fixed characteristics moving through time, we get an image of ourselves as "dissolved" and emergent. As Deleuze observes in Chapter 2 of *Difference and Repetition*, we are "larval subjects"; an irreducibly complex and precarious contraction of multiple actively and passively synthesized processes, habits, emotions, ideas, and bodily parts and sensation, always in a process of becoming, yet never achieving a secure stasis. "The self," he goes on to say, "does not undergo modifications, but is itself a modification" (Deleuze 1994, 78–79).

Justus Buchler offers a similar account of this processual understanding of ourselves, which he refers to as a "summed-up-self-in-process" (1979, 6). For Buchler, we "proceive" and have a "proceptive direction," moving and being inflected *in* the world (with an indefinite, permeable boundary between self and world) as a precarious complex of shifting, tenuously convergent processes *of* the world. We are a contingent "accumulating whole" that is ever-emerging, and are constituted (as groups and particular individuals) through our continuously revised history of encounters with shifting fields of asymmetrical power relations, institutions, and discourses, the material facts and forces of the wider universe, and no less importantly, through the unique moments which provide all of the defining details of a life (6–11). It is only in our reflective moments that a snapshot of a fragment of ourselves-in-process can be taken, and our self-images, commitments, identities, and life purposes can be crystallized to act as a summation of who we ostensibly are.

While not identical to each other (or Buchler), both Bergson and Deleuze (and Buchler) give us a view of subjectivity that is multiplicitous rather than straightforwardly unitary. Rather than rationally, endogenously ordered wholes, we are a complex confluence of disparately connected and intersecting processes and parts, containing irreconcilable contradictions. The unities we consciously and unconsciously attempt to construct out of this are real, in the sense that they certainly do manifest themselves in our experience, and concretely shape the direction (and our understanding) of our lives. They are also, however, tenuously maintained fictions sustained by psychological insecurity, biological necessity, and social convention, and lacking any overarching or deep unity as in Kant's transcendental ego.

By learning to think in time and recognizing multiplicity as a constitutive element of our subjectivity, we can begin to analyze time as it is lived. This means, in part, thinking about the complex ways that individuals and societies practically react to, mask, and structure time. It also entails inquiry into the manner in which those structurations are perceived. Following Deleuze's third identified rule of Bergson's method of intuition, analyzing time ultimately demands searching for the movement of time behind those spatialized stand-ins. Where is there difference and change being masked by an apparent unity and homogeneity? What social machines are operative behind an official representation? What are the effective political functions of different perceived projections

Time and Temporality 47

and shapes of time? Taken altogether, these ideas enable us to develop a critical analysis of political obligation by incorporating temporality as a dimension of investigation. This will allow us to re-trace the processes by which political obligation claims are constructed and sustained, and more specifically the manner in which they rely on subtle forms of temporal structuration in order for their theories to be comprehensible at all.

Other theorists or combinations of theorists could have potentially provided useful alternative frameworks for this project. Bergson has been called philosophy's "crown prince who never became king," and for good reason (Hoy 2009, 116). While he only briefly enjoyed the spotlight at the end of the nineteenth and beginning of the twentieth century, his influence on subsequent philosophy has been widespread. William James, Alfred North Whitehead, Martin Heidegger, Maurice Merleau-Ponty, Jean Paul Sartre, and of course, Deleuze and much of subsequent poststructuralism has felt his influence. Any number of offshoot formal and informal "Bergsonisms" – perhaps as filtered through Merleau-Ponty's phenomenology, or through James' pragmatism – could provide us with a distinct and potentially useful take on temporality and political obligation, though they would likely entail a somewhat different constellation of values and concerns as a result.

This project casts a wide net, and consequently we will not be able to do justice to all of the many different, detailed expressions and appeals of political obligation theorists. Nor will we be able to address all of the complex, diffuse, and radically particular ways that institutions, cultural conventions, political discourses, and unexpected irruptions of happenstance and newness constitute and modify actual perceptions of political obligation in groups and individuals. Engaging more fully with either of these would be worthy and valuable extensions of the project at hand. At present, our scope will be limited to that of analyzing and critiquing the prevailing discourse on theories of political obligation, and proposing an alternative theoretical framework that gives temporality a central place. We will primarily focus on the literature of formal academic political obligation theorists, but given the significance and ubiquity of many of their foundational concepts to modern liberal democratic thought, institutions, and culture, it is important to remember their wider political consequences.

Notes

1 This role of expectation in shaping perceptions of death and one's life is distinct, even if not wholly separate, from our actually proximity to death at any particular moment.

2   Without death there would be neither sex nor reproduction, no fatherhood or motherhood, no growing up, no maturation, no urgent call for love or intimacy or warm desire, and little enough of the strivings and ambitions and of the natural groupings that are the prime bonds of any society.... Without death, therefore, there would be no renewal in the world of life, no surge of disturbing energies, no fresh approaches to old problems, no new goals.... Without death the great evolutionary adventure could never have begun, and life itself would have remained unrevealed.... Why should anyone seek to redeem the time when there

48   Time and Temporality

can be no threat? Why should there be any urgency to achieve when there is an ocean of time ahead? What significance could there be in action were there an endless future in which to act?

(MacIver 1962, 98–99)

3 The ancient Sophists provide an early counterpoint to the Platonic hitching of thought with truth, and represent an alternative path not widely taken up in the history of philosophy until Nietzsche.

4 In *The World and the Individual* (1900), Royce contrasts the "wilderness" with the "city" as both geographical and mental spaces. As mental spaces, the city represents all of the received norms, everyday wisdom, and taken for granted prejudices that make social life possible. The wilderness is a mental place of retreat and reflection where one ventures in order to exercise doubt and question the givens of the city (and for Royce, attempt to rethink and strengthen the rational foundations for community).

5 This is not a universally recognized distinction, a fact that has created its own theoretical conundrums.

6 "Experience" can be a problematic word. We should be cautious here not to exclusively emphasize the role of mental and high cognition in talking about this intersection between time and our lives. While important, the role, for example, of habituation in shaping the unconscious and the body, and the consequences of this for affecting cognition, or in constraining possible futures, or bearing the marks of the past in the present is also an important temporal concern for "lived time."

7 Also adorning his tombstone, Kant expresses his wonder and admiration at the starry heavens above and "the moral law within" in the conclusion to his *Critique of Practical Reason* (2015, 129). This pairing of the universal and the individual is a powerfully simple image of his overarching philosophical project to bring the two into harmony.

8 Even scientific measurements of universal time are dependent upon aspects of temporality in order to make the world legible for such endeavors.

9 See, for instance, Kevin Birth's *Objects of Time: How Things Shape Temporality* (2012).

10 Despite the widespread convention and even value of its use, the notion of the "premodern" as a broad swathe of time and peoples – even societies presently existing – defined by an overall separation and dislocation from modernity is itself a product of a distinctly modern interpretation of temporality.

11 See Tenzin and Hopkins (1985).

12   The conviction that the universe and each of the wholes composing it have a cyclical nature, undergoing alterations, so dominated [Chinese] thought that the idea of succession was always subordinated to that of interdependence. Thus retrospective explanations were not felt to involve any difficulty. "Such and such a lord, in his lifetime, was not able to obtain the hegemony, because, after his death, human victims were sacrificed to him." Both facts were simply part of one timeless pattern.

(Needham and Wang 1956, 289)

13 Only the Heroic Age was a clear improvement over the prior age.

14 Ovid, the Roman poet, provides a similar account with the same metals in *Metamorphoses*, only omitting the Heroic Age.

15 The alternative is to let the future carry us along wherever it will, which Heidegger considers to be an "inauthentic" way of living.

16 None of this is to say that Bergson did not respect scientific inquiry, reason, or the significance of abstractly ordering our world for the purposes of understanding and practical life. Bergson was himself studying to be a mathematician before becoming a philosopher, and stayed abreast of scientific developments for much of his life, incorporating them regularly into his philosophical works. For more on Bergson's relationship to science, see Milič Čapek's *Bergson and Modern Physics* (1971).

Time and Temporality 49

17 Chapter 2 of *Time and Free Will* (2001) contains Bergson's most thorough discussion of duration and intuition.

18 The appeal to a common sense or reasonableness is a very common means of justifying the parameters of inclusion and exclusion of particular arguments and conclusions within modern political obligation theory. We will discuss this more in Chapter 2.

19   We can understand that material objects, being exterior to one another and to ourselves, derive both exteriorities from the homogeneity of a medium which inserts intervals between them and sets off their outlines: but states of consciousness, even when successive, permeate one another.

(Bergson 2001, 98)

Treating time as a homogeneous medium thus makes it impossible to appreciate the difference between actually lived sensory experience, and our rationalizations and *post hoc* distinctions imposed upon those experiences through categorization and language.

20 The relationship between experience and truth becomes more complicated within Bergson's framework. Concepts and distinctions are developed as practical responses to problems in order to facilitate action, rather than carrying either a perfect or imperfect reflection of truth. They are at the same time less than the Real by virtue of being reductive representations, and more than it, by virtue of containing the mental act entailed by the spatialization being imposed on duration.

21   We must thus distinguish between the perception of extensity and the conception of space: they are no doubt implied in one another, but, the higher we rise in the scale of intelligent beings, the more clearly do we meet with the independent idea of a homogeneous space.

(Bergson 2001, 96)

22 Bergson provides a variety of examples to illustrate this process. One example, based on Bergson's own experiences studying mathematics, is the process by which we hold numbers together when treating them as distinct pieces of formulae. Another example he asks us to consider is that of a flock of sheep. Insofar as we imagine each of the particular sheep as consisting of part of the set, we imagine them, in spite of their radical individual uniqueness, to share a fundamental homogeneous sameness as sheep of this set. We draw out what we consider to be similarities and hold each sheep together in our mind, suppressing the differences for the practical expedient of perceiving them together as one set.

23 The alternative is an inexpressible flow of experience without significance or unity, an impossible condition to maintain for the sustenance of active life.

24 "We might say, strangely enough, that duration would remain purely intuitive, in the ordinary sense of the word, if intuition – in the properly Bergsonian sense – were not there as a method" (Deleuze 1991, 14).

25 One example of a nonexistent problem that Deleuze points to is the concept of "disorder." Disorder is commonly thought of as an empty negation of a given order, and thus as something "less" than order. The perceived "problem" of establishing order depends on this assumption. However, the concept of disorder actually presupposes and contains an idea of order, the act of negation of that idea, *as well as* the motive for the act of negation. "The idea of disorder appears when, instead of seeing that there are two or more irreducible orders ... we retain only a general idea of order that we confine ourselves to opposing to disorder" (Deleuze 1991, 19).

26 One example of a badly analyzed composite would be the general idea of order implied in the previous footnote that makes the creation of the nonexistent problem of disorder possible. Another example would be the general conflation of time with space in Kantian thought, in spite of their difference in kind.

27 Bergson and Deleuze use the phrase "tending" or "tends to" here when talking about duration not as a suggestion that sometimes the character of duration and space switch

50 *Time and Temporality*

places, but to reinforce the understanding that duration is fundamentally processual, and can only "tend," rather than "be" in any stable sense.

28 Even simultaneity is a difficult term to use here, because it is so frequently thought of in terms of two objects existing within the same present. Bergson wants to challenge the way in which we think about the present, and what makes it distinct from the past and future.

29 At least, for those of us non-Trobriand Islanders who have been deeply habituated to modern Western conceptions of how time is partitioned.

30 This lack of a substantially retained past at work in building their lived present is why infants live only "in the moment," in probably the closest thing we ever experience to the idealized mathematical pure present.

31 Bergson heavily emphasizes the relationship between our physical embodiment, action, and our perception of the present. He says that "my body is a centre of action" (2004, 178) and that the present is "that which interests me, which lives for me, and, in a word, that which summons me to action" (176).

32 Given the circuit-like process we described, Bergson still wants to keep our imagination and projection of the future closely connected with our past perception.

33 It is this dichotomy that prompts Bergson to develop his famous memory cone diagrams (2004, 197; 211). In the diagrams, there is an upside-down cone, with the bottom point intersecting a plane. The plane represents one's "actual representation of the universe" (196). The point intersecting the plane represents one's restricted awareness to the here and now, and at its most extreme, to one's bodily operations alone. The wide base of the cone represents the whole accumulation of one's past memories, and the highest level of reflective abstraction. If we picture this cone moving along the plane as we move through life, we can think of the different ways in which we move up and down the cone in our regular interactions with the world, with these telescopic movements themselves contributing to the transformation of our representation and account of ourselves and the world.

34 Unamuno attempted to stabilize his conventional self and re-establish a cultural time perspective by making a leap of faith, not unlike Kierkegaard's.

35 Unamuno's agonized doubting attempted to do just this.

36 They overlap, but one of Deleuze's other principal targets of reaction within this context was the totalizing focus within the university system upon doing "history of philosophy" if one wished to do philosophy at all. This restricted the kind of "creative" work one could do to that of close readings of classic philosophical texts. See especially Daniel Smith's contextualization of this reaction and commentary upon Deleuze's reaction to Hegel in essay four of his *Essays on Deleuze* (2012).

37 It is in this early period, before and alongside his first "original" works, that Deleuze wrote his commentaries on Hume, Nietzsche, Kant, Proust, Bergson, and Spinoza, among others.

38 As Wendy Brown characterizes untimeliness:

> To insist on the value of untimely political critique is not, then, to refuse the problem of time or timing in politics but rather to contest settled accounts of what time it is, what the times are, and what political tempo and temporality we should hew to political life. *Untimeliness deployed as an effective intellectual and political strategy*, far from being a gesture of indifference to time, is a bid to reset time.
>
> (Brown 2005, 4)

39 In the preface to the English translation of *Difference and Repetition*, Deleuze makes a distinction between his earlier studies of and commentaries on individual philosophers, and his first attempts to really "do philosophy" (1994, xv).

40 "In either case, difference remains subordinated to identity, reduced to the negative, incarcerated within similitude and analogy" (Deleuze 1994, 50).

41 See Chapter 1 of *Difference and Repetition* for Deleuze's extended discussion of difference in itself.

Time and Temporality   51

42   Representation is a site of transcendental illusion. This illusion comes in several forms, four interrelated forms which correspond particularly to thought, sensibility, the Idea and being. In effect, thought is covered over by an "image" made up of postulates which distort both its operation and its genesis.

(Deleuze 1994, 265)

43   Though as we will see shortly, Deleuze has to go beyond Bergson to complete his conception of difference.

44   Their conjunction involves both the formation of concrete processes and systems in the world, and the conscious or (more likely) unconscious cognitive attribution of unity in the world.

45   Proust provides a powerful literary exploration of the human experience of time in his *In Search of Lost Time*, though it is not necessary for us to delve into his work here. In Proust, Deleuze finds a conception of thought and change (and their relationship to each other) that is quite different from Bergson's duration, with change appearing instead like "a defection, a race to the grave," marked by steady change, but also discontinuities, obliterations, and random re-emergences of the past into the present (Deleuze 2000, 18). The Proustian truth that Deleuze finds is less about seeking an accord between knowledge and reality, and more about the production of concepts that unground taken-for-granted perceptions of thought. For further comparison, see Moulard-Leonard (2008).

46   In *The Gay Science* (1974) Nietzsche presents the eternal return through a story:

What, if some day or night a demon were to steal after you into your loneliest loneliness and say to you: "This life as you now live it and have lived it, you will have to live once more and innumerable times more." ... Would you not throw yourself down and gnash your teeth and curse the demon who spoke thus? Or have you once experienced a tremendous moment when you would have answered him: "You are a god and never have I heard anything more divine."

(§341)

47   Deleuze's argument for this is rather nuanced, but he depends on the observation that Nietzsche wants to think about the world in terms of becoming, of change as the default, and of being as something produced (but never stable). The consequence of this (which we won't be able to explain fully here) for Nietzsche is that the past is infinite, and that the future has no ultimate end point. Deleuze rejects the endless "cyclical" interpretation of the eternal return precisely because it suggests the existence of an end point, and thus a contained, discrete existence that can be reproduced. If it did not have an end point, how could "the same" with presumed boundaries ever return? (Deleuze 1983, 47).

48   See especially Deleuze (1994, 54–58):

eternal return does not appear second or come after, but is already present in every metamorphosis.... Eternal return relates to a world of differences implicated one in the other, to a complicated, properly chaotic world *without identity....* The ultimate element of repetition is the disparate [*dispars*], which stands opposed to the identity of representation.

(57)

49   Rather than Bergson's own use of the term, which functions more as a synonym for duration. We will see why this difference matters shortly.

50   For an experiment in thinking about agency, complexity, and global systems by way of this understanding of becoming and temporality, see William E. Connolly's *A World of Becoming* (2011).

51   Which is why Deleuze limits Bergson to his "second synthesis" of time, and uses Nietzsche to develop his third synthesis.

52   In developing these syntheses, Deleuze is drawing a parallel to Kant's notion of "synthesis" as the means by which sensory input is processed and incorporated into experience.

52 *Time and Temporality*

53 Deleuze actually develops two separate vocabularies for his philosophy of time, which can lead to some confusion. In *Difference and Repetition*, Deleuze frames time in terms of the three syntheses. In *Logic of Sense* (1990), Deleuze instead frames time with the two concepts of "Chronos" and "Aion." While this might appear problematic at first glance, and as if Deleuze is abandoning his earlier theories, the shift is not as dramatic as one might think. I concur with James Williams who argues that the same distinct sets of relationships between the past, present, and future can be found in the relationship between Chronos and Aion as in the three syntheses, and that there is an "extraordinary consistency" between the two approaches (2011, 138; 154). The shift to the new terminology makes sense in the context of *Logic of Sense* given Deleuze's focused considerations of classical Stoic cosmology and ethics, which is the original source of the terms, and his concern for different problems alongside time, such as the nature of being wounded. In order to avoid confusion and the use of effectively redundant terms, I will focus solely on Deleuze's three syntheses approach to time. Hopefully, this will make his complex philosophy of time, as well as my appropriation of elements of it, a bit more manageable.

54 Deleuze does say in discussing the first synthesis that "the present alone exists," but it exists as an extended "living present" that contains the past and future within it (1994, 76).

55 Deleuze is providing his connection here between his ontology of the world and of the constitution of subjectivity, and his philosophy of time. This is necessary since, like Bergson, he views time and process as intimately intertwined.

56 Deleuze is not denying material causality as such here. He is contesting linear images of causality that deny any space for novelty and the unexpected.

57 Faulkner (2006) refers to all three syntheses of time as "passive," explaining that they are passive because they are beyond an individual's will or effective control. As noted by Widder (2008, 88), however, it is only the first two syntheses that Deleuze explicitly refers to as passive, while the third (as the virtual looming promise of dissolution) resists being classified as either.

58 See Badiou (2000); Hallward (2006).

59 Deleuze argues that Nietzsche's will to power is not simply a "power hungry" psychological mindset or impetus, as might be attributed to a politician. It is instead a virtual organizing and directive "principle" within a given relationship of forces (Deleuze 1983, 50). This kind of principle is not an overarching, Hegelian teleology, pushing the world along and attempting to "suppress chance" (53). Rather, it is an operative logic and process of unfolding, immanent within and limited to the arranged patterns and conditions of a particular body of force relations. It is "the element from which derive both the quantitative difference of related forces and the quality that devolves into each force in this relation" (50).

60 Although they do include human bodies, Deleuze's reading of Nietzsche was highly influential for Foucault's own development of the concept of "discipline," as developed in his *Discipline and Punish* (Foucault 1995).

61 As demonstrated creatively by Deleuze-inspired theorists like Manuel De Landa, Deleuze's concept of assemblages does not presuppose anything particularly central about humanity or life. It not only doesn't require the maintenance of the kind of Man-Nature distinction that defines much of modern philosophy, but actively challenges the coherence of such a division when engaging in social and political theory and analysis.

62 According to Deleuze and Guattari, "arborescent" thought emphasizes representation, identity, unity, rigid stratification, binary logic, stability, and hard distinction – it is a tree with clear roots, a rigid trunk, and clearly delineated branches. It is exemplified by the Platonic tradition. Rhizomatic or "nomad" thought is its counterpart, and celebrates the creation of a variety of connections across disparate areas of life, multiple nodes of ideas rather than a unitary foundation, heterogeneity, and remaining open to transformation.

Time and Temporality 53

63   I suppose the main way I coped with it at the time was to see the history of philosophy as a sort of buggery or (it comes to the same thing) immaculate conception. I saw myself as taking an author from behind and giving him a child that would be his own offspring, yet monstrous. It was really important for it to be his own child, because the author had to actually say all that I had him saying. But the child was bound to be monstrous too, because it resulted from all sorts of shifting, slipping, dislocations, and hidden emissions that I really enjoyed.

(Deleuze 1995, 6)

64 Further examples: Boundas (1996); Grosz (2005); Hodges (2008); Lefebvre (2008).

65 Both Bergson and Deleuze's work on temporality influenced a variety of different artistic movements. Bergson's *Creative Evolution* (1920) influenced a variety of early twentieth century French avant-garde artists, while Deleuze's *Cinema* books (1986; 1989) contain both his later reappraisals of Bergson's ideas on temporality and one of the first real efforts at developing a comprehensive philosophy of cinema. While there is overlap between these expressions of their temporal philosophies, they are not central for the problems we will be dealing with here. All of the significant features of Deleuze's philosophy of time can be found in his previous works, and arguably in a clearer form, while Bergson's later work, as mentioned previously, contains an undesirable emphasis on the role of "life" as a unifying force behind change that distracts from his early expressions of duration and intuition.

References

Al-Saji, Alia. 2004. "The Memory of Another Past: Bergson, Deleuze and a New Theory of Time." *Continental Philosophy Review* 37 (2): 203–239.

Anderson, Benedict. 1991. *Imagined Communities: Reflections on the Origin and Spread of Nationalism.* Revised Edition. New York: Verso.

Bachelard, Gaston. 2000. *The Dialectic of Duration.* Translated by Mary McAllester Jones. Manchester: Clinamen Press.

Badiou, Alain. 2000. *Deleuze: The Clamor of Being.* Translated by Louise Burchill. Minneapolis: University of Minnesota Press.

Benjamin, Walter. 1969. *Illuminations.* Edited by Hannah Arendt. New York: Schocken.

Bergson, Henri. 1920. *Creative Evolution.* New York: The Macmillan Company.

Bergson, Henri. 2001. *Time and Free Will: An Essay on the Immediate Data of Consciousness.* Mineola, NY: Dover.

Bergson, Henri. 2004. *Matter and Memory.* Mineola, NY: Dover.

Birth, Kevin. 2012. *Objects of Time: How Things Shape Temporality.* New York: Palgrave Macmillan.

Bodde, Derk. 1991. *Chinese Thought, Society, and Science: The Intellectual and Social Background of Science and Technology in Pre-Modern China.* Honolulu: University of Hawaii Press.

Boundas, Constantin V. 1996. "Deleuze-Bergson: An Ontology of the Virtual." In *Deleuze: A Critical Reader,* edited by Paul Patton. Oxford: Basil Blackwell.

Bourdieu, Pierre. 1992. *The Logic of Practice.* Stanford, CA: Stanford University Press.

Bourdieu, Pierre. 2000. *Pascalian Meditations.* Stanford, CA: Stanford University Press.

Brown, Wendy. 2005. *Edgework: Critical Essays on Knowledge and Power.* Princeton, NJ: Princeton University Press.

Bryant, Levi R. 2009. "Review of David Couzens Hoy, *The Time of Our Lives: A Critical History of Temporality.*" *Notre Dame Philosophical Reviews* 2009 (9). Available at: https://ndpr.nd.edu/news/24162-the-time-of-our-lives-a-critical-history-of-temporality/.

54 *Time and Temporality*

Buchler, Justus. 1979. *Toward a General Theory of Human Judgment*. Second Revised Edition. Mineola, NY: Dover.

Čapek, Milič. 1971. *Bergson and Modern Physics*. Dordrecht: D. Reidel Publishing Company.

Connolly, William E. 2011. *A World of Becoming*. Durham, NC: Duke University Press.

Deleuze, Gilles. 1983. *Nietzsche and Philosophy*. Translated by Hugh Tomlinson. New York: Columbia University Press.

Deleuze, Gilles. 1986. *Cinema 1: The Movement-Image*. Minneapolis: University of Minnesota Press.

Deleuze, Gilles. 1989. *Cinema 2: The Time-Image*. Minneapolis: University of Minnesota Press.

Deleuze, Gilles. 1990. *The Logic of Sense*. New York: Columbia University Press.

Deleuze, Gilles. 1991. *Bergsonism*. Translated by Hugh Tomlinson and Barbara Habberjam. New York: Zone Books.

Deleuze, Gilles. 1994. *Difference and Repetition*. New York: Columbia University Press.

Deleuze, Gilles. 1995. *Negotiations: 1972–1990*. Translated by Martin Joughin. New York: Columbia University Press.

Deleuze, Gilles. 2000. *Proust and Signs*. Minneapolis: University of Minnesota Press.

Derrida, Jacques. 1999. "Marx & Sons." In *Ghostly Demarcations: A Symposium on Jacques Derrida's Specters of Marx*, edited by Michael Sprinker. New York: Verso.

Faulkner, Keith W. 2006. *Deleuze and the Three Syntheses of Time*. New York: Peter Lang.

Foucault, Michel. 1995. *Discipline and Punish: The Birth of the Prison*. New York: Vintage Books.

Grosz, Elizabeth. 2005. "Bergson, Deleuze and the Becoming of Unbecoming." *Parallax* 11 (2): 4–13.

Guerlac, Suzanne. 2006. *Thinking In Time: An Introduction to Henri Bergson*. Ithaca, NY: Cornell University Press.

Hallward, Peter. 2006. *Out of This World: Deleuze and the Philosophy of Creation*. London: Verso.

Hawking, Stephen. 1998. *A Brief History of Time*. New York: Bantam.

Heidegger, Martin. 2010. *Being and Time*. Translated by Joan Stambaugh. Albany, NY: State University of New York Press.

Hesiod. 2006. *Theogony; and Works and Days*. Translated by Catherine Schlegel and Henry Weinfield. Ann Arbor: University of Michigan Press.

Hodges, Matt. 2008. "Rethinking Time's Arrow: Bergson, Deleuze and the Anthropology of Time." *Anthropological Theory* 8 (4): 399–429.

Hoy, David Couzens. 2009. *The Time of Our Lives: A Critical History of Temporality*. Cambridge, MA: The MIT Press.

Kant, Immanuel. 1996. *Critique of Pure Reason*. Translated by Werner Pluhar. Indiancreativeapolis: Hackett.

Kant, Immanuel. 2015. *Critique of Practical Reason*. Cambridge: Cambridge University Press.

Koselleck, Reinhart. 2004. *Futures Past: On the Semantics of Historical Time*. Translated by Keith Tribe. New York: Columbia University Press.

Lee, Dorothy. 1950. "Lineal and Nonlineal Codifications of Reality." *Psychosomatic Medicine* 12 (2): 89–97.

Lefebvre, Alexandre. 2008. *The Image of Law: Deleuze, Bergson, Spinoza*. Stanford, CA: Stanford University Press.

Time and Temporality 55

MacIver, R.M. 1962. *The Challenge of the Passing Years: My Encounter With Time*. New York: Pocket Books, Inc.

Moulard-Leonard, Valentine. 2008. *Bergson–Deleuze Encounters: Transcendental Experience and the Thought of the Virtual*. Albany, NY: State University of New York Press.

Needham, Joseph, and Ling Wang. 1956. *Science and Civilization in China: History of Scientific Thought, Vol. 2*. Cambridge: Cambridge University Press.

Nietzsche, Friedrich. 1968. *The Will to Power*. Translated by Walter Kaufmann and R.J. Hollingdale. London: Weidenfeld and Nicholson.

Nietzsche, Friedrich. 1974. *The Gay Science*. Translated by Walter Kaufmann. New York: Vintage Books.

Patton, Paul. 2000. *Deleuze and the Political*. New York: Routledge.

Rosen, Ralph M. 2004. "Ancient Time Across Time." In *Time and Temporality in the Ancient World*. Philadelphia, PA: University of Pennsylvania Museum of Archaeology and Anthropology.

Royce, Josiah. 1900. *The World and the Individual*. New York: The Macmillan Company.

Smith, Daniel W. 2012. *Essays on Deleuze*. Edinburgh: Edinburgh University Press.

Stagoll, Cliff. 2010. "Becoming." In *The Deleuze Dictionary*, edited by Adrian Parr, revised edition, 25–27. Edinburgh: Edinburgh University Press.

Tenzin, Gyatso, and Jeffrey Hopkins. 1985. *Kalachakra Tantra: Rite of Initiation*. Somerville, MA: Wisdom Publications.

Unamuno, Miguel de. 1954. *Tragic Sense of Life*. Translated by J.E. Crawford Flitch. New York: Dover.

Weinstein, Michael A. 1979. *Structure of Human Life: A Vitalist Ontology*. New York: New York University Press.

Widder, Nathan. 2008. *Reflections on Time and Politics*. University Park, PA: Pennsylvania State University Press.

Widder, Nathan. 2012. "Deleuze on Bergsonian Duration and Nietzsche's Eternal Return." In *Time and History in Deleuze and Serres*, edited by Bernd Herzogenrath. New York: Continuum.

Williams, James. 2011. *Gilles Deleuze's Philosophy of Time: A Critical Introduction and Guide*. Edinburgh: Edinburgh University Press.

Wood, David. 2007. *Time After Time*. Bloomington, IN: Indiana University Press.

Zerubavel, Eviatar. 2003. *Time Maps: Collective Memory and the Social Shape of the Past*. Chicago: University of Chicago Press.

2 Modernity and Political Obligation

One of the defining characteristics of humanity is our capacity to temporalize, to create structured times and pattern our lives in accordance with those creations. It seems unlikely that we are the only species that does this, but we are arguably the species that does so the most ubiquitously, and in the most complex fashion. For all of their ubiquity, they are nevertheless quite fragile enterprises. Individuals try to maintain their own synchronic projections of a past-present-future that anchors their perception of a unified self over time, and gives their life purpose and direction. Such autobiographical narratives may also be conjoined with the more immediate and possibly unexpected demands, accidents, and urgencies of everyday life, as well as the temporalities of the dominant large-scale organizations, institutions, and systems in a social order. These macro-temporalities can both powerfully condition and unsettle life's rhythms and possibilities.[1] Continual encounters with each of these can reinforce or destabilize an individual's past-present-future projections at each moment. Kinship and local networks, among other relatively durable relationships frequently categorized under the label of "civil society," can generate their own temporalities that cut across those of the personal and macro-organizational. Family lineage, local traditions, and the identity and shared memories of cultures can be just as, or more powerful in people's lives than the temporalities of officialdom, and their disruptions even more wrenching.

Beyond these more easily visible temporalities – and of particular importance for our understanding of political obligation – are the temporal constructs which attempt to knit each of these distinct and potentially antagonistic elements into a cohesive and harmoniously patterned complex. Jean-François Lyotard's concept of the "metanarrative," Pierre Bourdieu's "*doxa*," and most usefully, Michael Weinstein's concept of "cultural time"[2] are each suggestive of the manner in which this kind of temporality operates, and the function it serves. A cultural time provides an overarching temporality that makes the perception of a common social order, a shared history, and a sense of collective purpose toward common objects and goals possible. Public life doesn't simply demand a cultural time; a cultural time makes a cohesive public with a mutually legible interior membership and sense of shared existence over time possible. Cultural times (as long as they are stable) provide a way of delivering transpersonal meaning, connecting an individual to something beyond themselves, and giving the comfort of taking

Modernity and Political Obligation 57

one's place and direction in the world (as an individual and a member of a group) for granted. As MacIver observes,

> The community is far more enduring than its individual members, and within its relative immortality the individual can find some assurance against the fragility of his private existence. That of which he is a part abides. He is moored in the continuity of that to which he belongs.
>
> (MacIver 1962, 77)

Within a cultural time, the past and future become reminders that the duration of the world persists beyond the limited brackets of one's mortal existence. They also serve as guarantors of one's access to a "larger" significance, integrating one's personal temporal projections with the projects of others and transforming them into something transcendent.

In this chapter, we will examine the relationship between cultural times and theories of political obligation more closely. We will identify the major elements that feature in the arguments of political obligation theorists (discussing specific theories of obligation more closely in Chapters 3 and 4), and pay special attention to the role that political obligation theories have filled for modern political philosophy following the collapse of pre-modern cultural times. The state plays a crucial role here as the principal figure of modern political authority. By outlining the manner in which modern political obligation theorists conceptualize the state and comparing this to Deleuze's account of the state as a kind of "social machine," we can identify the particular ways in which political obligation theorists implicitly temporalize the state in order to render it serviceable for their projects. This will also require us to examine concepts like "legitimacy" and "justification" in order to make sense of their role in securing obligation theorists' visions of the state and its associated obligation claims. Finally, we will introduce the concept of "time-binding" as a way to usefully frame the intersection between the processes of temporal structuration described by Bergson and Deleuze, and the diverse operations of political power, institutions, and discourses in which they are implicated in the creation and enforcement of political obligations.

Modernity and Cultural Time

The particulars in the shape and content of a cultural time are largely immaterial (as far as categorization is concerned), as long as it fulfills the function of transpersonal temporal cohesion and orientation. In Ancient Egyptian religion, a complex polytheistic hierarchy ruled the heavens, while their divine will was manifested, mediated, and appeased through the rituals and body of the Pharaoh. Often portrayed as bearing the symbols of Maat (the goddess and principle of social and universal order, justice, and unity), the Pharaohs were the living symbols of a cultural time that provided a totalizing principle of order and purpose for an ancient Egyptian's place in society and the universe (Pinch 2002, 159–160). During the European Middle Ages, roughly from the latter half of the

58　*Modernity and Political Obligation*

first millennium CE through the first half of the second millennium, Christendom and its adaptation of Platonic conceptions of the Great Chain of Being[3] provided a powerful cultural time in Europe with no serious interior rivals that could displace it. While it was never absolutely totalizing in its strength and reach, it nevertheless provided the means of rationalizing feudal social structures, framing intellectual exploration, and delivering a system of meaning that connected everyday activities and social conduct to a more expansive cosmic purpose and order. Consequently, as the strength of this cultural time began to waver under successive assaults from multiple quarters, it generated shockwaves that left many disoriented, and searching for something to fill the void. It is out of the steady collapse of the cultural time of Christendom that what we now call modernity emerged, both as a symptom and a successor.

Modernity is a nebulous concept that has been made to include many different processes and moments of social change under its purview. The experiences of dislocation, contingency, and change are commonly identified as significant elements of modernity, and are commonly identified perhaps the only things that unify all of its purported dimensions. Marshall Berman describes modernity as

> a mode of vital experience – experience of space and time, of the self and others, of life's possibilities and perils – that is shared by men and women all over the world today.... To be modern is to find ourselves in an environment that promises adventure, power, joy, growth, transformation of ourselves and the world – and at the same time, that threatens to destroy everything we have, everything we know, everything we are ... modernity can be said to unite all mankind. But it is a paradoxical unity, a unity of disunity; it pours us all into a maelstrom of perpetual disintegration and renewal, of struggle and contradiction, of ambiguity and anguish.
>
> (1983, 15)

The expanding reach and predominance of markets and capitalism in the transformation and constitution of societies is one of its more commonly associated elements. The social disruptions and disintegrations caused by the enclosure of peasant commons lands and the rise of market institutions in fifteenth and sixteenth century England,[4] the emergence of rationalized industrial practices in Caribbean sugar plantations and their importation and expansion throughout Europe,[5] and the massive shifts that this industrial expansion posed for patterns of production (ever and rapidly increasing), labor (increasingly waged), and consumption contributed to the experience of rapid change and uncertainty. It is this experience that evoked Marx's observation that under the capitalist mode of production, "all that is solid melts into air" (Marx and Engels 1998, 38).

The emergence of Enlightenment thought and its celebration of reason, skepticism, science, and anti-absolutist government was pivotal in the formation of European modernity, both in the ideals of its early, exuberant celebrants, and in the reactions of its critics. In Kant's principal essay on the Enlightenment, he states quite bluntly that "*Enlightenment is man's emergence from his self-imposed immaturity*" (emphasis in original). Finally becoming more than dumb

Modernity and Political Obligation   59

"domestic livestock" kept by paternalistic guardians,[6] Enlightenment is an as-yet incomplete process of mankind becoming increasingly capable of and willing to question and reason freely, rather than being comfortable in their own subjugation (Kant 1983, 41–42).[7] Building off of the influence of the Enlightenment – and receiving renewed energy with the maturation of industrial capitalism – was the increasing valorization of science and technological progress, which was itself accompanied by a growing sense of separation between mankind and nature. Bruno Latour argues that to be truly modern entails (among other things) being able to believe in the separateness of humans and culture on the one hand, and nonhumans and nature on the other (1993, 10). This perception is not timeless, but rather the result of a convergence of historical projects and processes of "purification," both of ontological and epistemological perception, and of "radical" and "terrifying revolutions" in the areas of "science, technology, administration, economy and religion" which transformed societies and "bulldozed" away the "barbarian medley" of the past (130). Finally, modernity has also been associated with the rise of secularism, the relative decline of organized religion, and the emergence of the "crossed-out God."[8] When Nietzsche declared that "God is dead!" he was not referring to the disappearance of religious believers. Rather, his death of God points to the collapse of any authentic belief in Providence or the transcendent, and the circumstances in which we are left attempting to live amidst the wreckage. Max Stirner, too, saw God dethroned by the Moderns, only to surreptitiously re-emerge through their reification and idealizations of Man; a grasping effort to reclaim the universal and the timeless that God had previously secured.[9]

Each of these are real but partial reflections of the changes and anxieties which accompanied and instigated the rise of Western modernity, precipitated by the collapse of the cultural time that had been dominant in Europe in the Middle Ages. Reinhart Koselleck argues that modernity entails a particular "temporalization" of our perceptions of history, and that both a "compression" and "acceleration" of time distinguish the boundaries of its emergence. In *Futures Past* (2004), he observes that until well into the sixteenth century, "the history of Christianity is a history of expectations, or more exactly, the constant anticipation of the End of the World on the one hand and the continual deferment of the End on the other" (11). In the religious and political turmoil of this period, the signs of this End could be seen everywhere and by many different parties to the struggles.[10] So poignant was the sense of an imminent End that Luther frequently declared his expectations that the Fall would come by the current year or the next (12). If we fast forward to 1793, we find Robespierre able to say in a speech on the Revolutionary Constitution: "The time has come to call upon each to realize his own destiny. The progress of human Reason laid the basis for this great Revolution, and you shall now assume the particular duty of hastening its pace" (ibid.). How, Koselleck asks, is such an "inversion of the horizon of expectations" possible? Increasingly, the temporal compression Luther felt in perceiving a God-willed oncoming future marked by the End of Days was replaced by a sense of more optimistic (or at least more open-ended) futural temporal acceleration, whose speed and direction could be driven by the will and actions of humanity (2004, 12–13).

60 *Modernity and Political Obligation*

Spurred on by the Reformation and concurrent socio-political struggles and transformations, modernity emerged in Europe at a point of temporal disjuncture. Latour echoes Koselleck, arguing that modernity designates a "revolution" and asymmetrical "break in the regular passage of time," with victors and vanquished in this temporal combat (Latour 1993, 10). The English astronomer Jeremy Shakerley exemplifies this sense of victory, rhetorically asking the ancients in 1649:

> Heaven and Stars! How much hath our age triumphed over you! Neither doth our victory end here, still new miracles adde to the number of the old, and no day passeth without a triumph.
>
> (Shakerley 1649, iii, cited in Corfield 2007, 136)

Modernity thus implies a shift in the projected past-present-future perceived by those who either consider themselves modern, or (for those who perceive their society and/or themselves as "backwards") accept some account of modernity's reality. It is a "culture of time" that "valorizes the new" through a process of continuous future-oriented negations of the lingering residues of the past, and thus which understands itself as distinct from that past (Osborne 1995, xii; 13–17). Whether or not modernity has ever been as totalizing a phenomenon as its own internal narrative suggests – or even "been" at all[11] – the perception of modernity's reality plays a vital role in its efficacy as a means of structuring perceptions of time and its passage.

In all of its manifestations, the phenomenon of the experience of modernity is comprised of a dialectic, which Weinstein breaks down into three "moments." The first moment of this dialectic is the "unselfconscious unity" of the self in relation to the wider world, both of other selves and the cosmos. The second moment is a "radical separation" of the self from this unity. The third moment is completed through the achievement of reunification, and an accord between the separated self and the whole without losing the distinction of that self (Weinstein 1982, 3). Modern philosophy in general – but especially its normative political projects – are perennially caught between the shoals of the second and third moment, trying, yet continually failing to produce a durable synthesized unity (ibid.).

Modernity thus entails the sense of a break with what is considered "past." The most optimistic early Enlightenment thinkers embraced this fully, drawing a clear line between the present and an ignorant, superstitious, and tradition-bound past.[12] Critics of this exuberance recognized the rupture, yet were not content to simply sing praises to a futural telos, or to being set adrift in history. In aghast reaction to the French Revolution, Edmund Burke argued that society was a sacred contract made between the dead, the living, and the not-yet-born. To rashly cast aside this temporal bond was akin to destroying one's parent, collective cultural inheritance, security, and the possibility of a rich and meaningful life, as well as to rend asunder one's connection with "eternal society" and the timeless God that authored it (Burke 1986, 194–195). Coming from a very different philosophical tradition and writing after the emergence of fascism,

Modernity and Political Obligation   61

totalitarianism, and total war in the twentieth century, Max Horkheimer and Theodor Adorno traced a connection between the culmination of these horrors and their origins in the Enlightenment celebration of instrumental rationality in their *Dialectic of Enlightenment* (2002). By subordinating the present to the demands of the future under the banner of the pursuit of rational progress, rationality itself has become irrational, and has destroyed the possibility of freedom in both the present and the future.

With modernity's separation from the past, the future in turn frequently functions as a realm wherein attempts to reclaim a cultural time are made. Such attempts can, at their grandest, posit a clear trajectory for history, and at their most modest offer a limited hope for the achievement of surrogate piecemeal projects in the near future. One's progress toward the future is gauged by how far each person, group, or society has traversed along the charted arc of improvement, development, or actualization. Consequently, the present functions as a semi-elastic zone of retreat upon which individuals can "fall back" when denied a cultural time or an effective surrogate, a maneuver entailing both possibility and anxiety. Modern subjects can attempt to hitch their present to new past-present-future projections; a teleology of dialectical progress, a link to a primordial past and durable future through civilizational belonging, or perhaps a millennial revolution. Already separated from the unselfconscious unity noted by Weinstein, even projects of "traditionalism and reaction are distinctively modern forms" of political temporalities (Osborne 1995, xii). In so far as modern subjects remain modern, however, lacking an unselfconsciously sustained cultural time that connects them with something beyond themselves, and being faced with the practical (and existential) problem of developing a temporality (or collection of temporalities) to structure their actions, goals, and self-understanding, any solution seized upon will always be a tenuous one, without a guarantee of success.

The methodical doubting of René Descartes is commonly used to identify the onset of modern philosophy in Europe.[13] It was not the doubting itself, of course, but the scope of his doubts, and the method of their resolution that distinguished him from his predecessors. The collapse of the medieval worldview left Descartes without an overarching cultural time that could act as a vehicle for the provision of transpersonal meaning. He did not have the luxury of taking for granted his own purpose and place in a grand scheme of things. Instead, as he traveled around Europe he found a world of increasingly obvious temporal diversity and fragmentation. This world appeared to be full of disparate peoples, traditions, customs, and ways of life. Consequently, he felt compelled "to believe nothing too certainly of which [he] had only been convinced by example and custom" (Descartes 1927, 9). The prevailing dogma-bound theological and philosophical systems offered by the scholastics rang hollow to him, since they appeared insufficiently critical and took too much for granted. It is in this context that Descartes developed his argument regarding the Cogito, wherein at the very least he could rest assured that he existed, because the act of thinking required a thinking subject. It was not simple epistemological curiosity that led him to pursue a solid foundation upon which he could comfortably stop doubting.

62   *Modernity and Political Obligation*

Rather, he was filled with an "excessive desire to learn to distinguish the true from the false, in order to see clearly in [his] actions and to walk with confidence in this life" (ibid.). In other words, his searching doubts as well as his conclusion that he could at least rely upon the existence of his own questioning self were eminently practical responses to the disorienting effects of the collapse of the medieval cultural time. Descartes posited a unified, foundational Self moving within a continually renewed present as a surrogate for the grander, unifying temporality he was denied. He also attempted to supplement this with a "provisional moral code" whose first maxim advocated deference toward law and convention, transforming accommodation to the present into a moral virtue for practical personal and political guidance. Descartes had the misfortune of being situated at God's deathbed. While he could clearly feel the litanies of the old order turn to ash in his mouth, he could not find true succor in a comparably totalizing replacement for transpersonal meaning and life orientation.

Like Descartes, Jean-Jacques Rousseau felt the gnawing anxieties opened by the faltering temporalities in his own life. Especially in his "Reveries of a Solitary Walker" (2013), written near the end of his life after having faced a slew of bitter frustrations, he opines:

> Everything on Earth is in continual flux. Nothing keeps a fixed and constant form, and our affections, which attach themselves to external things, invariably pass and change as they do. Always before or behind us, they recall the past that no longer exists or foretell the future that often is not to be: there is nothing firm to which the heart can attach itself.
>
> (491)

In this condition, we are faced with the uncertainties, ephemeral concerns, and pains of individual mortal lives, with no guarantee of "happiness that lasts." The past and future are not sites of certainty or contentment, but hollow and uncertain shades toward which our affections feebly grasp. We grasp (not just consciously, but at a subconscious and affective level), because the present in which we reside is, even at its "most intense pleasures," not a place where we feel we can be satisfied remaining forever. This is the case even though it is only in a pure embrace of the present wherein "time is nothing"[14] that one can be "sufficient unto oneself, like God" (491–492). Time itself, he recognizes, operates as a force of unrelenting change and dissolution, and exhibits little care for our attempts to glean some persistence and unity out of the flux. As ominous as this condition might be for an individual in such an existential conundrum, Rousseau also saw the problems this continual flux posed for the stability and continuity – or even the possibility – of social and political life.

For Rousseau, social life is essentially defined by its precarious position in the face of time.[15] The iconic "savage man" in the state of nature that Rousseau presents to conceptualize humanity outside of and prior to its modern social existence is not simply an attempt at philosophical anthropology (although there is plenty of that). One of the primary characteristics Rousseau grants the savage man is a unique relationship to time. In discussing the existence of the savage

Modernity and Political Obligation   63

man, Rousseau does present it as a historical and chronologically prior figure (as an ideal type, if not necessarily in all details). We can also understand that priority as an ontological one. Life in the state of nature is a struggle for survival, but not only against starvation, weather, and other animals of the wild. As Mabel Wong argues, savage man represents the primordial significance of our attempts to survive in the face of time itself. It also represents a particular way in which humanity can organize their "temporal economy" in order to secure that survival (Wong 2012, 181). In Rousseau's philosophy the savage man is a figure living not "timelessly" as a purely instinctual being (something Rousseau flatly denies) but rather within a "durational economy" that synthesizes experience into a flexible (rather than isolated and momentary) present (180). This "pre-reflective temporal synthesis" is what principally distinguishes savage man from social man, and the state of nature from modern society (ibid.). The savage man serves, in other words, as a kind of transhistorical ideal and strategy of living thoroughly in the present, which as noted is the place where Rousseau identifies the possibility of contentment and happiness in the face of time.

The social man that supersedes the savage man upon his entrance into society is similarly identified by its relationship to time. While the savage man survives its encounter with time by virtue of living strictly in the present, the social man is burdened by a troublesome concern for the past and the future, burdened by active "memory and foresight" and thus possessing a greater awareness of time's passage. Stretched and fragmented, social man's identity requires a sense of self that ties memory with expectations into the present, the consequence of which is that we "no longer exist where we are; we only exist where we are not" (Rousseau, cited in Wong 2012, 182). We are unable to hold onto a stable sense of presentness and unity as social man. For Rousseau this is what society and the recognition of one's relationship within the "general will" can offer; a shoring up of one's temporality, and a securing of one's sense of presentness by offering a way to merge with a larger social aggregate.[16] Yet, as a tenuous congregation of already-fragile, distracted, and mortal individuals, the general will of society is still an ideal that is impossible to absolutely maintain.[17] In spite of its impossible totalization, it nevertheless provides the promise of a bulwark against time's dissolving effects, and is one of our best practical hopes of securing it (short of an impossible return to the position of the present-grounded savage man).

The question for Rousseau becomes how to secure this impossible temporal unity. Social belonging, political order, and temporal organization become fundamentally intertwined expressions of this singular problem. It is in Rousseau, I argue, that we see one of the fullest modern expressions of "the problem" of social cohesion, belonging, and political obligation emerge specifically as a reaction to our encounter with time and the individual and social alienation that this has generated. In his "Reveries," he points to the timeless present as a state of mind that can be the source of true, stable happiness and contentment. It can do so by virtue of its negation of one's anxieties regarding lived time. In lieu of this pure present, Rousseau's solution is to extol membership and a sense of belonging within a unified and enduring social order operating in accordance with the general will, and to negate the possibility of dissonance and

64 *Modernity and Political Obligation*

disobedience toward a just form of state through the inculcation of patriotism, an internalized personal identification with the needs of society and the state, and a comprehensive regime of human nature transformation. It is his concern for temporal unity that informs his theory of obligations toward the general will and a just state. Although most contemporary theorists of political obligation would not identify as Rousseauians in the details of their arguments or solutions, they share these fundamentally similar concerns. Rousseau represents one of the purest modern expressions of social and individual anxiety in the face of time, and his theories of and prescriptions for political obligation and social cohesion serve the same temporal functions as those developed by subsequent obligation theorists.

Theories of political obligation can thus be usefully interpreted as attempts to exercise control. As discursive weapons in political rhetoric and struggles, that control can be interpreted in a more conventionally coercive fashion. In so far as Rousseau attempts to make our chains legitimate, he is indeed trying to make them feel lighter and more tolerable, as well as strengthen their power *as bonds* in relation to an ideal state. The practical implications of this include strengthening the ramparts of authority (of a particular kind), enhancing its legitimacy, encouraging compliance toward its prerogatives (removing, in fact, the *thinkability* of deviation from the general will), and, overall, making the processes of ordering and controlling populations and resources easier for a state. That control can also be understood, however, in the more vitalistic and existential fashion derived from Bergson: as a defensive securitization effort intended to spatialize time and ward off the anxieties and uncertainties that accompany time's flow. In lieu of the complex, fragile, and mutable ties, alliances, and struggles of social and political life, obligation theories act as representations of an ideal or desired social order, and a bulwark against the precarity of time. In so far as those who encounter them grant them moral weight, obligation theories not only compel bodies and minds toward some degree of obedience by functioning as disciplinary constructs, but do so by means of structuring time. Theories of political obligation are, in part, attempts to reclaim the unity of a convincing cultural time by providing rationalized mechanisms of ordering duties, expectations, and a sense of place within an integrated and cohesive social and political order.

The onset of modernity elevated anxieties over the foundations of social order and meaning to a new pitch – or perhaps more accurately, these anxieties were constitutive of that which we now call modernity – but it certainly does not have a historical monopoly on the urge for control or the fear that generates it. The unselfconscious sense of temporal unity maintained by pre-moderns through stable cultural times can be an effective manner of sublimation, but it does not truly negate these challenges and tensions. There is thus an important continuity between pre-modern and modern obligation theorists. Anxieties over the foundations of social order, personal and transpersonal meaning, and simply wanting to "walk with confidence" in life are magnified in modernity, but the urge for spatialization, temporal structure, and Bergsonian control, and the psychological struggles and practical demands upon which they rest run throughout human history.

Modernity and Political Obligation 65

Contemporary political obligation apologists find themselves confronted with the same basic dilemmas of modernity felt by Descartes and Rousseau before them. The cultural time of pre-modernity is already rent asunder, and humanity granted a new domain of freedom. That freedom, unfortunately, is not a straightforward cause for celebration. It can entail the notion of choice regarding obedience and disobedience, and opens up possibilities for new futures beyond the old temporal horizons. It also, however, holds properties shared by flotsam; an unmoored, directionless drifting of shattered parts without function and proper place, cast upon the waves. How are we to reconcile this assumed freedom with the sense of right orientation, purpose, and place that has been lost? For most modern obligation apologists, the answer has been the positing of regulative ideals and disciplinary constructs through the method of time-binding.[18] Individuals are seen as free, yet they must also be properly bound for social and political order to be secured, and for attempts at reconstituting cultural times and shared temporalities to have a chance at success – preferably voluntarily and without seeing the binds as restrictions at all. It is by attempting to develop a comprehensive rationalizing representation of our proper political behavior and place within a political order that political obligation theorists have tried to secure this.

The State

As the locus of where political obligations are generally considered to be owed (or where those obligation claims are contested), the state is an object of immense theoretical significance for modern obligation theorists, both apologists and philosophical anarchists alike. For both, a "successful" theory of political obligation would compel a willing compliance to some specified range of demands imposed by the "legitimate" political authorities of the state, and disallow resistance to those demands, castigating that resistance as illegitimate. The price of "failure" for political obligation theories is, at minimum, a removal of any reason for obedience to a state (at least, beyond the desire to avoid the wrath of its monopoly on violence). At most, this failure becomes a normative justification for armed insurrection, with the state's demands being understood as illegitimate and its compulsions being little more than the violent usurpation of a prior autonomy.

The modern state, with its familiar police, office holders, bureaucracies, courts, and social services is a relatively recent invention. Although, as Deleuze argues, there are some fundamental continuities between the nature of earlier city-states or empires and the modern state that should be recognized, there are also differences that must be appreciated, especially if we are to understand how modern and pre-modern conceptualizations of obligation diverge. The Athenian *polis*, for example, was not conceived of as a distant body of rulers by Athenians. At least those few who were citizens thought of themselves collectively as the *polis*, and their immediate loyalties to *each other* were contested and understood in terms of familial allegiance, reputation, and honor (Pateman 1985, 99). Much of ancient pre-modern political life was interpreted as a problem of virtue,

66 *Modernity and Political Obligation*

honor, or piety rather than explicitly as a problem of political obligation and legitimacy (Salkever 1974). It is, as we might expect, primarily modern theorists who have placed such a heavy emphasis on the institutions and authority of the modern state as the proper claimant of our political obligations (although we will see shortly that this is not an uncontested norm).

Retroactively, however, many modern obligation theorists have made use of terms like "the state" in their discussions of ancient political institutions. As Carole Pateman notes, this kind of retroactive projection has been especially common in discussions of the polity of ancient Athens, where a figure like Socrates is presented as if he were facing off against a modern, distant ruling state as "the first civil disobedient and his arguments ... those of a contemporary liberal democrat" (1985, 98). There are certainly empirical and theoretical problems with this kind of heavy-handed, direct grafting of modern concerns, worldviews, and priorities onto a pre-modern context. More interesting, perhaps, is the way in which this kind of transhistorical universalization of the modern state allows these theorists to establish a virtual continuity (and implicit comparability) between this real or imagined past and the problems and circumstances of the present. This continuity allows them to then rummage through the past in search of tools and weapons that they can bring to bear on the present and future. Out of difference, they may uncover (or rather, string together) the "ancient problem" of law, authority, or obligation as if it were a universal form that only underwent circumstantial modifications. Through efforts to establish these continuities, the state can sometimes appear in contemporary political obligation scholarship as the complex machine of comprehensive rule that so worried Weber and Kafka, and at other times be reduced to a few skeletal principles, facets, or instruments of collective life ("law," "collective rule-making," "community"). Often enough, the lines between the two become blurred, and the imagined present begins to seep into the represented past.

Most modern obligation theorists conceptualize the state in terms that – at first glance – don't depart terribly far from those articulated by Weber, who described the state as "a human community that (successfully) claims the monopoly of the legitimate use of force within a given territory" (1946, 77). The state is some specific group of people that have the dominant ability to wield violence in a particular territory with people in it, and – if that monopoly is to be sustained – are recognized by a critical mass of the residents in that territory as being justified, legitimate, or right in wielding that coercive power. There are technical variations on this formula, but this is the standard image of the state adopted within modern political obligation discourse. The state certainly has other implied or derivative elements that have received attention from obligation theorists,[19] but it is this overwhelming coercive power of the state that has been their primary concern, the element that has most compelled a defense among apologists, and faced criticism by philosophical anarchists. The state can present a more benign face when it is building roads (setting aside the violence behind eminent domain claims) and hospitals. Even these provisions, though, emerge from its primary capacity (even among the most "liberal" and "democratic" of states) to summon armed individuals in uniforms who are willing to threaten,

Modernity and Political Obligation   67

beat, cage, or even kill others on command to enforce its rule and rules, domestically or abroad, and to have the word of its agents be the final effective determinant of right and wrong.

All states rest upon their ability to govern, and in the words of Pierre-Joseph Proudhon, one of the first modern anarchist political theorists,

> To be governed is to be kept in sight, inspected, spied upon, directed, law-driven, numbered, enrolled, indoctrinated, preached at, controlled, estimated, valued, censured, commanded, by creatures who have neither the right, nor the wisdom, nor the virtue to do so.... To be governed is to be at every operation, at every transaction, noted, registered, enrolled, taxed, stamped, measured, numbered, assessed, licensed, authorised, admonished, forbidden, reformed, corrected, punished. It is, under the pretext of public utility, and in the name of the general interest, to be placed under contribution, trained, ransomed, exploited, monopolised, extorted, squeezed, mystified, robbed; then, at the slightest resistance, the first word of complaint, to be repressed, fined, despised, harassed, tracked, abused, clubbed, disarmed, choked, imprisoned, judged, condemned, shot, deported, sacrificed, sold, betrayed; and, to crown all, mocked, ridiculed, outraged, dishonoured.
>
> (2011, 538)

This conjunction of the state's capacity to project violence, its claimed right to do so, and the effective recognition of that claim by a ruled populace implies the existence of *authority* in political relationships. There are many kinds of authority, such as epistemic or expert,[20] moral,[21] or parental.[22] Setting these forms aside for our present purposes,[23] it is the concept of political authority, understood as the right to command and expect obedience, which underwrites the unique powers claimed by the state.[24] It can be helpful to think of the problem of political obligation as a necessary correlate to the problem of authority. Whether we are empirically attempting to understand how authority functions within a given political system, or we are attempting to morally justify some particular kind of authority, the effective exercise of authority depends upon either the existence or justifiability of political obligations. The (perceived) right to rule depends upon the (perceived) necessity of obeying those with the right to rule. As Robert Paul Wolff argues, political obligation implies that one obeys the command of a person in authority "because [they tell] you to do it," rather than because of the specific content of the command, or alternatively, that one follows the laws of the state "simply because they are the laws" (1970, 9; 18). There have been a variety of different obligation apologist critiques of the phrasing that Wolff has deployed (and, of course, of his philosophical anarchist conclusions regarding the incompatible relationship between obligation and autonomy),[25] but I accept that this basic relationship between authority and political obligation holds true in so far as we are discussing the state as a discrete body of persons wielding this authority over its ascribed subjects.[26]

Beyond these conventional minimal definitions emphasizing violence, authority, or membership, obligation apologists frequently argue that the state is also

68   *Modernity and Political Obligation*

functional in character. According to this line of reasoning, the provision of certain public goods or social functions is necessary and the state is the only available, possible, or optimal institution for providing or protecting those necessary functions. Consequently, some form of general political obligations are owed in order to secure the state's existence and ability to provide those necessary functions. The necessity of the state or state-like forms of political organization is a nearly universally held position among obligation apologists that is rooted, as George Klosko observes, in many of the basic premises of the liberal tradition (2005, 3; 17).[27] Following Locke, the state is treated as, at minimum, a defense against the inconveniences and troubles imagined as being the properties of the state of nature (17). Both the ends to which the state is supposedly oriented to serve and the necessity of the state itself are thus functional in character. Elizabeth Anscombe, one of the primary proponents of this view of state necessity, argues that a state is essential for the establishment and maintenance of a minimal level of general well-being, especially the protection of life and limb. Authority is itself the domain of necessary social function, and those fulfilling these necessary functions are owed the sanction required to carry them out (Anscombe 1978). Anscombe finds that "the world is less of a jungle because of rulers" being able to exercise these necessary functions, with the alternative being chaos and disarray (Anscombe 1981). Christopher Wellman provides one of the more comprehensive arguments regarding the state's role as a guarantor of the fulfillment of certain minimally necessary social functions, arguing that "political states are necessary to avoid the extreme perils of the state of nature," and that

> It does not require a full Hobbesian account of human nature to recognize that an environment with no political state would be an insecure place in which peace would be unavailable and moral rights would be disrespected. Put plainly, there will always be people unwilling to honour the moral rights of others if there were no legal repercussions of violating them. Moral rights will be respected and peace will be ensured only if police effectively protect individuals and recognized judges impartially adjudicate conflicts according to established rules.
>
> (1996, 216–217)

He develops his theory of necessary functions through three steps of argument that are representative of the reasoning of others who make this appeal (even if the specified functions and grounding moral principles differ).[28] In the first, Wellman argues in the spirit of Hobbes that a minimal degree of security and order are required for any acceptable quality of life to be possible, and that the state is a vital institution for securing this in modern society. A system of law with homogeneously applied rules for behavior and secured rights is of fundamental importance for this. The second step argues that obedience to the state's authority is a requirement for its laws to have force and for order, security, and the necessary social functions and goods to be preserved. In the third step, Wellman argues (drawing from a broader appeal to our "Samaritan" duties to

Modernity and Political Obligation 69

save others from peril, in this case the peril of the state of nature) that we have duties of political obligation which we must discharge in deference to the state so that it may fulfill the necessary functions required to defend the minimal well-being of others (1996; see also 2001, 743).

The exact content of the necessary functions of the state can vary between obligation apologists, although they can be overwhelmingly identified with the principal concerns of liberal democratic traditions broadly construed. A minimal overall well-being, the prevention of harm to others, the defense of property and the enforcement of contracts,[29] and the pursuit of justice are commonly ascribed necessary functions. While the pursuit of justice is a goal seized upon in a variety of different theories of political obligation, its most notable use in relation to the concept of necessary social functions can be found in the "natural duty" theories associated with the work of John Rawls. Given Rawls' influence over liberal theories of political obligation over the last few decades, we will hold off on discussing the functional appeal to justice until Chapter 3. Necessity is fickle, however, and can just as easily be used to appeal to an expansive list of values that demand fulfillment. John Finnis argues that there are certain "self-evident" and "basic forms of human good" that political and legal frameworks must aim to either satisfy or secure, including life, play, knowledge, friendship, and aesthetic experience (1980). We can address why necessity – a concept that itself suggests a kind of absolute limit – can be so malleable when we discuss the temporality of necessity later in this chapter.

While the state as an apparatus of rule enforcement and guarantor of necessary functions is usually the primary target of apologists' justifications, it is not necessarily the only one (nor is the definition of "state" always limited to the institutions and elements of the modern state[30]). Bhikhu Parekh argues that focusing on obligations to the state and the law can actually be de-politicizing, and distract us from the manifold obligations a citizen has, such as "to take an active interest in political life, to promote the well-being of his community and to help redress its injustices" (1993, 240). What is commonly called political obligation is instead cast as a form of "civil obligation," while political obligation properly understood refers to those duties that citizens owe to one another and to their polity through active participation in political life (ibid.). Parekh's distinction is an important one to make, not necessarily because of the semantic line drawn, but rather because it highlights the complex concerns, values, and social relationships that motivate much of modern political obligation theory. It isn't simply a great love of the state that motivates apologists, but rather (or also) a concern for the maintenance of the fabric of social life in all of its richness and a fear regarding its sustainability without the modern state. As John Horton argues, it is concern for the relationship between people and their political community as a whole that commonly drives questions regarding political obligation (2010, 1). It is arguably out of these extended concerns that theories of membership, fairness, and justice especially find much of their moral force and appeal. Although Parekh critiques the state-centric theories of political obligation as being an unfortunate consequence of much of "post-Hobbesian" political reasoning, it is worth remembering Hobbes' own fears regarding what the

70   *Modernity and Political Obligation*

lack of a Sovereign and generalized obedience would entail. Beyond making life "solitary, poor, nasty, brutish, and short," it would also destroy humanity's capacity for sustaining industry, culture, sea trade, engaging in collaborative projects for moving or building things, accumulating knowledge of the world, and keeping a common account of time, art, letters, or society generally (Hobbes 1987, 186). For obligation apologists, the whole tapestry of human experience appears to be at stake, even while the state is treated as the keystone of its security.

The State and Political Subjectivity

Consequently, a theory of political obligation entails a theory of the characteristics and nature of the political subjects that corresponds to its conception of the state. There have been far too many different accounts of human nature to discuss all of them adequately here, though we can identify some of the most common elements that unite modern political obligation discourse in spite of these differences (we will discuss more of these differences in greater depth in subsequent chapters). Questions regarding the conception of political subjects include issues of human nature, but also go beyond them, we will see, to provide certain implicit forms of temporal structure in the relationship between the state and those under (and beyond) its scope of authority. We can identify three particularly significant features attributed to the subjects of states within modern theories of political obligation: morality, rationality, and lack. While there are certainly many more attributes granted to political subjects, I consider these to be significant owing to the role they play in structuring the temporality of the state within obligation theories, and thus the form and content of those obligations. Each of these features overlaps with the others in ways that will become clearer later in this chapter.

Given that political obligation is principally understood as a moral problem in one way or another, it is no surprise that one of the most common features ascribed to political subjects within modern political obligation discourse is that they are moral creatures. How can we begin to pose the question of why one should obey legitimate authority, or what one owes to a polity if subjects are not "capable of choice and autonomy and responsible for the consequences of their actions," or able to consider and reflect upon a political demand and decide whether or not it would be right for them to obey or disobey (Parekh 1993, 240)? Kant's influence here is tremendous. Political subjects cannot simply obey, but must see the rightness of obeying (or disobeying) to satisfy modern obligation theorists. Even for more communitarian obligation theorists inspired by Aristotle and Hegel,[31] the necessity of conceiving of individuals as moral creatures inseparable from a moral community only further entrenches the necessity of their moral capacity (even if it alters the accepted conclusions).

Political subjects are also usually portrayed as rational. The quality of that rationality may vary,[32] but the appeal to subject rationality almost always contains the attribution of a certain set of given or assumed interests, values, or desires in relation to which subjects are rational in their pursuit. Klosko provides

Modernity and Political Obligation 71

a broadly representative account of given subject interests in assuming that those subjects (conflated with "the majority of inhabitants of modern societies") would only really find "acceptable" the kind of lives found in "modern industrial societies." These societies "are relatively safe, have functioning economies, and allow travel and a wide range of occupations, activities, and modes of life." Some small change is allowed, but "change must be within reasonable bounds and the resulting societies acceptable to contemporary citizens with preferences much like those they currently have" (Klosko 2005, 19–20).[33] Even with the highly abstract thought experiment initiated by Rawls in *A Theory of Justice* (1999), the kinds of rationality, interests, and values that the representative subjects of the original position possess once they emerge from behind their veil of ignorance looks not-so-surprisingly like those of the modern, Western, liberal democratic, secular, capitalist(-ic) subject imagined by Klosko. That rationality is thus organized as a way to constrain subjects' permissible motivations, expectations, concerns, and their horizon of imaginable or acceptable alternatives. The trait of rationality reinforces the "responsibility" of subjects entailed through their morality. Subjects are treated as a terminal moral source in part because – again following Kant – their purported rationality appears to reinforce their capacity for morality.

Aside from our moral characteristics, we also appear as subjects imbued with a constitutive lack. We are presented as beings that require something that we cannot have in isolation, but instead must find within a social situation or in relation to a political institution (almost always the state). This lack is not simply an absence, but an absence that compels us to fill it, and that we must fill if we are to be complete, happy, or achieve the requirements that the obligation theorist has deemed significant. By and large, this lack can be understood as that which is implied by the "necessary functions" that the state is supposed to fulfill, whichever functions those might be. The necessary functions are rendered necessary precisely because we are creatures that lack. This lack thus appears as a motor force for our rationality and assumed interests. If our interests and evaluation of what constitutes an acceptable life are defined up front as including the desire for all of the components of "modern societies," and our lack compels us to pursue these necessities, then we as subjects appear telically primed to behave in ways that make the justification of obligation (and our deference to authority) an easier feat.

Each of these attributes, as we will see later, plays an important role in preparing the temporal features of political subjects within modern obligation theories. While they are distinct, each of them overlaps with and reinforces the others in making this temporal structuration possible. Morality opens the possibility of a subject viewing obligations as necessary. Rationality constrains the subjects' relevant interests and operative methods of thinking as such, circumscribing the conditions under which obligations could be accepted, and providing the subject with their orientation toward the world. Finally, lack provides the motivation, the need, and the grounds for the teleology that – lo and behold – is completed and fulfilled by the subject's recognition of their proper political obligations toward the state.

72   *Modernity and Political Obligation*

Because of its significance as a node for all theories of political obligation, the state can become a complex conceptual artifact. This complexity is not primarily a result of any particular variations on its delineated or proposed constitutional or institutional architecture. Rather, it is a consequence of the significant temporal structurations that render it serviceable to any particular theory of obligation; a kind of virtual constitution. These structurations can take the form of broad past-present-future projections, implications of "necessary functions," telic or teleological attributions, and de-historicizing abstractions. As a consequence, the hypothetical subjects that correspond to these hypothetical states are subject to these same processes of structuration. We will return to the specifics of these temporal structurations within political obligation theories of the state shortly. First, however, we will consider Deleuze's conception of the state in order to understand how these processes of temporal structuration fit in relation to other important processes that constitute contemporary political institutions and authorities.

Deleuze and the State

As Daniel Smith (2012) observes, the concept of "flow" is uniquely central in Deleuze's understanding of social and political life (160). In *Anti-Oedipus* (2009), Deleuze and Guattari state outright that their "general theory of society is a generalized theory of flows" (262). It is not hydrology, but rather economics that informs Deleuze's use of this term, especially in its development by John Maynard Keynes, and its similarities in the work of Karl Marx. Keynes produces a theory of flow as a form of transmission and movement, primarily of money and economic value. The counterpart to flow is the concept of "code." A code is a "form of inscription or recording" that marks, sorts, orders, measures, and imbues with meaning a flow. It is what makes a flow recognizable as a particular kind of entity at all. For Keynes, the exemplary coding mechanism of capitalism is the accounting system, but money itself can be essentially understood as a kind of code. Deleuze, in turn, effectively universalizes the concept of flow, not by giving it any specific content, but rather by making it "unqualified" and "undetermined." It is not that the concept of flow has no meaning, but rather that its meaning is established indirectly and retrospectively through association with different phenomena. Flows are not only comprised of conventionally liquid materials, but also

> *economic* flows such as money and capital, along with the control of markets. There are *material* flows of raw matter and utilities such as oil and electricity, along with the control of the grid and the oil supply. There is the flow of *commodities*, along with their marketing and transport. There is the flow of *traffic*, along with the regulation of the highways and circulation (avoiding traffic jams), as well as the mastery and control of speed. There are *social* flows such as flows of populations, the flow of immigrants and foreigners over borders, along with the ability to control and monitor those borders (issuing passports, customs, and so on). There are flows of *sewage*

Modernity and Political Obligation   73

and *refuse*, and the question of what to do with them. There are *somatic* flows such as urine, blood, sperm, sweat, faeces, milk, menstrual blood, and so on, with their various codings.... One can even think of flows of *thought*, and the attempt to code and control the flow of thought via marketing, advertising, and the media.

(Smith 2012, 160–161, emphasis in original)

Flows are an endemic feature of our world, and thinking principally in terms of flows allows us to pose new problems and think in new ways.

This elevation of the importance of flows should be understood in the context of Deleuze's project of developing a more comprehensive materialist empiricism (what he refers to as "transcendental empiricism"). Deleuze agrees with Marx in emphasizing the centrality of understanding capitalism as a prerequisite for understanding modern political life, and even agrees with the significance Marx places upon tracing the flows, production, and interactions of labor and capital, but wants a materialist empiricism that is not limited by orthodox Marxism's conventionally economistic reductions. For this reason, Deleuze's approach often speaks more to Bergsonian duration (minus Bergson's problematic tendencies toward conceiving of duration with continuity) than conventional dialectical materialism. While Deleuze does not give us a straightforward definition of flows, opting instead to suggest its meaning by virtue of the phenomena with which it is associated, we could say that they are the particular and real expressions of movement and newness in the world. Flows are the instantiation of becoming and difference that we then judge to be concrete and discrete objects. They are not the movement of given unified things, but the processes of transformation that produce patterns which we retrospectively treat as unified objects, signs, people, or goods.[34]

These flows, then, are not simply an unfolding of pure chaos, but in practice exhibit "consistency"; they "hold together" and in so doing produce particular patterns and shapes of interaction (Deleuze and Guattari 1987, 327). All of the forms, divisions, and structures we perceive in the world are a consequence of the construction of different material and symbolic kinds of consistency. We perceive and project the homogeneity and sameness of some collection of flows, as with Bergson's notion of spatialization, but at the same time there are also very real, material interactions and interlocking functions and systems being produced. It is through processes of "coding" and "striating" the "socius"[35] that consistencies, unities, and structured divisions among flows can be created and reproduced. Through these, social and political life becomes imaginable and possible. The production of consistency transforms flows into a combination of still-heterogeneous yet interacting and interlocking elements that Deleuze and Guattari refer to as "assemblages" (1987, 503). Graham Livesey (2010) characterizes assemblages in this way:

Assemblages, as conceived of by Deleuze and Guattari, are complex constellations of objects, bodies, expressions, qualities, and territories that come together for varying periods of time to ideally create new ways of

74 *Modernity and Political Obligation*

functioning. Assemblages operate through desire as abstract machines, or arrangements, that are productive and have function; desire is the circulating energy that produces connections.

(18)

An assemblage emerges through the production of the consistency of different flows and force relations. As suggested in their use of the concept of flows, assemblages are not restricted to individual humans, or to large social structures, although these are themselves kinds of assemblages. Rather, they are comprised of all forms of consistency wherein otherwise heterogeneous elements coalesce and function together, such as ecosystems, migratory patterns, speech patterns, government institutions, psychological habits, traditions, discourses, social stratifications, and consciousness. What is significant is their character as convergent interacting processes.

By giving flows and assemblages a central place in his theory of individuals and societies – a consequence of his concern for putting difference before unity – we get a rather different image of the state, its functions, and its consequences. For Deleuze, rather than being defined as a given kind of structure, the state is first and foremost a kind of *machine of capture*. Deleuze uses the term "machine" as a literal descriptor, not simply a metaphor. Following a definition supplied by Franz Reuleaux and applied by Lewis Mumford (with the concept of the social "megamachine"), Deleuze understands a machine to be made up of a "combination of solid elements, each having its specialized function and operating under human control in order to transmit a movement and perform a task" (Mumford 1966, cited in Deleuze and Guattari 2009, 141). The state is such a social machine, and like all social machines, its principal endeavor is to code and codify the flows within its reach, sorting, dividing, merging, and generating functions and tasks for the objects and individuals that serve as its parts. Organizing flows of people entails sorting them into castes, categories, and roles, and marking their bodies and flesh through what Foucault would refer to as processes of inscription.

The codification of people's desire itself, and thus the "apportioning of production" (not just economic, but all forms of production and reproduction of the social machine) is key to the operations of these state machines. Codification extends to all flows of people, materials, objects, and other machines within the scope of this socius: "Flows of women and children, flows of herds and of seed, sperm flows, flows of shit, menstrual flows: nothing must escape coding" (Deleuze and Guattari 2009, 142). For Deleuze, the whole of the world (including individual persons) is a dynamic system of flows, assemblages, and machines that are always combining, dispersing, and recombining. The state is one kind of social machine (comprised of many smaller machines, and operating in a complex of other social machines that comprise and constitute a given socius) whose function and operative logic is to continually attempt to "capture," "cut," and "break" these endless flows into forms of consistency and unity by instrumentally functionalizing them in relation to each other and to itself.

Deleuze presents a kind of "universal" history of society and the state, though this universality is not used as a way to deny the complexity of actual forms of

Modernity and Political Obligation 75

social and political organization, or reduce them to a shadow of the European nation-state. He is keenly aware of the research of political anthropologists and the details of the historical emergence of the modern state system. This universal history instead functions as a parodic take on the Hegelian *bildungsroman* of civilizational development, and a general critique of attempts to reduce the complexity of history into discrete epochs, ages, or forms unfolding across a progressive teleology. While Hegel tracked the *movement* of a unified rationality through history, folding the details of the world into an account of the development of Spirit, Deleuze tells us of the *production* of unities through an account of the mechanisms by which flows and assemblages become captured, altered, and reproduced. In this way, Deleuze's history resembles Marx's own modified version of Hegel's dialectic. Marx turned Hegel on his head and provided a materialist history that interpreted the production of social forms through processes of economic production and class conflict. Deleuze does not overturn Marx as much as expand the idea of historical materialism to include all forms of social production, rather than principally economic, and all forms of inequitable power struggles, rather than principally class conflict.[36]

While Marx's history of social development has five stages, Deleuze gives us only three. He argues that with regard to the state as a special, distinct category in social formations, "Marxism didn't quite know what to make of it" (Deleuze and Guattari 2009, 219). In Marx's social history the state became fragmented, passive, perfunctory, and confused across the five evolutionary social stages when, in fact, there has only ever been one state which historically "appears fully armed, a masterstroke executed all at once" (217). The state is not simply one kind of institutional arrangement appearing and then disappearing in a historical relay as a function of economic transformations, but an operational logic of organizing and capturing flows that manifests in many different kinds of institutions of social ordering and political rule. By understanding the state as a social machine whose primary function is to code flows – people, symbols, resources, meaning – Deleuze's three stage history of society becomes more, rather than less useful for understanding the distinct social machines operative in a given socius than Marx's five stage history.

Territorial, Despotic, and Capitalist Machines

The first form of socius in Deleuze's history is the "primitive territorial machine." This machine is "primitive" not simply in the sense that allegedly primitive societies are representative of its operation, but because it is primary and primal in the constitution of societies as such. The territorial machine is principally geared towards the organization of people into systems of social production, especially the production of the social body itself. It "codes flows, invests organs, and marks bodies," involving both bodily modification as well as the infusion of symbolic categorization and significance into different behaviors and appearances (Deleuze and Guattari 2009, 144). Ritual rites of initiation, tattooing, and scarifying are historically common examples of this, but so too are the legal vestments, mechanisms of determining membership, methods of

76 *Modernity and Political Obligation*

identification and recognition, and processes of cultural and institutional habituation found in modern nation-states. All of these are techniques and processes that both Deleuze and Nietzsche identify as a form of cruelty, through which "the movement of culture ... is realized in bodies and inscribed on them, belaboring them" (145). The territorial machine is thus the ontologically basic means, the political "founding act," through which the bodies of people are symbolically and materially "hewn into the socius" and rendered as serviceable "parts and wheels of the social machine" (144–145). It operates primarily through kinship systems; horizontal alliances and relations of filiation corresponding roughly to the primitive communism of Marx's social history (147).

The second form of socius is the "barbarian despotic machine," and corresponds closely to Marx's concept of the "Asiatic" modes of production. It is principally defined by its absorption and subordination of these lateral relationships under a stratified system of castes and classes, and a hierarchical structure of rule. It is this form of socius that inaugurates the State apparatus as a distinct machine. The despotic machine creates a "new alliance and direct filiation" with the despot positioned as the central nexus of all political relations, possessing a direct connection to a deity (192).[37]

> And new perverse groups spread the despot's invention (perhaps they even fabricated it for him), broadcast his fame, and impose his power in the towns they found and conquer. Wherever a despot and his army pass, doctors, priests, scribes, and officials are part of the procession.
>
> (193)

Although they are at odds with each other, the lateral relationships that comprise the basic ground of social life and the territorial machine are not destroyed through the despotic machine. Instead, they are integrated as "working parts" of the new state machine, with their prior inscriptions of meaning and purpose being "bricked over" and "overcoded," in order to mobilize them for new ends. This overcoding – the "essence of the state" – is a means of maintaining the forms of coding, capture, and consistency established through the territorial machine, yet also of going beyond them, harnessing them to "make desire into the property of the sovereign" and appropriating "all the forces and agents of production" into this hierarchical system (198–199). The invention of money, rather than being a spontaneous creation among barterers seeking a more efficient means of exchange, was primarily a means of facilitating precisely this kind of appropriation.

> The role of money in commerce hinges less on commerce itself than on its control by the State. Commerce's relationship with money is synthetic, not analytical. And money is fundamentally inseparable, not from commerce, but from taxes as the maintenance of the apparatus of the State. Even where dominant classes set themselves apart from this apparatus and make use of it for the benefit of private property, the despotic tie between money and taxes remains visible.
>
> (197)

Modernity and Political Obligation   77

While the territorial machine depends upon an economy of blocks of mobile and finite moral and economic debts and disequilibrium in order to maintain its network of alliances,[38] the despotic machine transforms this into a system of infinite debt owed to the despot. Money, and in particular its circulation, is a means of rendering the debt infinite. While taxation is one material manifestation of this infinite debt, it also manifests in the form of an irremediable duty to the sovereign despot, the god to which it claims filiation, and the machine of which it is a part. The debt to the sovereign despot becomes a "debt of existence, a debt of the existence of the subjects themselves" (197).

The third form of socius is the "civilised capitalist machine" which corresponds to Marx's capitalist stage of social development. While the territorial and despotic machines allow certain kinds of decoded flows to exist, they are always within highly circumscribed forms. The territorial machine establishes designated social spaces for aberrant individuals, such as the social position of the mystic, as a route for them to remain incorporated even while being on the outside of the normal social field of activity, while the despotic machine allows some money circulation in order to establish taxation systems and harness social production. Both, however, are still haunted by a persistent "dread of decoded flows," of order collapsing, of proper roles and places becoming confused, of a disintegration of unity, and of forces and flows that exceed capture and sorting (197). It is the capitalist machine alone which rests upon the "generalized decoding of flows" (Deleuze and Guattari 2009, 224).

It is only when the decoded flows of money, markets, private property, and unbonded labor coalesce into a critical "conjunction" of forces that the despotic machine falters, and the capitalist machine can emerge.[39] Forms of these decoded flows can and have existed throughout history without creating a capitalist machine, and their conjunction in Europe was the result of accidents and contingent factors, rather than a developmental destiny (226).[40] Deleuze says that the reason that China did not become a capitalist power in the thirteenth century even though all of the apparent conditions were there is precisely the lack of conjunction of these flows. Without their convergence and transformation into a new "desiring machine" successfully operating according to a new endogenous systemic logic ("production for production's sake" and for the benefit and reproduction of capital as a class and logic of collective organization) these flows may transform the appearance and some of the operations of a despotic state, but it will not create a capitalist machine (224). This conjunction occurs when capital becomes the full organizing "body" and principle of the socius (thus effectively creating a new form of socius), when it "directly appropriates production" instead of being marginal to the despotic machine's system of social and economic production, and when (following Marx) "money begets money" and "value a surplus value" (226–227). Much of this follows directly from Marx's analysis in *Capital*.

On top of this account of the capitalist machine's continuous auto-production of surplus value, Deleuze identifies another significant element that pertains directly to his conception of a generalized social theory of flows. The capitalist machine diverges fundamentally from the despotic machine in its "*transformation*

78 *Modernity and Political Obligation*

of the surplus value of code into a surplus value of flux" (228, emphasis in original). It produces dissolution and a decoding of flows across society in order to mobilize and re-harness them for the purpose of continual production for production's sake. Again following Marx's observations, capital is a force, a "universal cosmopolitan energy which overflows every restriction and bond" and can't help but attempt to do so since that is its systemic logic of operation and survival (Marx 1964, 129, cited in Deleuze and Guattari 1987, 453).[41] Such efforts of overcoming and dissolution will operate even when their operation leads to conditions of potential self-destruction.[42]

It is no surprise, then, that this relentless push for deterritorialization[43] and overcoming resistance runs up against the state's efforts to code and structure everything within its purview. Indeed, in a purely ideal form, it can seem like capital is opposed to the state (which is part of the reason why some of its celebrants imagine that capitalism could exist without it). Yet, in spite of its deterritorializing and sometimes catastrophe-inducing character, within the modern capitalist *machine* we can see that capital depends utterly on the state, even as it transforms it and undoes the state's reterritorializing efforts.[44] The state rescues capital from its self-destructive impulses (as seen with bailouts, and buying peace through welfare and labor concessions in periods of intense class war), secures the institutional conditions for its basic operations (its legal enforcement of property rights claims), opens up new areas for capital's exploitation (through war, imperialism, public works projects, "public-private partnerships"), absorbs surplus value (through standard state operations and the military-industrial complex), and even enhances capital's ability to more closely approach full productive and extractive capacity within the limits of particular conditions by integrating people and populations into the social machine, imposing a general lack through taxation mechanisms, and training populations to have utility and operability within the capitalist system. In spite of the conflicting processes, the state is still the ally of capital, because in rescuing capital from itself and securing the conditions for its operation (and even enhancement), it is able to harness its productive powers to expand its own capacities (at least relative to the purely despotic state) by taking a share of the surplus value produced. Consequently,

> The social axiomatic of modern societies is caught between two poles, and is constantly oscillating from one pole to the other. Born of decoding and deterritorialization, on the ruins of the despotic machine, these societies are caught between the Urstaat that they would like to resuscitate as an overcoding and reterritorializing unity, and the unfettered flows that carry them toward an absolute threshold. They recode with all their might ... while decoding – or allowing the decoding of – the fluent quantities of their capital and their populations.
>
> (Deleuze and Guattari 2009, 260)

Consequently, when "the historian says, no, the Modern State, its bureaucracy and its technocracy, do not resemble the ancient despotic state," Deleuze agrees (261). They do not entirely mirror each other, since they are engaged in different

Modernity and Political Obligation 79

kinds of coding and territorializations of flows. "The paradox," however, "is that capitalism makes use of the Urstaat for effecting its reterritorializations" (ibid.). Modern capitalist states, in other words, are torn between the modern machine of capitalist deterritorialization (a process captured perfectly by Marx's observation that under capitalism, "all that is solid melts into air") and what Deleuze calls the Urstaat, the transhistorical principle of state efforts to capture flows, ever trying to reterritorialize that which breaks loose of its diagrams and codifications.[45] The Urstaat becomes an "internalized limit" mechanism of the modern capitalist machine (Deleuze and Guattari 2009, 261). By virtue of this relationship with a kind of institutionalized, yet never quite controlled process of deterritorialization and decoding, the modern capitalist machine is distinct from the territorial and the despotic. When it comes to the question of political obligation, however, the differences are not as radical as they might appear.

Even though each of the three social machines – territorial, despotic, capitalist – have generally first emerged in a historically successive fashion, this succession should not be folded into a teleological narrative. These machines are not simply historical instances that exist for a time, only to be superseded through some operation of progress or the unfolding of history. Rather, Deleuze uses them to exemplify virtual kinds of social machines whose operative logic can be co-operative within a given socius and in a particular state. When comparing them to extant forms of social organization, we can say that particular "concrete social formations are then specified by the extent to which the different abstract social machines are actualised within them in varying combinations" (Patton 2000, 88). Even though the modern capitalist machine has succeeded and displaced many territorial and despotic machines, it did not wholly brush away the systemic function of political obligation and rationalized obedience that were a part of these prior systems of capture. The decoding and destabilizing pole of the modern capitalist state has intensified the dislocations and anxieties that have been constitutive of modernity, including the displacement of prior cultural times. While this accelerating force of decoding dissolves some social bonds, institutions, and temporalities, it also creates new conditions (and threats) that compel the other pole, the machine of the Urstaat, to intervene with new reterritorializations and impositions of stability and order, and new "axioms" to facilitate this.[46]

Deleuze's analysis lets us theorize the nature of the state beyond the confines of simple juridical or sovereign conceptions of power and rule. We are given an account of the state as a "system of desire and destiny" that incorporates assemblages of land, objects, signs, and bodies into a complex – if never quite stable – social machine (Deleuze and Guattari 2009, 142). As a system of desire and destiny, however, Deleuze focuses quite heavily on the ways in which those desires are plugged into what we could call more strictly "functional" destinies; the ways in which people and objects become incorporated into the telic operations of particular combinations of social machines. In his *Capitalism and Schizophrenia* books written with Guattari, the more broadly perceptual element of temporality is de-emphasized in favor of the analysis of flows, machines, and assemblage. This analysis of flows certainly derives from and depends upon his

80 *Modernity and Political Obligation*

earliest appropriations of Bergson's insights into temporality (especially the connections between duration and difference), but it does not exhaust those connections. We can elaborate on this system of destiny entailed in the state processes of capture by incorporating and emphasizing the broader ways in which temporality is structured in the demands and justifications of political obligation claims.

Temporality and the State

The state is a thoroughly spatialized concept among political obligation theorists. It has to be in order to function as the defense against the force of time we identified earlier with the efforts of Rousseau, but also to be used as a recipient of obligations owed by particular subjects. While the state actually does appear "all at once" and "fully armed" within modern theories of political obligation, that appearance is not through the historical operations of machinic capture prioritized by Deleuze. Instead, it appears through the active forgetting of this process. This amnesia is achieved in two movements that occur distinctly but usually simultaneously. The first movement is a form of *excision*, while the second requires a telic *projection*.[47] The state is excised in the first movement in the sense that it is isolated and treated as a given unity rather than a convergence of distinct processes (it is Being excised from becoming). It is considered as something wholly formed and given with properties that do not require explanation. This is not something that is intrinsically objectionable. Taking the state as given allows us to practically consider our relationship to it, and can be especially necessary in cases requiring immediate and urgent action. Political obligation theorists tend to crystallize and universalize this excision, however, rendering it more rigid than any ad hoc heuristic measure.[48] Excised, the state is then grafted into a projected teleology wherein it appears as the culmination point that completes the necessary functions required by (our carefully pruned) political subjects. Through repetition and an emergent amnesia wrought of this spatialization, the moment of excision is forgotten. The idealized movement of subjects finding their constitutive lack completed through their recognition and enactment of their obligations toward the state can then appear to possess a self-sufficient cohesion.

As I claimed earlier, morality, rationality, and lack overlap and reinforce each other within political obligation theorists' conceptualizations of the political subject. More than this, however, I argue that these ascribed traits converge to form a distinct amalgamation that serves its own vital function within their teleology between political subjects and the state. In effect, these traits converge to form a kind of *doxa*. This *doxa* functions as a means to bind the subject and the state together within the teleology I described. It provides the "movement" to complete the teleology that begins at a given political subject (which, again, is distinguished by its delineated morality, rationality, and lack), and is fulfilled through that subject's recognition of an obligation's necessity and their corresponding obedience. This recognition and obedience is then taken to retrospectively affirm the state's attributed necessary functions.

Modernity and Political Obligation   81

Critiques of *doxa* go back to at least Plato, who contrasted it with Reason. In the *Gorgias* (1987) dialogue, Plato criticizes the Sophists for appealing to the common sense and popular beliefs of *doxa* rather than truth in their argumentation. Pierre Bourdieu uses the concept of *doxa* to mean that which is taken for granted in a society, and what in "the natural and social world appears as self-evident" (1972, 164). Within modern political obligation discourse, *doxa* is not passively accepted belief. Rather, it functions as a mobilization of assumed sentiments and forms of reasoning toward a conception of moral truth and right behavior. The problem with obligation theorists' deployment of *doxa* is not, then, its doubtful relationship to a particular account of truth. Instead, the problem lies in the fact that much like the state itself and the hypothetical subjects who live under it, the existence of some particular collection of sentiments, interests, and directed rationality is treated as a given. As a given, it then functions as a foundation upon which obligation theorists can develop their model architecture of political life, rather than as something whose very emergence requires explanation. Even when cursorily treated, the political conditions, institutions, legacy of struggles, and contingent and accidental particulars that played a part in the creation of shared sentiments and assumptions are excluded from subsequent arguments regarding their validity. Even when obligation theorists are accurate in their empirical assessments regarding the commonality of a particular set of beliefs or desires, their construction of a functional *doxa* within their subject-state teleology operates by isolating a particular (real or hypothetical) social configuration – what, on this account, amounts to merely a momentary distribution of difference and captured flows. Obligation theorists then excise that configuration from its conditions of historical production, obscure its contemporary processes of emergence, and project it into the future as part of the teleological link between a now effectively timeless and originary political subjectivity, the futural pull of the state's attributed necessary functions, and their mutual culmination through the fulfillment of the subject's political obligations, spurred on by their purported doxic characteristics.

Even when they do explicitly acknowledge and reflect on the historical emergence of the state in their work, modern obligation theorists are compelled to divorce the state from the processes of its historical *and ongoing* emergence as soon as they attempt to make it do any argumentative work. The problem with this is not simply one of a lack of appreciation for historical nuance as such. The primary problem with political obligation theorists' uses of the state is not its ahistoricity, but rather that the state is treated as an object outside of time. Regardless of any historical context brought to bear in describing the emergence of the state, once it is actively put to use in service of a particular theory of political obligation it is given to us as an ontologically pre-formed, packaged unity. In treating the state as an already-formed object – starting from a theoretical position of given unity and wholeness – modern obligation theorists block off our ability to account for the assemblages that constitute actual states, as well as the processes of capture required to sustain them.

By beginning from this position of given unity, obligation theorists (primarily apologists) also conflate the state with order as such, and dichotomize this state

82   *Modernity and Political Obligation*

order against an inverse conception of disorder, generating the kind of false problem discussed by Deleuze in *Bergsonism* (1991),

> [behaving] as though nonbeing existed before being, disorder before order, and possible before existence. As though being came to fill in a void, order to organize a preceding disorder, the real to realize a primary possibility.... In the false problem ... being, order, and the existent are supposed to precede themselves, or to precede the creative act that constitutes them, by projecting an image of themselves back into a possibility, a disorder, a non-being which are supposed to be primordial.... The idea of disorder appears when, instead of seeing that there are two or more irreducible orders ... we retain only a general idea of order that we confine ourselves to opposing to disorder and to thinking in correlation with the idea of disorder.
>
> (18–20)

The most obvious instance of such a clear dichotomy is Hobbes' conception of the state versus the state of nature, but this retro-projection maneuver is by no means limited to this kind of formal construct. It is only upon being denuded[49] of the temporal that the state can be presented by obligation theorists as a bundle of (pre-captured) functions, and offered up to hypothetical subjects who have already had their desires primed and pruned, and their imaginations helpfully misplaced.

Legitimacy and Justification

Even when the state and its subjects are ontologically prepared in this way, theorists of political obligation have to integrate the state with the political obligations that they argue are owed. This integration is accomplished through the establishment of two qualifying standards that function to exclude some kinds of obligation claims, and reinforce others. The first qualifying standard is a set of conditions of "legitimacy," the rightness of a state's claim to rule and demand obligations within some domain of activity.[50] The second qualifying standard is the set of parameters for evaluating the "success" of a particular theory of political obligation; its method of proper "justification" as such. They are occasionally implicit and unexamined, but they are universal features of formal theories of obligation. Although practical political discourses regarding expected duties and behavior usually sustain themselves by rendering such justification unnecessary, equivalent functions operate there as well.[51] Rather than objective or impartial measures of evaluation, legitimacy and justification are inextricable from the theoretical assumptions and goals of any particular obligation theorist, and function to reinforce the perceived validity and temporal organization of their account of political obligation.

Few theorists of political obligation posit the necessity of blanket obedience to all existing authorities in all circumstances. Requisite obedience is conditional, and subject to questions regarding the legitimacy of either a state, or the particular demands of a state. Legitimacy as A.J. Simmons defines it is "the

Modernity and Political Obligation 83

complex moral right a state possesses to be the exclusive imposer of binding duties on its subjects, to have its subjects comply with these duties, and to use coercion to enforce the duties" (2001, 130). In terms of the exercise of individual reason, the existence of legitimacy in a state's rule implies that you should substitute the judgments of the state for your own when it pertains to a domain in which a state properly legislates (Raz 1985). In political obligation theory, legitimacy thus operates as a delimiter of what kinds of obligation claims are considered valid or invalid, when, and where. It is a standard appealed to in order to evaluate claims regarding the force of obligations in any particular context.

In defending his philosophical anarchism,[52] for instance, Simmons argues that legitimacy follows from voluntarily assumed obligations between individuals and institutions. Because no existing states meet satisfactory standards for genuine consent to be possible, no existing states can possess legitimacy (2001, 155–156). Dudley Knowles, an obligation apologist, argues for the importance of certain "domain-limiting principles" in order to establish absolute limiting principles on the proper boundaries of legitimate state action and obligation claims. If the actions or demands of authority are "immoral," would force you to cause harm to yourself, or are "absurd," then they are no longer legitimate (Knowles 2010, 40–45). Each of these boundaries is defined in relation to a particular account of pluralistic liberal morality characterized by a dialectic between the reasoning of the state and its citizens.[53] Carole Pateman argues that the problem of political obligation is irresolvable in liberal democracies, because those obligations can only be given expression within participatory self-managing democracies. Legitimacy follows only from the obligations one accrues through active political participation in such institutional arrangements (Pateman 1985, 1).

Legitimacy is treated for each of these theorists as a standard for evaluating obligation claims. Although most modern obligation theorists certainly recognize that there is no universal standard of legitimacy, it is nevertheless treated within a given obligation theory *as if* it were a kind of independent arbiter. We thus see a curious kind of disassociation occurring. The assumptions operating within any particular conceptualization of legitimacy, as we can see from our examples, are clearly hitched to the values and goals of the theorists who set out to establish an obligation theory or evaluate the particular claims of an idea or political circumstance in relation to that theory. Knowles' domain-limiting principles are clearly tied to his conception of liberal morality while Simmons wields legitimacy as an extension of his conception of ideal conditions of consent. Moral questions of legitimacy as used within contemporary political obligation discourse are not impartial descriptions or measures by which a state and its obligation demands can be evaluated. Nevertheless, legitimacy is regularly cast as one of the primary qualities that states ostensibly must have in order for their authority to be "genuine" and for their obligation claims to hold.

What function does legitimacy serve in political obligation theory, then, and why is it shown such concern? What work is it doing for these scholars? I argue that within this discourse, legitimacy functions as part of a closed-loop conceptual circuit whose sole purpose is to affirm the validity of the principles and

84   *Modernity and Political Obligation*

commitments that any particular theorist begins with. No obligation theorist is ever surprised at the kind of political order that they end up judging to be legitimate. They may, perhaps, have to evaluate the details of a particular state or set of laws in order to fully understand what it is that they are assessing, but they invariably conclude that those orders which repeat their values and ideal conditions back to them convincingly are "legitimate," while those who deviate sufficiently from the ideal value or conditions are illegitimate.

In an influential 1966 article, Hanna Pitkin considered the meaning of legitimacy alongside other concepts that frequently appear in modern obligation theory:

> Now the same line of reasoning can be applied to the question "why does even a legitimate government, a valid law, a genuine authority ever obligate me to obey?" As with promises ... we may say that this is what "legitimate government," "valid law," "genuine authority" mean. It is part of the concept, the meaning of "authority," that those subject to it are required to obey, that it has a right to command. It is part of the concept, the meaning of "law," that those to whom it is applicable are obligated to obey it. As with promises, so with authority, government, and law: there is a prima facie obligation involved in each, and normally you must perform it.
>
> (Pitkin 1966, 48)

For Pitkin, this observation was a way to forestall an infinite doubting as to the validity of any particular obligation claim. If a government is legitimate, then you have an obligation toward it by definition. While A.J. Simmons was deeply unsatisfied with this way of approaching legitimacy in his critique of Pitkin in his *Moral Principles and Political Obligation* (1979), and sought to develop a *stronger* account of legitimacy as a defense of his own philosophical anarchism, I actually think that Pitkin's observation here is extremely apt, though not for the reasons she wishes. It is the case that legitimacy and validity imply some conditions for acceptable political obligations and obedience as "part of the concept." Legitimacy and validity each clearly affirm the "correctness" and acceptability of the institutions they qualify (government, the law) as part of the function of the description. Even government, law, and authority (as well as sovereignty) in their normalized conceptualization and popular use contain the trace of these sanctifying qualifiers. The fact that a government is usually treated as radically different in kind than organized crime syndicates, street gangs, or large-scale piracy, *even when it is engaged in overt war-making or plunder*, is a testament to the power of these sanctifying elements.[54] The concept of legitimacy functions as a means of closing off endless possible doubting of one's obligations through the imposition of an echo of the obligation theorist's commitments and values, or from another angle, a delayed tautology of their theory as such. Simmons identifies a common criticism of the "circularity" of Weber's account of legitimacy that usually arises when it is treated as a normative standard (Simmons 2001, 133). While Simmons dismisses this critique as a misunderstanding of Weber, he does not seem to recognize the circularity intrinsic to the function of the concept of legitimacy itself within the moral discourse of political obligation.

The methods and standards of justification used by political obligation theorists determine the way in which the success of a theory itself is evaluated. They establish what counts as a successful or unsuccessful theory of political obligation, and the kinds of reasoning and evidence that are pertinent to determining this success. There is no uniformly accepted standard of success among contemporary obligation theorists. Some build a complex architecture of what constitutes justice from explicit first principles, while others appeal to more informal methods of establishing theoretical consistency. Margaret Gilbert appeals to a nuanced set of criteria for the theoretical justification of her plural subject theory of associative obligations, including its explanatory depth and breadth, its "intuitiveness," an "intelligible grounding" of theoretical obligations in one's real political membership, the "puzzle-solving" ability of a theory to address immediate concerns and puzzles pertaining to obligation theory, as well as other criteria.[55] John Horton appeals to a more flexible "hermeneutic" approach to justification, proposing four criteria that he argues follow from this: a theory's ability to make sense of obligation while respecting other valued ideas and "ordinary thought about these matters," to account for the "standard case" in which obligations would apply, to explain cases where obligation is thought to be significant, and to meet Simmons' "particularity requirement," which demands that a theory explain why obligations must be owed to the particular polity of which someone is a member, rather than any other (Horton 2010, 9). Others propose more minimalist forms of justification, such as Dudley Knowles through his "good reasons" thesis, which argues that obligations are valid if citizens can find good moral reasons to support them (Knowles 2010, 53). The most straightforwardly minimalist method of justification is arguably that of Thomas McPherson who claims that the idea of political obligation requiring justification at all is "absurd."[56]

There is no point here in attempting to evaluate the relative validity of any of these standards of justification. To attempt to do so would simply involve deploying (either implicitly or explicitly) an alternative justification mechanism to joust with the rest. Invariably, of course, our little jouster would defeat its opponents by virtue of the rules that it has defined for itself – as would each of the others. *Justifications are self-justifying*. Or rather, justification presents itself as self-evident, while it actually rests upon an act of pure decree by the theorist (or in practical political discourse, by the voice of "common sense"). This is not to say that justification is pointless, or "false."[57] All philosophical, theoretical, empirical, and argumentative endeavors – any attempt to draw conclusions about anything – require justifications of some sort. Justification defines admissible forms of evidence and reasoning, and is thus eminently practical in nature. What this highlights, however, is not the intrinsic truth value of any particular form of justification, but rather the function it serves within discourse generally, and political obligation theory in particular. Given Bergson's analysis of the practical nature of most spatializations, we should not rest at the recognition that a spatialization is practical. Practicality, we can say, inevitably entails closure.

86 *Modernity and Political Obligation*

Closure is functional. In terms of justification, it draws boundaries, blocks off lines of questioning, and rebuffs some kinds of evidence while exalting and including others, all in order to render certain collections of personal experience, values, concepts, and data usable as a cohesive and stable "body" of thought at all. In terms of its role in grounding any theory of obligation, if legitimacy acts as a delayed tautology by echoing the theorist's assumed values and goals back to them once they appear, justification acts as a form of indirect question begging, structuring the conceptualization of the problem of obligation so that it arrives at a foregone conclusion.

Theories of political obligation thus depend on the development of a systematic consistency between concepts in order to ground themselves and produce the appearance of stability and certainty. They develop, we can say, an "endo-consistency" within the conceptualization of obligation itself, and an "exo-consistency" between obligation and other concepts (legitimacy, sovereignty, necessity, etc.) (Deleuze 1994, 19–20). Legitimacy reinforces an ideal vision of the state, its political subjects, and the form of doxic reason that binds them together by echoing the value assumptions and ideals of the obligation theorist and closing the loop of potentially endless doubt over the validity of those values and ideals. The legitimized state may further appeal to associated sub-concepts that sanctify dimensions of its rule, such as authority or sovereignty to further articulate and reaffirm its moral correctness, and, of course, the weight of its obligation demands.[58] Justification sanctifies the entire conceptual and discursive assemblage by virtue of its establishment of the accepted standards of proof and admissible forms of reasoning and problematization. It receives its justification through a fiat declaration of the correctness of that form of reasoning on the part of the obligation theorist. This creates an insulated, self-referential system of concepts, each of which justifies itself by reference to the recognition granted to it by the other concepts. It is no coincidence that the creation of this homogeneous and self-referential discourse is a part of a spatializing project to secure a vision of social order, purpose, and moral certitude against time.

Conclusion: Time-binding

In spite of their ostensible differences and divisions, both the apologists of political obligation and the philosophical anarchists can only maintain their existing parameters of argument through the theoretical move of spatializing time. It is in this sense that the traditional dichotomy posed between the two positions – and thus the contours of their discourse as such – obscures their commonalities, shared assumptions, and shared blind spots. As argued by Bergson in the previous chapter, spatialization is a ubiquitous temporal phenomenon. Language, identity, and other fundamental elements of practical life depend on it utterly. Yet, not all spatializations are equal or identical, either in their outcomes or in the manner in which they are approached and maintained by individuals and groups. Bergson discusses ways in which spatializations constitute social and political life, but the term is a bit too baggy for our present purposes. It makes it difficult to distinguish between distinct material and symbolic

Modernity and Political Obligation   87

processes, perceptual transformations, and large-scale consequences of different spatializing operations. Using his ideas on memory and synchronic time from *Matter and Memory* can help us incorporate temporal transformations and projections into our understanding of spatialization, but even then we are limited by Bergson's heavy emphasis on the role of contiguous memory, and his lack of a more comprehensive political theory that can conceptually bridge his account of synchronic temporal projections and spatializations with a theory of social production, and the role of collective discourses of political discipline and order. Deleuze's theory of time and assemblages provides a better general framework for thinking about the complex and diffuse processes of organization, discipline, and capture which can structure and create distinct and multiplicitous temporalities. Combinations of concepts from Deleuze's toolbox can get us very close to what we need (we will draw upon them in subsequent chapters), but he does not give us a single ready-made concept that is entirely adequate for addressing the perceptual and discursive processes of temporal structuration that we find occurring among theories of political obligation.

In order to fill this need, we will use the concept of "time-binding" to designate the primary mechanism whereby temporalities are generated, shaped, and deployed in order to compel people to comply with some goals or ends. Time-binding is not exclusively a mechanism of states or philosophers of state, but it is on the compelling of individuals to obey the state via appeals to their political obligations that we will focus. Time-binding is a mechanism of spatialization, projection, and discipline geared toward the pursuit of effecting certain behavior, perspectives, or outcomes in individuals and populations. It produces the temporal structuration (the emergent structure and shape of a temporality or collection of interlocking temporalities) that shapes our perceptions of time and of our conventional selves – the representations, personal history, and identities that constitute the symbolic dimension of our overall "self" – across time, and does so in order to facilitate compliant behavior. Through time-binding, the past, present, and future can be projected, segmented, rendered timeless, or shrouded entirely, and these transformations can be either limited or attached to larger temporalities.

Among theories and practical discourses of political obligation, this time-binding maneuver is generally performed in two related yet distinct ways. In the first method, *vertical time-binding*, obligation theorists develop a universalizing, homogenizing, and atemporal notion of political obligations, and debate those obligations or lack thereof as appendages of competing stratified images of properly distributed roles, institutions, axiologies, behaviors, and burdens. They create what I will refer to as a "vertical co-temporality" in their attempts to justify their obligation claims and time-bind our conventional selves to the parameters of this construct. In the second method, *horizontal time-binding*, obligation theorists do not attempt to make this kind of overtly imperative merger of an individual's conventional self into an image. Rather, they attempt to bind one's concrete self to and through their conventional self across time. This is achieved through a multi-stage process of extracting, crystallizing, and extending a (real or hypothetical) moment from a person's life, and using it as a

88   *Modernity and Political Obligation*

disciplinary tool to justify and compel the compliance and obedience entailed in an obligation claim.

Over the next two chapters, we will examine these processes of time-binding found throughout the literature on political obligation. We will outline their major features, and identify elements of these processes that are problematic analytically, practically, and at times even according to the standards and commitments of the obligation theorists themselves. Most importantly, following the third rule of Bergsonian intuition, we will attempt to frame these processes in terms of time rather than space. While it is important to map out the illusory shape that a particular method of time-binding creates, we must also explain the underlying material and phenomenological processes upon which it depends.

Notes

1 Among theorists of modernity, capitalism, and democracy, concern for time and especially speed and "social acceleration" has been steadily increasing. Zygmunt Bauman's *Liquid Modernity* (2000), Robert Hassan's *Empires of Speed* (2009), Daniel Innerarity's *The Future and Its Enemies* (2012), and Sarah Sharma's *In the Meantime* (2014) are just a very small sampling of a wide variety of attempts to grapple with the many-faceted and oft-disruptive consequences of post-modernity, liquid modernity, post-Fordist capitalism, late capitalism, or any number of other designations for the complex and intensifying changes in markets, technology, communication, and class relations over the last half-century or so.

2   The time of everyday life, when it is maintained, is a collective product that functions to integrate the projects and contributions of human beings into a context transcending the personalized time of the individual. The time of everyday life, which might best be called cultural time, is unified by a transpersonal meaning linking human beings to a past that happened before they became aware and to a future that will occur after they die.

(Weinstein 1978, 11–12)

3 The Great Chain of Being is a hierarchical conception of the cosmos that provides a place and order of priority for the contents of the cosmos, from the most mundane to the divine. In its Christian variant, God is at the top of this order, followed by angels of various rank, humans, other animals, plants, and then minerals. Within humanity there could be further subdivisions, with Kings at the top, and other social ranks falling into line, symmetrical to the overarching Chain. See Arthur Lovejoy's *The Great Chain of Being* (1964).
4 See Karl Polanyi's *The Great Transformation* (1957).
5 See Eric Williams' *Capitalism and Slavery* (1994) and Sidney Mintz's *Sweetness and Power* (1985).
6 The "guardians" are those who enable one to abstain from using the "natural gift" of reasoning by providing easy surrogates in the form of unquestionable rules, structures, and the replacement of "alien guidance" for one's own. Examples he gives include physicians, priests, tax collectors, military officers, and rulers of states.
7 This is not to say that Kant's support for the use of one's ability to doubt and question translates into an actual support for radical insubordination. Distinguishing between one's "public" ability to freely reason as a particular individual, which should be inviolate, and one's "private" reason, which is limited when one is occupying a position of institutional or civic authority, Kant argues that we should be free to question without obstacle, but when it comes to fulfilling our oaths and duties to a legitimate government, "one certainly must not argue, instead one must obey" (1983, 42–43).

Modernity and Political Obligation 89

8   A fourth guarantee [offered by the Modern Constitution] had to settle the question of God by removing Him forever from the dual social and natural construction, while leaving Him presentable and usable nevertheless. Hobbes's and Boyle's followers succeeded in carrying out this task – the former by ridding Nature of any divine presence, the latter by ridding Society of any divine origin. Scientific power "no longer needed this hypothesis"; as for statesmen, they could fabricate the "mortal god" of the Leviathan without troubling themselves further about the immortal God whose Scripture was now interpreted only figuratively by the Sovereign. No one is truly modern who does not agree to keep God from interfering with Natural Law as well as with the laws of the Republic. God becomes the crossed-out God of metaphysics, as different from the God of the Christians as the Nature constructed in the laboratory is from the ancient *phusis* or the Society invented by sociologists from the old anthropological collective and its crowds of nonhumans.

(Latour 1993, 33)

9 See Stirner's *The Ego and His Own* (2005).

10   The mythical investment of the Apocalypse could be adapted to a given situation, and even noncanonical prophecies presented little variation from the figures that were supposed to appear at the Judgment, such as the Emperor of Peace, the Engelspäpste, or harbingers of the Antichrist such as Gog and Magog who, according to oriental tradition (also then current in the West), remained confined to the Caucasus by Alexander until the time came for their irruption. However the image of the End of the World was varied, the role of the Holy Roman Empire remained a permanent feature: as long as it existed, the final Fall was deferred. The Emperor was the katechon of the Antichrist. All of these figures appeared to emerge into historical reality during the epoch of the Reformation. Luther saw the Antichrist in possession of the "holy throne," and for him Rome was the "Whore of Babylon"; Catholics saw Luther as the Antichrist; peasant unrest and the growing sectarian militancy of diverse sections of the declining Church appeared to foreshadow the last civil war preceding the Fall. Finally, the Turks who stormed Vienna in the year of Altdorfer's painting appeared as the unchained people of Gog.

(Koselleck 2004, 11–12)

11 Latour argues that "we have never been modern." Our perception of modernity, he argues, is predicated upon our belief in the distinction between "purification" on the one hand (creating entirely distinct ontological zones, such as a realm of man versus a realm of nature), and translation on the other (creating "mixtures between entirely new types of beings" such as the creation of a conception of a comprehensive ecological chain). He argues that they both actually depend entirely on each other, so once we recognize this we are no longer modern, then simultaneously we recognize that we have never actually been modern in the sense of ever actually being able to keep them separate (1993, 10–11).

12 Latour argues that the concepts of the modern, modernization, and modernity are held distinctly in contrast to an "archaic and stable past" (1993, 10).

13 Modernity is often portrayed as an event that straightforwardly (at least in the West) superseded an older order that had met its inevitable fate. This narrative is itself, however, a product of modernity. It was in fact a slow and uneven spreading of several distinct processes, even in Europe. The emergence of markets as an increasingly dominant force of social dissolution and reconstitution began around the fifteenth century, but it often isn't until the nineteenth century that it is characterized as having matured. Social accommodation and resistance to these changes varied across regions. In terms of the spread of Enlightenment ideas, and the dislocation of religion in people's lives, these also varied widely by country and class makeup at different times.

90　*Modernity and Political Obligation*

14　Rousseau's description of this sporadically accessible absorption with the present resembles Bergson's descriptions of duration, as well as the ideal of being purely present in Zen meditation:

> But if [happiness] is a state in which the spirit finds a base solid enough on which to rest and gather there all its being without needing to recall the past or step into the future; a state in which time is nothing for the spirit, in which the present lasts forever without, nevertheless, marking its duration, and without a trace of succession, without any other feeling of deprivation or delight, pleasure or suffering, desire or fear, except that of our mere existence: such a feeling alone can fill the soul completely. As long as this state lasts, he who finds himself in it can call himself happy, not with an imperfect happiness that is poor and relative, of the kind one finds in the pleasures of life, but a happiness that is sufficient, perfect, and complete, that leaves in the soul no emptiness that it feels it must fill.
>
> (Rousseau 2013, 491–492)

15　For the rest of this paragraph on Rousseau, I rely on Mabel Wong's (2010; 2012) creative interpretation of Rousseau as a highly sensitive social theorist of temporality.

16　It is the role of the Legislator in Rousseau's work, Wong argues, to initially forge this temporal unity through a willingness to transform human nature, and to bind people to a common cause and a common future through the founding of a social order. Patriotism and other methods of social discipline serve to maintain this unity (Wong 2012, 182–183).

17　As Wong notes, "the advent of industry and commerce, the increase in population size and density, the introduction of property" and other socially disruptive developments intensified the sense of temporal fluctuation for Rousseau (Wong 2012, 181).

18　Bergson discusses "binding time" and its social significance. He seems to understand this phrase itself as more of a synonym for the mental act of spatializing and imagining connections between moments in spite of their lack of necessary relationship. It is R.M. MacIver, however, who discusses processes by which we can become the "bondsmen of time," and seems to suggest a much more politically charged understanding of the dimension of power operative in the configurations of our experience of time and temporality (MacIver 1962, xxiv).

19　Robert Nozick, for instance, also focuses on the state's claimed right to levy taxes, critiquing that from a position of (a modified interpretation of) Lockean property rights and a libertarian ethic (1974). Ilan Zvi Baron focuses on the state's ability to ask us to die for its goals or existence, discussing both overtly compulsory and ostensibly non-compulsory elements of the ability (2009).

20　Such as the authority of the scientist or the auto mechanic.

21　By this I mean those people who are perceived as influential moral exemplars, and whose opinions are supported by prestige and respect.

22　It would be dangerous to call this "natural" authority as some have, since the Western atomic family unit is by no means the only or default way in which children are raised. Nevertheless, within this arrangement, parents are able to exercise a profound form of authority over children that is not conventionally bound to institutions of rule.

23　We will also, for the moment, ignore the patriarchalist theory of the Divine Right of Kings defended by philosophers like Robert Filmer.

24　See Wolff (1970, 5); Beran (1987, 12); Klosko (2005, 21–22).

25　One especially common response has been to defend the possibilities of retaining some individual decision-making discretion with the existence of both obligations and authority. For examples of this, see Winch (1972); Klosko (2004, 76–77); Horton (2010, 126–127).

26　When the state is used in a more expansive fashion to include all of a society as such, or when the claimant of obligations is presented as friends, family, bosses, or those in need, the nature of this relationship can change. Those who appeal to the "Samaritan" justification for political obligation often position our obligation to help those in need

Modernity and Political Obligation 91

as primary, and argue for our obligation to the state itself as a derivative of the primary, presumably horizontal duty to other individuals who don't necessarily occupy any position of authority. We will address the Samaritan appeal more fully in Chapter 3, and how we can think about other informal kinds of obligations in Chapter 5.

27 Most contemporary obligation theorists, both apologists and anarchists, are operating within the liberal tradition. Even among communitarian advocates of membership theories who de-emphasize the role of consent in establishing obligations, there is a general concern for the rights and freedoms of individuals, limitations on what the state can legitimately do, and other hallmarks of liberal political thought. Philosophical anarchists generally reside here as well, although the priority they place upon certain principles, such as moral autonomy, leads them to opposed conclusions.

28 George Klosko structures his argument in a similar way, arguing that states are necessary to provide certain necessary goods of modern society, and obligations (grounded in the principle of fairness, alongside others) follow in order to achieve or sustain these goods (2005, 18).

29 See Nozick (1974).

30 Rousseau, for instance, has a quite idiosyncratic definition of state. The state, for him, is the full, collective body and will of a people who together make up the sovereign (ideally within a direct democracy). The government, on the other hand, is the specialized group of people operating as a kind of executive branch, and tasked with actually carrying out the sovereign people's will (see his *Social Contract*).

31 See especially Sandel (1998), MacIntyre (1984), Taylor (1989), Walzer (1971; 1983).

32 Rationality is usually interpreted as at least a minimally Kant-inspired conception of autonomy: the ability to conceive of morality and act upon it (or not), and to reflect upon evidence calmly and not simply through "emotion" or "passions." It may also extend up to the hyper-calculative conception of the unbounded rational-actor.

33 As he observes, this account is something that even philosophical anarchists like Simmons accept, and which anti-state libertarians frequently attempt to provide in their arguments for non-state alternatives for goods distribution. Klosko cites Friedman (1973), but also see Huemer (2013) for a more extensive discussion of attempts to justify largely market provisions of traditionally public services and goods.

34 "Every 'object' presupposes the continuity of a flow; every flow, the fragmentation of the object" (Deleuze and Guattari 2009, 6).

35 The socius is not "society" as such, since the concept of society tends to focus on people alone, and already tends to assume a degree of consistency, interaction, and endogeneity among people, culture, resource flows, and symbolic exchanges. It takes them as a given, essentially unified aggregate. The socius is understood instead as the whole terrain of bodies and objects which are constantly in the process of being assembled, disassembled, and reassembled according to certain patterns and processes of consistency.

36 This also has the rather important consequence of obliterating the evolutionary teleological dimension of Hegel's dialectic which Marx had tried to preserve. Nevertheless, Deleuze explicitly positions himself as operating in a way that is consonant with Marxist theory, in spite of jettisoning or radically modifying most of its major concepts (Deleuze 1995, 171).

37 This deity can be a conventional one, as under Christendom. Much more important is the function this deity serves as a kind of "despotic signifier" that both represents and justifies the social machine of which it is a part, and which it helps to continually create. Thus, a conventional deity could be – and has been – replaced by any number of symbols or collection of symbols that are capable of fulfilling this position, to which the despot lays a privileged relationship; sovereignty, legitimacy, general will, and popular consent are no different in this regard than Providence or God's Will.

38 In some gift economies (the "kula" ring exchange in the Trobriand Islands, or the Pacific Northwest "potlatch"), for example, although we find a constantly imbalanced exchange

92   *Modernity and Political Obligation*

of goods, ritual objects, or prestige, a debt is completely discharged once one side completes its traditional exchange, hand-off, or part of the cycle, shifting to the other party.

39 This conjunction is necessary for the capitalist machine to emerge and transform the despotic state. Each of these flows can "strike" the despotic state and "submerge the tyrant," only to result in its return and transformation in new forms when lacking the conjunction: "they democratize him, oligarchize him, segmentize him, monarchize him, and always internalize and spiritualize him" (Deleuze and Guattari 2009, 222–223).

40 For Deleuze, "universal history" is a history of chance encounters rather than fate.

41 These restrictions that capital seeks to overcome can certainly be thought of in spatial terms. The forces of globalization which intensified in the latter half of the twentieth century enabled markets, commodities, corporations, and finance capital to move around the world more easily and rapidly, and often in spite of any single state's wishes. We can also think of them as obstacles to the maximum extraction of profit. Attempts to cut labor costs, or get around state regulations are classic efforts by capital to overcome them.

42 The 2007–2009 Great Recession in the United States, for instance, was largely a product of conditions that finance bankers, hedge funds, and their lobbyists created for themselves in attempting to overcome obstacles to profit. The increasingly ponderous size and destabilizing force of finance capital itself, the allowance of credit default swap derivatives, a burst bubble in housing prices, and the sizable domestic private debt were products of this relentless logic, as well as contributors to their convergent effects in the Recession.

43 Deleuze uses the concept of "territorialization" (and reterritorialization) to mean essentially the consolidation, convergence, coding, and unification of flows, and the concept of "deterritorialization" to mean the dissolution, molecularization, and loosening or rearranging of flows.

44 Deleuze also appeals here to Marx's hypothesis of the tendency of the rate of profit to fall in capitalism, wherein markets continually become more saturated, unemployment rises, and stagnation ensues until new opportunities for profit can be opened up. Marx saw this as indicative of capitalism's self-destructive capacity. The state, Deleuze says, operates within the capitalist machine as a limiting mechanism that constantly defers and resets capital's theoretical limitless urge toward expansion and comprehensive exploitation (Deleuze and Guattari 2009, 230–231).

45 The concept of the Urstaat is a reference to

> the city of Ur, the point of departure of Abraham or the new alliance. The State was not formed in progressive stages; it appears fully armed, a master stroke executed all at once; the primordial *Urstaat*, the eternal model of everything the State wants to be and desires. "Asiatic" production, with the State that expresses or constitutes its objective moment, is not a distinct formation; it is the basic formation, on the horizon throughout history.
>
> (Deleuze and Guattari 2009, 217)

46 Deleuze understands "axioms" as concessions and modifications that the state incorporates into the capitalist machine in order to secure that machine's overall stability when faced with threat. Deleuze points to the establishment of union and labor concessions in capitalist countries as a stabilization and threat reduction response to the Russian Revolution and "a powerful working class that required a high and stable level of employment." Axioms alter some features of the machine in order to leave essentials unchanged (Deleuze and Guattari 2009, 253).

47 Both apologists and philosophical anarchists spatialize the state through excision, though it is usually only the apologists that adopt the projected teleology. Philosophical anarchists adopt a different form of temporal structure, which we will discuss more in Chapter 4.

48 Kant's insistence on a universal, categorical morality as opposed to a particularistic ethic rears its head again.

Modernity and Political Obligation   93

49 This denuding should not be taken to preclude the possibility – indeed, the extreme like-lihood – that an official *history* will form to replace the state's substantive *temporality*.

50 Political obligation theorists generally distinguish between an empirical, sociological analysis of legitimacy, such as Weber's (where legitimacy is seen as a kind of "reservoir of loyalty on which leaders can draw" (Tyler 1990, 26)) and their own normative accounts.

51 The power of "common sense" and the internalized voice of the *doxa* usually render overt justification of ubiquitous norms unnecessary. That is their function.

52 As we will discuss more in Chapter 4, while the philosophical anarchists draw different conclusions than the apologists, the means by which they do so are susceptible to many of the same critiques being brought against apologists themselves.

53 This dialectic is summed up by Knowles' phrase, "the state proposes; the citizen disposes" (2010, 53).

54 A fundamental difference is not to be taken for granted as obvious. Aside from political anarchists judging them to be deeply similar, Charles Tilly (1985) has drawn his iconic comparison between the emergence of European nation-states and the operation of organized crime protection rackets. Augustine (hardly an anarchist) provides this parable in Book 4 Chapter 4 of *City of God* (1958):

> Justice being taken away, then, what are kingdoms but great robberies? For what are robberies themselves, but little kingdoms? The band itself is made up of men; it is ruled by the authority of a prince, it is knit together by the pact of the confederacy; the booty is divided by the law agreed on. If, by the admittance of abandoned men, this evil increases to such a degree that it holds places, fixes abodes, takes possession of cities, and subdues peoples, it assumes the more plainly the name of a kingdom, because the reality is now manifestly conferred on it, not by the removal of covetousness, but by the addition of impunity. Indeed, that was an apt and true reply which was given to Alexander the Great by a pirate who had been seized. For when that king had asked the man what he meant by keeping hostile possession of the sea, he answered with bold pride, *What you mean by seizing the whole earth; but because I do it with a petty ship, I am called a robber, while you who does it with a great fleet are styled emperor.*

55 See Gilbert 2006, 43–47 for a more thorough discussion of these criteria.

56   [W]hy should I obey the government is an absurd question. We have not understood what it *means* to be a member of political society if we suppose that political obligation is something we might not have had and that therefore needs to be *justified*.

                                 (McPherson 1967, 64)

57 Categories of true and false are themselves only secondary products of particular standards of justification.

58 Both of which, when "genuine" – and legitimacy already defined the state's possession of them as genuine – carry the trace of the tautological echo that Pitkin sees in legitimacy. What is the concept of "sovereignty" but a special category for distinguishing overwhelming power and force in a given territory, setting this manifestation of force aside as something different in kind? As Carl Schmitt argued in *Political Theology* (1985),

> All significant concepts of the modern theory of the state are secularized theological concepts not only because of their historical development – in which they were transferred from theology to the theory of the state, whereby, for example, the omnipotent God became the omnipotent lawgiver – but also because of their systematic structure.

As theology was designed to sanctify the despotic signifier of God, modern political theory is structured to repeat this affirmation of not only the state, but rule (*archê*) as such.

94   *Modernity and Political Obligation*

References

Anscombe, Elizabeth. 1978. "On the Source of the Authority of the State." *Ratio* 20 (1): 1–28.

Anscombe, Elizabeth. 1981. *The Collected Philosophical Papers of G. E. M. Anscombe, Volume Three: Ethics, Religion and Politics*. Oxford: Blackwell.

Augustine. 1958. *The City of God*. New York: Image.

Baron, Ilan Zvi. 2009. *Justifying the Obligation to Die: War, Ethics, and Political Obligation with Illustrations from Zionism*. New York: Lexington Books.

Bauman, Zygmunt. 2000. *Liquid Modernity*. Malden, MA: Polity.

Beran, Harry. 1987. *The Consent Theory of Political Obligation*. London: Croom Hill.

Berman, Marshall. 1983. *All That Is Solid Melts into Air*. New York: Verso.

Bourdieu, Pierre. 1972. *Outline of a Theory of Practice*. Cambridge: Cambridge University Press.

Burke, Edmund. 1986. *Reflections on the Revolution in France*. New York: Penguin Books.

Corfield, Penelope J. 2007. *Time and the Shape of History*. New Haven, CT: Yale University Press.

Deleuze, Gilles. 1991. *Bergsonism*. Translated by Hugh Tomlinson and Barbara Habberjam. New York: Zone Books.

Deleuze, Gilles. 1994. *What Is Philosophy?*. New York: Columbia University Press.

Deleuze, Gilles. 1995. *Negotiations: 1972–1990*. Translated by Martin Joughin. New York: Columbia University Press.

Deleuze, Gilles, and Felix Guattari. 1987. *A Thousand Plateaus: Capitalism and Schizophrenia*. Translated by Brian Massumi. Minneapolis: University of Minnesota Press.

Deleuze, Gilles, and Felix Guattari. 2009. *Anti-Oedipus: Capitalism and Schizophrenia*. New York: Penguin Books.

Descartes, Rene. 1927. "Discourse." In *Descartes: Selections*, edited by Ralph Eaton. New York: Charles Scribner's Sons.

Finnis, John. 1980. *Natural Law and Natural Rights*. Oxford: Clarendon Press.

Friedman, David. 1973. *The Machinery of Freedom*. La Salle, IL: Open Court.

Gilbert, Margaret. 2006. *A Theory of Political Obligation: Membership, Commitment, and the Bonds of Society*. New York: Oxford University Press.

Hassan, Robert. 2009. *Empires of Speed: Time and the Acceleration of Politics and Society*. Boston: Brill.

Hobbes, Thomas. 1987. *Leviathan*. Edited by C.B. Macpherson. New York: Penguin Classics.

Horkheimer, Max, and Theodor W. Adorno. 2002. *Dialectic of Enlightenment: Philosophical Fragments*. Edited by Gunzelin Schmid Noerr. Translated by Edmund Jephcott. Stanford, CA: Stanford University Press.

Horton, John. 2010. *Political Obligation*. Second Edition. New York: Palgrave Macmillan.

Huemer, Michael. 2013. *The Problem of Political Authority: An Examination of the Right to Coerce and the Duty to Obey*. New York: Palgrave MacMillan.

Innerarity, Daniel. 2012. *The Future and Its Enemies: In Defense of Political Hope*. Stanford, CA: Stanford University Press.

Kant, Immanuel. 1983. "An Answer to the Question: What Is Enlightenment?" In *Perpetual Peace and Other Essays*. Indianapolis: Hackett Publishing Company.

Klosko, George. 2004. *The Principle of Fairness and Political Obligation*. New York: Rowman & Littlefield.

Modernity and Political Obligation 95

Klosko, George. 2005. *Political Obligations*. New York: Oxford University Press.

Knowles, Dudley. 2010. *Political Obligation: A Critical Introduction*. New York: Routledge.

Koselleck, Reinhart. 2004. *Futures Past: On the Semantics of Historical Time*. Translated by Keith Tribe. New York: Columbia University Press.

Latour, Bruno. 1993. *We Have Never Been Modern*. Translated by Catherine Porter. Cambridge, MA: Harvard University Press.

Livesey, Graham. 2010. "Assemblage." In *The Deleuze Dictionary*, edited by Adrian Parr, Revised Edition. Edinburgh: Edinburgh University Press.

Lovejoy, Arthur O. 1964. *The Great Chain of Being*. Cambridge, MA: Harvard University Press.

MacIntyre, Alasdair. 1984. *After Virtue*. Second Edition. Notre Dame, IN: University of Notre Dame Press.

MacIver, R.M. 1962. *The Challenge of the Passing Years: My Encounter With Time*. New York: Pocket Books, Inc.

Marx, Karl, and Frederick Engels. 1998. *The Communist Manifesto: A Modern Edition*. New York: Verso.

McPherson, Thomas. 1967. *Political Obligation*. New York: Routledge & Kegan Paul.

Mintz, Sidney W. 1985. *Sweetness and Power: The Place of Sugar in Modern History*. New York: Penguin Books.

Nozick, Robert. 1974. *Anarchy, State, and Utopia*. New York: Basic Books.

Osborne, Peter. 1995. *The Politics of Time: Modernity and Avant-Garde*. New York: Verso.

Parekh, Bhikhu. 1993. "A Misconceived Discourse on Political Obligation." *Political Studies* 41 (2): 236–251.

Pateman, Carole. 1985. *The Problem of Political Obligation: A Critical Analysis of Liberal Theory*. New York: John Wiley & Sons.

Patton, Paul. 2000. *Deleuze and the Political*. New York: Routledge.

Pinch, Geraldine. 2002. *Egyptian Mythology: A Guide to the Gods, Goddesses, and Traditions of Ancient Egypt*. New York: Oxford University Press.

Pitkin, Hanna. 1966. "Obligation and Consent – II." *American Political Science Review* 60 (1): 39–52.

Plato. 1987. *Gorgias*. Translated by Donald J. Zeyl. Indianapolis: Hackett.

Polanyi, Karl. 1957. *The Great Transformation: The Political and Economic Origins of Our Time*. Boston: Beacon Press.

Proudhon, Pierre-Joseph. 2011. "General Idea of the Revolution in the Nineteenth Century." In *Property Is Theft!: A Pierre-Joseph Proudhon Anthology*, edited by McKay Iain. Oakland: AK Press.

Rawls, John. 1999. *A Theory of Justice*. Revised Edition. Cambridge, MA: The Belknap Press.

Raz, Joseph. 1985. "Authority and Justification." *Philosophy and Public Affairs* 14 (1): 3–29.

Rousseau, Jean-Jacques. 2013. "The Reveries of a Solitary Walker." In *The Essential Writings of Rousseau*, edited by Leo Damrosch, translated by Peter Constantine. New York: The Modern Library.

Salkever, Stephen G. 1974. "Virtue, Obligation and Politics." *American Political Science Review* 68: 78–92.

Sandel, Michael. 1998. *Liberalism and the Limits of Justice*. Second Edition. New York: Cambridge University Press.

Schmitt, Carl. 1985. *Political Theology: Four Chapters on the Concept of Sovereignty*. Translated by George Schwab. Cambridge, MA: The MIT Press.

96 *Modernity and Political Obligation*

Sharma, Sarah. 2014. *In the Meantime: Temporality and Cultural Politics*. Durham, NC: Duke University Press.

Simmons, A. John. 1979. *Moral Principles and Political Obligations*. Princeton, NJ: Princeton University Press.

Simmons, A. John. 2001. *Justification and Legitimacy: Essays on Rights and Obligations*. New York: Cambridge University Press.

Smith, Daniel W. 2012. *Essays on Deleuze*. Edinburgh: Edinburgh University Press.

Stirner, Max. 2005. *The Ego and His Own*. Mineola, NY: Dover.

Taylor, Charles. 1989. *Sources of the Self: The Making of the Modern Identity*. Cambridge: Cambridge University Press.

Tilly, Charles. 1985. "War Making and State Making as Organized Crime." In *Bringing the State Back In*, edited by Peter Evans, Dietrich Rueschemeyer, and Theda Skocpol. Cambridge: Cambridge University Press.

Tyler, Tom R. 1990. *Why People Obey the Law*. New Haven, CT: Yale University Press.

Walzer, Michael. 1971. *Obligations: Essays on Disobedience, War, and Citizenship*. New York: Simon & Schuster.

Walzer, Michael. 1983. *Spheres of Justice*. Oxford: Blackwell.

Weber, Max. 1946. *From Max Weber: Essays in Sociology*. New York: Oxford University Press.

Weinstein, Michael A. 1978. *Meaning and Appreciation: Time and Modern Political Life*. West Lafayette, IN: Purdue University Press.

Weinstein, Michael A. 1982. *The Wilderness and the City: American Classical Philosophy as a Moral Quest*. Amherst: The University of Massachusetts Press.

Wellman, Christopher Heath. 1996. "Liberalism, Samaritanism, and Political Legitimacy." *Philosophy and Public Affairs* 25 (3): 211–237.

Wellman, Christopher Heath. 2001. "Toward a Liberal Theory of Political Obligation." *Ethics* 111: 735–759.

Williams, Eric. 1994. *Capitalism and Slavery*. Chapel Hill: University of North Carolina Press.

Winch, Peter. 1972. "Authority and Rationality." *The Human World* 7.

Wolff, Robert Paul. 1970. *In Defense of Anarchism*. New York: Harper Torchbooks.

Wong, Mabel. 2010. "Belonging in the Midst of Time: Temporalities of Community from Rousseau to Deleuze." PhD diss., Johns Hopkins University.

Wong, Mabel. 2012. "Struggling with Time: A Rousseauian Caution to the Politics of Becoming." *Contemporary Political Theory* 11 (2): 172–191.

3 Vertical Time-binding

For good or ill, modernity has left shattered cultural time perspectives in its wake. One of the primary features of modern political thought has been the attempt to reclaim the sense of security and temporal orientation those cultural time perspectives had provided. It is through the process of time-binding in particular that modern theorists of political obligation have attempted to complete this dialectic of modernity. While it is already a more refined distinction than Bergson's spatialization, time-binding itself can be carried out in a variety of different ways. The first significant form of time-binding deployed by many political obligation theorists is what we can call vertical time-binding. It is "vertical" in that it entails the production of stratified images of ideal roles, burdens, norms, institutions, and subjects – images of vertical political co-temporality – and evaluates the various problems of political obligation according to how well they emulate the stratifications in the image. Included in this approach are most of the major justifications for political obligation that modern obligation apologists have to offer.[1] Appeals to fairness, membership, natural duty, and, the most recent development, the multiple principles approach, can all be considered exemplary projects of vertical time-binding. Significantly, and certainly likely to elicit protest from these theorists, we can also include that most decidedly unmodern of appeals under the same banner: the appeal to divine right, broadly construed.

Some may consider it negligent or sloppy to corral together so many subdivisions within political obligation theory. I should state at the outset that I do not mean to suggest that there are not notable differences between these different positions, either in terms of how their particular conceptualizations of obligation are constructed, or in terms of their practical political implications. A Rawlsian appeal to our natural duties would likely entail different kinds of acceptable political institutions, social norms, and requirements for obedience than those advocated by a membership theorist. It isn't that there are no significant distinctions to be made as such, but rather that these distinctions are of little value to our project at hand. Many questions or problems that have been considered vitally important points of disagreement and distinction between schools of obligation theorists – such as whether or not one has an obligation to die for the state – are on this account largely beside the point; they are distinctions without a significant difference for the problems we are presently concerned with. When it

98　*Vertical Time-binding*

comes to making sense of how these political obligation theories function as disciplinary constructs to bind time, the traditionally demarcated theoretical positions will be helpful as evidence, but of little use as a guide.

Nevertheless, we must lay out the basics of each of these positions if we are to make sense of their key commonalities. We will begin this chapter by briefly outlining each of the primary theories of political obligation pertinent to our discussion of vertical time-binding. We will then discuss vertical time-binding as a particular method of synthesizing the dialectic of modernity discussed in the previous chapter, drawing from Deleuze and Jacques Rancière to develop an account of the relationship between politics and aesthetics, and the production of images of social ordering. Finally, we will reconsider the relevant theories of obligation in light of our concept of vertical time-binding and account of political aesthetics, and discuss the implications, paying special attention to the kinds of continuities and discontinuities this interpretation can make visible.

Political Naturalism

Following A.J. Simmons, what we can call "political naturalism" has been tremendously influential in informing the ways in which political order and life have been perceived and justified, especially with regards to the nature of authority and political obligation. The basic proposition of political naturalism is that "it is part of the natural condition of humankind for persons to be politically organized, for some to be subject to the political authority of others" (Simmons 2006, 251). In ancient Greek thought, this is exemplified by Aristotle's assertion that humanity is "by nature a political animal," with political societies thus also existing "by nature."[2] In medieval European thought, Thomas Aquinas and Marsilius of Padua developed theories of political naturalism out of Aristotle's ideas, but further grounded the "nature" appealed to by Aristotle in the will of God. While political naturalism posits the essential and given character of political life for humanity, that naturalism can appear in both secular and religious forms. Aristotle's largely secular political naturalism appealed for its authority to a set of given and durable facts of the human condition, such as group belonging, while the religious political naturalism of Aquinas, Krishna, or Confucius established political life as an extension of the nature of divinity and the cosmos, and/or the will of God.

While few contemporary obligation theorists openly defend the idea of a divine right to rule as the primary foundation of their position, it is one of the oldest grounds for justifying political authority and political obligations to that authority. Even today, it is common to find political regimes appealing to the special favor or blessing of a deity, or proclaiming the coincidence between their policies and the said deity's will in speechwriting, nationalist narratives, and other propagandistic endeavors. Beyond these explicit appeals, figures such as Max Stirner, Carl Schmitt, and Friedrich Nietzsche have observed the genetic continuation of religious conceptual frameworks and categories of thought within liberalism and its discourses on sovereignty, law, legitimacy, and rights.[3] Even when latent and unrecognized, its influence persists.

Within religious political naturalist theories of obligation, obedience to a political order is traditionally intertwined with the perceived validity of a religious belief system or other supernatural ordering principle. Political disobedience can be seen as an act of religious disobedience and a divergence from the proper or natural arrangement of the world more broadly. Within the Christian kingdoms of medieval Europe, the idea that God had ordained the necessity of political authority in the institution of the monarch who was to rule by divine right was ubiquitous and foundational to the legitimating narratives of the prevailing order. St. Paul's doctrine played a pivotal role in grounding divine right claims in the medieval period, arguing that

> there is no authority except from God, and those that exist have been instituted by God. Therefore he who resists the authorities resists what God has appointed, and those who resist will incur judgment.[4]

For Thomas Aquinas, God is the author and sustainer of the essential nature of all beings in the world, both as particular kinds of beings and in their relationships with each other. The essential natures which God authors can collectively be understood as the universal and knowable "natural law," which is distinct from the various imperfect laws and polities set up by humanity. Not only is the natural law universal and knowable, it is eternal, "since Divine Reason's conception of things is not subject to time" (Aquinas 1981, I–II, 91.1). Aquinas argues that political life is an end we naturally pursue as a result of what God has authored us to be, and that membership in a polity has the potential to help us become more virtuous individuals. Further, through the form of monarchy we may be able to effectively reproduce, as best we can, the natural order sustained by God.[5] Following Aristotle, he does not refuse the possibility of permissible rebellion against tyrants, but the bulk of his argument supports the idea that our moral adherence to natural law should tend us toward deference to authority. Even into the seventeenth century, Robert Filmer's patriarchalist[6] theory of divine right carried enough political currency to be one of the primary targets of John Locke in his *First Treatise of Government* (Locke 2003). Political obligation within this kind of system entails understanding and acting in accordance with one's social and cosmic place within a vertical distribution of roles, expectations, and duties that itself mirrors the hierarchical relationship between God and humanity.

A comparable justification for political obligation can be found in the classical Chinese concept of the Mandate of Heaven. The concept of the Mandate has its inspirational roots in the ideal of a unified Ancient China developed during the Zhou Dynasty. Confucius drew from this ideal, and argued that the natural condition of the universe was one of harmony among all things. Confucius identifies five "fundamental human relationships" – husband and wife, father and son, older and younger brother, friend and friend, and ruler and subject – which he argues deserve particular respect (Bozeman 1960, 134–135). Beyond respect, "when the timeless patterns of these associations were fully understood and realized, peace, order, and happiness were to prevail in the entire community, however great its scope" (135). This harmony is mostly hierarchical in its

100 *Vertical Time-binding*

expression (with the exceptional relationship being "friend and friend"), yet it is ideally a hierarchy defined by benevolence from superiors, and a reciprocity of obligations rather than pure domination and oppression (Glanville 2010, 329). The legal cosmology upon which it was based saw a world divided into three parts, "the world of spirits, the realm of human beings, and the emperor" (Yonglin 2010, 175). The role of the emperor was that of mediator between spirits and humanity. While this granted the emperor the privilege of being a ruler, it also demanded the responsibility of maintaining harmony within the realm of humanity and between the realms of spirit and humanity. This was a task that required providing for the practical and moral education of the populace, as well as securing its material prosperity (ibid.). The Mandate of Heaven provides for a broader right to rebel against an unjust ruler than the divine right of kings found in medieval Europe. The conduct and virtue of the ruler is fundamentally in question, and the mere fact of rebellion challenges the leader's ability to appeal to the Mandate as a buttress to their legitimacy. For the Confucian scholar Mencius, the Mandate granted both Heaven and the ruler's subjects the authority to depose an unjust ruler. Indeed, the will of Heaven is said to be discernible through the "response in the people's hearts to their ruler" (Glanville 2010, 331). Still, the emphasis within this form of religious political naturalism rests upon a hierarchically structured understanding of order and stability. That understanding entails generalized political obligations owed toward the order and its rulers, as long as they meet the proper conditions of virtue and fulfill their role in helping sustain cosmological harmony.

In the West, explicit appeals to political obligations accruing from the divine rights of authority began to dissipate as a result of several significant challenges to the *ancien regime*. The emergence of liberalism and pushes for constraints on the power of the monarchy, the collapse of the feudal order and relative power of the church, and the rise of the Enlightenment each played a role in chipping away at the force of the justification. Thomas Hobbes and John Locke provided early expositions against the derivation of legitimacy and political obligation from divine right in their reflections on the social contract. As we will discuss in the next chapter, this early modern movement against dependence upon the direct justification of political authority and obligation should not be taken as a rejection of the divine as such, nor even a rejection of the importance of theological reasoning for political thought. Interpretations of the relationship between humanity and the divine were changing in this period, and with those changes (which were themselves imbricated with the political and economic transformations and struggles of the time) came shifts in interpretations of the character and foundations of political rule.

The secular political naturalism of Aristotle still provides the basic conceptual architecture for many contemporary theorists of political obligation, particularly for those who appeal to principles of "natural duty," and "membership." For these theorists, Aristotle's arguments regarding our fundamentally political nature (especially with regards to the telic character of our belonging to groups) is an especially powerful insight into the human condition and the significance of obligations for the fulfillment of our individual and collective aspirations.

Natural Duty

The appeal to the "natural duties of justice"[7] (usually shortened to "natural duty" theory) was initially developed by John Rawls in *A Theory of Justice* (1999).[8] In this work, he develops his most well-known thought experiment for defending his vision of justice known as the "original position" (102). The original position is a hypothetical scenario wherein representative individuals would meet, under specific constraints, in order to decide upon the moral principles and practical general rules that would apply to everyone. In order to prevent these hypothetical representatives from simply advocating rules and principles that would advantage themselves given their particular lot in life, they would operate behind a "veil of ignorance" (118). This veil would prohibit them from accessing information about what their station in life would be, including their income, intellectual abilities, religion, age, or other particulars. As a result, the representatives would have to decide upon the moral requirements and "primary goods" that any person would want while lacking knowledge of their personal characteristics or particular circumstances in the world (78). Natural duties are one such kind of derived moral requirement that apply to people generally. Rawls argues for several kinds of natural duties, including a duty to avoid harming others, and a "mutual aid" duty to help others when they are in jeopardy (assuming that one can do so without facing excessive personal risk) (98). He also argues that

> the most important natural duty is that to support and to further just institutions. This duty has two parts: first, we are to comply with and to do our share in just institutions when they exist and apply to us; and second, we are to assist in the establishment of just arrangements when they do not exist, at least when this can be done with little cost to ourselves.
>
> (293–294)

For Rawls, supporting and complying with just political institutions is something every person would hypothetically agree to in the original position. This is in large part because "the maintenance of public order" is a "necessary condition for everyone's achieving his ends whatever they are." He goes on to say that

> the government's right to maintain public order and security is an enabling right, a right which the government must have if it is to carry out its duty of impartially supporting the conditions necessary for everyone's pursuit of his interests and living up to his obligations as he understands them.
>
> (187)

While Rawls does offer provisions for legitimate civil disobedience in cases of serious violations of principles of fairness, equality, and justice generally,[9] he ultimately concludes that we have the duty to support generally just governments so that they may protect the conditions under which a decent minimum standard of life can be possible, because this is what "everyone" would hypothetically agree to in the original position (186).

102 *Vertical Time-binding*

Given the scope and conceptual complexity of his work, the literature both expanding upon and critiquing Rawls' project is massive, and would be impossible to cover here. One of the most famous of Rawls' critics is Robert Nozick, who objects to Rawls' theory of justice on libertarian grounds. For Nozick, Rawls' call for a justice based on a proper distribution of goods, especially material goods, overlooks questions regarding the justice of the procedures of distribution themselves. Most importantly, it overlooks questions of individual rights, with property rights (and the ability to both possess and freely exchange that property, as long as it was acquired legitimately) being of primary importance. It is not the outcome that we should be concerned with in thinking about questions of justice, then, but the history of the transactions and interactions that led to an outcome, and whether those transactions and interactions occurred in a just way. Nozick consequently desires a "night-watchman" minimal state designed to enforce contracts and protect against "violence, theft, and fraud" rather than a state concerned with securing a more equitable distribution of wealth (Nozick 1974, 26). Rejecting Rawls' conception of distributive justice as a violation of natural rights casts doubt on the legitimacy of a state that demands obligations in order to pursue that vision of justice. Others have criticized Rawls for perceived defects and limitations in his unique philosophical devices (the original position, veil of ignorance, etc.), the details of his conception of justice, his conception of public reason, and the value assumptions at the root of his project.[10] Criticisms of Rawls' conception of justice or the concepts he devises to defend it attempt to undermine the connection between that conception of justice and the obligations we owe to see it actualized by any particular state.

Christopher Wellman provides an alternative form of natural duty theory that appeals to a principle of what he calls Samaritanism. While he argues that this Samaritan principle holds as a strong rule for decent human behavior in general, it is especially important as a means of grounding political obligations in order to ward off the threats of the Hobbesian state of nature. As mentioned in the previous chapter, Wellman argues that the state is necessary because it alone is seriously capable of providing the minimal social safety and security required in order to lead a decent life, particularly through its provision of a uniformly applied system of law guaranteed through its coercive capabilities (1996, 215–216; 2001, 743). It is not for our own individual benefit, however, that we should accept the necessary functions provided by the state. Framing the issue of necessity in terms of individual interests, will, or need introduces some messy problems in terms of the ambiguities of consent theory, and the problem of free riders on public goods that Wellman wants to overcome (2001, 735–737). Instead, he argues that we have an obligation to obey a just state because we have a natural Samaritan duty to aid those who are facing danger or are in extreme need. Unique to this duty is the claim that it is not for our own benefit that we must accept a general obligation to obey legitimate political authority, but in order to fulfill our natural duty to prevent harm to others.[11] Since the state of nature – or whatever we would like to call the circumstances without a lawful political order that protects people's basic needs – would presumably be highly

Vertical Time-binding   103

dangerous and a threat to the well-being of others, we have political obligations to obey a just state in order to prevent these circumstances.

Critiques of Wellman's Samaritanism have focused on its scope and strength of moral compulsion, and the unique way in which costs are calculated for others rather than oneself. Wellman argues that our duty to prevent harm to others who are in peril is limited by this posing "no unreasonable cost to oneself" (2001, 744). Heavy or risky costs will thus mitigate the duty we have to help others in need. George Klosko argues that, as a result, Samaritanism can ground only a "weak duty." As a weak duty, it fails to justify obligation for "central state benefits" that may be onerous, including demands to pay "burdensome taxes" or "obey other costly laws, let alone to undertake military service – to fight, possibly to die – for one's country" (Klosko 2003, 837–838). Massimo Renzo (2008) argues on the other hand that Wellman's theory can indeed justify our duty to help others who are in dire situations, but that it fails to consistently ground why there should be any special political obligation between a citizen and the state that rules over them. This would especially be the case if you could personally help people in a worse situation than that of your fellow citizens, such as by evading taxes and giving this money to those needier persons outside of your political community (provided that your personal disobedience did not threaten the overall stability of the state to which you belong).

Membership

"Membership" or "associative" theorists argue that simply by being a member of a group one is morally bound, independent of intervening variables, to respect and conform to the prescribed limits and laws of that group. Samuel Scheffler expresses the core observation of associative obligation theory when he says:

> Ordinary moral opinion ... continues to see associative duties as central components of moral experience. In so doing, it recognizes some claims upon us whose source lies neither in our own choices nor in the needs of others, but rather in the complex and constantly evolving constellation of social and historical relations into which we enter the moment we are born. For we are, after all, born to parents we did not choose at a time we did not choose; and we land in some region we did not choose of a social world we did not choose. And, from the moment of our birth and sometimes sooner, claims are made on us and for us and to us.... And if, in due course, we inject our own wills into this mix – straining against some ties and enhancing others, sometimes severing old bonds and acquiring new ones – the verdict of common moral opinions seems to be that we can never wipe the slate entirely clean.
>
> (Scheffler 2001, 64)

We are born into obligations to friends, family, colleagues, and political communities, then, as a simple fact, and these conditions of obligation are constitutive of our very sense of self. For associative theorists, questions of "voluntariness" regarding our obligations misconstrue the issue at hand (Horton 2010,

104　*Vertical Time-binding*

148). Associative theorists consider analogies between political communities and families to be especially apt. As Horton argues, "on a similar basis to the obligations that people have to their families, notwithstanding the many and undeniable significant differences between families and polities, it can be argued that people have an obligation to their polity" (149). Ronald Dworkin mirrors this sentiment in claiming that "political association, like family and friendship ... is in itself pregnant of obligation" (1986, 206). Political obligation, ostensibly like obligations one owes to one's family, are simply given, and for some associative theorists, beyond requiring justification as such (McPherson 1967, 64). Associative theorists have largely attempted to solve the problem of justifying political obligation by tying political obligation explicitly to membership, assuming the sense of obligation owed to family is comparable to political membership, and appealing to the basic validity and integrity of common sentiment regarding collective attachment and identification (thus removing the possibility of interrogating the sources and historical genealogy of such feelings of membership).

This has not stopped others from vigorously criticizing this position from a variety of angles. One such angle, such as that advanced by Alasdair MacIntyre, questions the validity of conflating obligations toward community or family with obligations to the "government which happens to rule me" when there is no moral consensus in the community being ruled. He argues that while there may be a virtue in communal patriotism, the modern state can be bureaucratic, alienating, and lack a true moral community with which it could derive a proper fit in order to generate associative obligations (MacIntyre 1984, 236–237). Another questions the membership theorists' conflation of a *sense* of obligation with an *actual* obligation, arguing that while there are obligations, their existence is independent of any particular individual's recognition of them (Wellman 1996). Richard Dagger questions what the adherence to membership theory would entail for oppressed groups within a polity that are nevertheless then obligated through membership to obey the wishes of the dominant groups and that control said polity (2000, 110). There is an intuitive connection made by membership theorists between our sociality and the necessity of it for the maintenance of modern states. As critics have observed in various ways, however, there is a slippage between – and potential danger in – membership theorists' aspirational image of a sociopolitical entity as a cohesive unit, and the messy excesses and remainders of actual people who don't neatly fit within actually existing political communities and their requirements for belonging.

Fairness

Fairness-based theories of political obligation remain one of the most common forms. Although they share a family resemblance to some forms of membership and natural duty theory, they are not straightforwardly a form of political naturalism.[12] Theorists of fairness or "fair play" extol the importance of sharing burdens for shared benefits in cooperative enterprises. H.L.A. Hart provides the classic statement of this position:

Vertical Time-binding   105

When a number of persons conduct any joint enterprise according to rules and thus restrict their liberty, those who have submitted to these restrictions when required have a right to a similar submission from those who have benefited by their submission.

(1955, 185)

To the extent, then, that one has agreed to bear certain costs and burdens cooperatively with others in pursuit of a goal, one possesses an obligation to bear those costs fairly with the others, and not seek to enjoy the benefits without bearing the burdens (this is known as "free riding"). Drawing in part on the concept of consent, but primarily emphasizing the imperative of maintaining promises and upholding agreements, fairness theorists identify the particular importance of not abridging expectations entailed in collective efforts for the pursuit of particularistic ends. Obligation is generated as a binding expectation at the point of cooperative agreement, not because of the sanctity of the agreement (as in consent theory), but by virtue of the principle of fair play.[13]

Drawing implicitly from the conclusions of social contract theorists, advocates of the principle of fairness see political communities as primarily cooperative and beneficial enterprises (at least compared to the perceived alternative of a state of nature). Since these political communities (if they are "just") provide non-excludable[14] benefits to all members, a political obligation is garnered by a need to do one's part to at least maintain the political community. Opposing the law of the land or shirking one's fair share of burdens ostensibly does not achieve this, and thus one has a duty generally to obey the law. Fairness theories of political obligation also then share significant theoretical overlap with rule utilitarianism.[15] Some fairness theorists, like Klosko, argue that the principle of fair play applies to both excludable and non-excludable goods (2004, 36). While the state's provision of non-excludable public goods is particularly important for justifying obligations to the state, fair play also (even especially) applies to the excludable cooperative enterprises in which we engage in civil society.

If *A*, *B*, *C*, and *D* cooperate to dig a well, other individuals who partake of the benefits have obligations to share the burdens. Thus the cooperators would be justified in refusing to provide benefits to *E*, who did not share in the labor. This would be especially clear if *E* had been asked to cooperate but had declined.

(Klosko 2004, 36)

The principle of fairness can thus be applied to thin or thick conceptions of political obligation to a political order (meaning either to the state alone, or the community and its institutions more comprehensively), with a "mutuality of restrictions" based on one's effort and sacrifice in relation to the efforts and sacrifices of others being of utmost moral importance (34). In terms of obedience to the state in particular, however, the principle of fairness is intended to demonstrate that "noncooperators also have obligations to cooperate" by virtue of the

106 *Vertical Time-binding*

importance of the state's provision of vital public goods that cannot be guaranteed otherwise (ibid.).

Traditional critiques of fairness theories have taken two general forms. Articulated by M.B.E. Smith, and also situated within the spirit of rule utilitarianism, the first critique has held that fairness cannot be used as grounds for *political* obligations, because no significant "benefit or harm turns on whether [one] obeys" (in Edmundson 1999, 81). Fairness may indeed generate an obligation when a group is small enough that violation of the group rules might produce harm or deny potential benefits to group participants. Political communities are generally large, however, and individual defections may produce negligible costs (ibid.). Negligible costs associated with generally isolated defections are not terribly convincing grounds for securing political obligation claims. Simmons argues for the second form of critique by asserting that the fairness principle does not produce *political* obligations, because the provision of non-excludable goods does not produce goods that can be refused. Simmons draws a distinction between the simple receipt and the active acceptance of a good. If one does not have the option to actively accept a good and the burdens or responsibilities entailed to that good in a cooperative enterprise, then one cannot be said to have acquired an obligation (Simmons 1979, 129). Political life is one that regularly fails to meet this excludability criterion. Robert Nozick makes a similar argument, surmising that the fairness principle would produce obligations whenever a benefit is bestowed on someone, willing recipient or not, which would "surely not" be acceptable (1974, 90–95). These theorists prize the importance of choice and consent, and reject the moral force of appeals to fairness in the compulsory conditions that define our relationship to the state.

Multiple Principles

Many recent attempts to justify political obligations tend to incorporate (consciously or not) a variety of the approaches previously discussed. George Klosko has openly advocated a "multiple principles" approach to justifying political obligation (2005, 98), while Jonathan Wolff similarly calls for a "pluralistic" approach (1995). Chaim Gans (1992) also implicitly advances a pluralistic approach by arguing for political obligations with multiple distinct lines of defense.[16] As these theorists see it, the complexity and diversity of political circumstances and social relations necessitate a more complex approach to thinking about political obligation. The weaknesses of individual theories of obligation are their inability to account for this diversity and complexity (Klosko 2005, 120–121). As Wolff argues, rather than multiple principles being necessarily conflictual or contradictory, they can be mutually supportive, and obligation theorists can identify their main insights and combine "the best of each" (1995, 10). Klosko similarly argues that if "a successful theory [of political obligation] establishes a strong presumption in favor of obedience," then the combination of theories may provide a position "that is stronger than any of the original theories on its own" (2005, 99–100). The multiple principles approach does not necessarily consider all theories of political obligation to be of equal worth. Klosko

Vertical Time-binding 107

and Wolff each primarily advocate versions of fairness theory, and appeal to principles of justice, the common good, and self-interest at various points to supplement that core approach.

There is currently little by way of focused critiques of the multiple principles approach to justifying political obligation. The likely trajectory of such a critique is not, however, too difficult to imagine. Amongst the obligation apologists, there would likely be disagreement regarding which of the multiple principles is of greatest importance within a proposed constellation of justifying principles of political obligation. Amongst philosophical anarchists, there is no reason to believe that advocating a slew of principles that they have already rejected as unconvincing will be any more persuasive. The multiple principles approach occupies a somewhat unique place among these theories, since it attempts to redress problems of method and justification more than articulate a particular theory of obligation.

Vertical Time-binding

Each of these conceptualizations of political obligation shares a commitment to completing or synthesizing the dialectic of modernity (with the exception of the religious naturalists, who reject the dialectical moment of separation and individuation in the first place), and providing a justification for political order, legitimate rule, and obedience as means of doing so. The method by which this set of obligation apologists pursues this, I argue, is through the mechanism of vertical time-binding. As mentioned in the previous chapter, vertical time-binding is one of the two primary methods by which this dialectical synthesis is pursued. Time-binding may entail the creation of homogeneity, but it is by no means homogeneous in all of its various manifestations across and within societies. Time, as we have already discussed, is regularly cast and tempered into a variety of shapes that can profoundly impact collective and individual lived experience. The shapes generated through processes of time-binding are no exception, and must be delineated if we want to understand the related conditions and structure of experience of those living within particular temporalities. Since all sociopolitical orders and institutions depend upon a host of temporal structurations, understanding social and political life as such depends upon making sense of the time-binding processes that produce them. Tracing the processes of time-binding deployed by political obligation theorists can help us make sense of what implicitly grounds each of their particular discourses and conceptualizations of obligation, revealing obscured commonalities, differences, and limits.

With this in mind, we can say that this method of time-binding is "vertical" in so far as it involves the construction of a distinctly stratified image of co-temporality. Anderson's analysis of nationalism that we noted in Chapter 1 traces the historical construction of the nation as a form of what we can here consider to be a "minimal co-temporality." Changes in capitalism, technology, and language made the basic perception of a common belonging and temporal co-existence through "the nation" possible. The nation-*state*, however, as with prior institutions and orders of rule, requires more elaborate specifications than

108 *Vertical Time-binding*

simple belonging. In relating to a system of hierarchical rule, a body of formal rules, and an infinite array of less formal (yet no less important) norms, social divisions, and distributive systems of honor and status,[17] people require more focused and actionable[18] orientation and direction if they are to be incorporated fully. Vertical time-binding specifies and enables the idealized representative images through which individuals and groups are to perceive, interpret, and live their social lives, and in relation to which they will be ordered, disciplined, and evaluated. Like the stained glass church windows of medieval Europe, these images are intended to provide a representative account of the hierarchies of the world and a corresponding guide for how the viewer should relate themselves to the account and act in that world. These representative hierarchies can be comprised of individuals, institutions, and categories of people, as well as the reified values of an axiology, potent icons or symbols within a given discourse, or the prolific "conceptual personae" (Machiavelli's Prince, Hobbes' Leviathan, Nietzsche's blonde beast, economists' rational actor, etc.) that grant flesh and weight to words in so much of political theory.[19] Also like that stained glass, from the position of the believers sitting in the pews, they color perception of the outside world.

Between different vertical time-binding obligation theorists, this stratification can involve varying degrees of actual specification of these differentiated elements. Some theorists focus on only a few strata, elevating, for instance, the importance of particular institutional procedures in anchoring their justifications.[20] Others provide more detailed or totalizing accounts of different strata in their image. Plato's thorough description of the features of the ideal Republic, the duties and divisions of responsibility required for its operation, down to its mirroring of the human soul is a classic example of this. What distinguishes vertical time-binding theorists from each other are the differing details and motifs in the images they construct.

Consequently, what principally distinguishes vertical time-binding from horizontal time-binding, which we will discuss in the next chapter, is what is done to a person's conventional self. If you will recall, the conventional self is the agglomeration of spatialized and refracted elements and partial representations of one's self that constitute one's identity, sense of life direction, and places within a social order. It is personally experienced as one's "sense" of a discretely defined self, and is continuously (if not always wildly) modified by the particularities of one's lived experiences. Through the process of vertical time-binding, one's conventional self is situated within a particular vertical co-temporality; it is placed within a particular image of social order that portrays some form of idealized and stratified roles and types of persons, a structuring and grounding axiology, and admissible forms of individual behavior and institutional procedures. Elements of concrete selves that do not fit within this image may be cut to match, ignored, overcoded, or otherwise removed from visibility.

In constructing such stratified images to which people will be bound, objects organized, and resources distributed, these theorists of obligation provide an important opening for us to think through the relationship between politics on the one hand and aesthetics on the other.[21] Insofar as all obligation theorists are engaged in projects of spatializing time, and all efforts at vertical time-binding

Vertical Time-binding 109

express that spatialization through the production of explicit or implicit images of proper or desirable social order, a critical temporal account of vertical time-binding must account for the role of aesthetics in the production, maintenance, and disruption of such endeavors. While perhaps the most well-known treatise on politics and aesthetics is Walter Benjamin's essay "The Work of Art in the Age of Mechanical Reproduction," it is limited in focusing on the application and manipulation of forms and criteria of beauty to authoritarian regimes.[22] Benjamin takes beauty as the primary concern of aesthetics, and diminishes the importance of other forms of sense, perception, and sensibility. Instead of using Benjamin, I would like to draw from the semiotic analyses developed by Deleuze and Guattari throughout their *Capitalism and Schizophrenia* books, as well as the political theory of aesthetics developed by Jacques Rancière. Deleuze and Rancière differ in significant ways in their broader works on aesthetics, especially with regards to literature and cinema. When it comes to theorizing the relationship between politics and aesthetics, however, especially where this connects with our concerns for temporality, spatialization, semiotics, and stratification, their insights and concepts can complement each other well. By discussing Deleuze alongside Rancière, we can better see the aesthetic dimension present in Deleuze's own analysis of the symbolic social field and the stratified images that help order it (as well as the formal theories which appeal to these images), and the political nature of that aesthetics.

Deleuze and Rancière: Politics and Aesthetics

While they are not simply reducible to each other, aesthetics and politics are intimately intertwined in Rancière's philosophical oeuvre. Aesthetics, for Rancière, is not simply a domain concerned with art or beauty, but rather pertains to the whole field of perception, sensation, and sensibility that constitutes political life, which he refers to as the "distribution of the sensible." The distribution of the sensible is the "system of self-evident facts of sense perception that simultaneously discloses the existence of something in common and the delimitations that define the respective parts and positions within it" (Rancière 2004, 12). We don't simply sense what is there in the world objectively. Our sensations and sensibilities are structured by prior normalized partitions that we become accustomed to and take for granted. Such partitions of sensibility (and the struggles over them) are the very stuff of politics, and consequently, politics has an intrinsically aesthetic dimension.

> What really deserves the name of politics is the cluster of perceptions and practices that shape this common world. Politics is first of all a way of framing, among sensory data, a specific sphere of experience. It is a partition of the sensible, of the visible, and of the sayable, which allows (or does not allow) some specific data to appear; which allows or does not allow some specific subjects to designate them and speak about them. It is a specific intertwining of ways of being, ways of doing, and ways of speaking.
>
> (Rancière, in Rockhill 2009, 199)

110 *Vertical Time-binding*

The struggles of politics are over who appears or doesn't within a political order, who has a voice and who can only be perceived as producing noise, and, for those who have a recognized "part" within this order, how those parts will be distributed.[23] These struggles entail inevitable conflict between those forces that seek to construct "consensus" – the reinforcement of hegemonic norms and interpretations of reality, taken-for-granted institutions and arrangements of privilege, unexamined and ossified distributions of social roles and identities, and their retroactive theoretical justifications – and forces creating "dissensus," challenges to the official consensus that seek to redistribute parts, roles, visibility, and the distribution of the sensible as a whole (Rancière 2004, 85).

In order to clarify the difference between the conventional, hegemonic consensus processes of politics (such as state politics operating through contained electioneering with minimal challenges to normalized political behavior) and the kind of politics that Rancière sees as making actual redistributions of the sensible possible, Rancière makes a distinction between "politics" and "the police." The arrangement and distribution of organized and institutionalized powers and social roles, their implementation systems, and their conceptual mechanisms of legitimation – that which is normally considered to be politics in contemporary societies – is better understood as "the police." Rancière's police is not simply the "petty police" with truncheons and uniforms, and is not simply "the state apparatus" (Rancière 1999, 28). The police is rather the complex order and ordering of bodies that defines and distributes social roles and tasks, disciplines the boundaries of sociopolitical discourses, acts to ensure that some groups, activities, and thoughts are visible while others are not, and ensures that some "speech is understood as discourse and another as noise" (29). Scholars and philosophers who emphasize and think within the terms of the police are not, on Rancière's account, engaging in "political" theory at all, but are rather only supporting various arrangements and distributions of the police and policing of society. Politics, on the other hand, "is always a mode of expression that undoes the perceptible divisions of the police order by implementing a basically heterogeneous assumption, that of a part of those who have no part" (30). Politics is the dissensual assertion and substantive enactment of inclusion, presence, and empowerment of those who have been excluded, hidden, and oppressed in opposition to the given distribution of the sensible. For Rancière, politics is thus a relatively rare occurrence, manifesting when the police order's distribution of sensibility is actually disrupted and the previously marginalized and downtrodden make themselves and their desires known, seen, and heard.

Although not usually paired, Deleuze's account of the operations of systems of "signifiance," "subjectification," and "majoritarianism" overlap together with Rancière's understanding of political aesthetics in significant ways. I argue that these elements of Deleuze's philosophy also effectively constitute a theory of political aesthetics that incorporates both the sensorium and discourses of a social field and the more discrete, normalizing, disciplinary images that serve to anchor that social order. Deleuze, like Rancière, recognizes a dominant field of signification, discourse, and sensibility as being a fundamental component in the maintenance of political orders and stratified social relationships. Individuals do

Vertical Time-binding 111

not simply decide what is meaningful about their world in a vacuum. What counts as reasonable, exceptional, and normal, or is even something that can be recognized at all – in other words, what generally makes sense, and *counts as making sense* – is in large part a product of the regimes or systems of signifiance in a society. Systems of signifiance are chains of symbols and meaning that suffuse the world in which we live, including, yet also involving more than language alone (Deleuze and Guattari 1987, 154). They are ubiquitous, and function not primarily as a means to convey a pure descriptive truth about the world, but rather to orient and direct us, to condition that which receives our attention, and that which compels certain actions and reactions (77). These systems of signifiance exist alongside systems of subjectification, which function by structuring and constraining what kinds of individual and collective subjects and identities people recognize in each other and themselves, and how they understand their social positions in relation to each other (128–130). Although they certain have distinct effects on the world, these systems should in no way be thought of as substantially separate from operations of material power relations, social assemblages, and state machinery. Deleuze says explicitly that

Very specific assemblages of power impose signifiance and subjectification as their determinate forms of expression, in reciprocal presupposition with new contents: there is no signifiance without a despotic assemblage, and no mixture between the two without assemblages of power that act through signifiers and act upon souls and subjects.

(180, emphasis in original)

Systems of signifiance and subjectification are thus expressions of concrete social relationships of inequality and rule, as well as constitutive of those relationships, helping to discipline, habituate, and sort people and their understanding of themselves, their world, their place in it, and their place in relation to others. These systems constitute sense and understanding in relation to a stratified social order generally, but that stratified order (especially under capitalism[24]) produces a further means of structuring our sense of the world to great political effect: the production of a "majority." Deleuze's majority is not a numerical majority.[25] It is instead the qualitative "standard measure" according to which other deviating or different elements of the world can be judged to be minorities (105). The standard of "majority implies a state of domination" in relation to subordinated, excluded, inferior, or less-than-the-ideal groups (291). This standard could hypothetically manifest itself as any dominant ideal type, but in our present world is clearly treated as "the average adult-white-heterosexual-European-male-speaking a standard language" (105). It "appears twice," standing in for itself, as well as for Mankind as such, and functions as an anchor for normalizing relationships of relative dominance within a society (ibid.).

Beneath these systems of signifiance and subjectification, and the majoritarian image are the elements of "difference" and "becoming" discussed in previous chapters. Any particular system of majoritarian production is constituted through the capture and masking of particular flows of difference. No given majoritarian

112 *Vertical Time-binding*

system is inevitable, therefore, or eternal, but instead must constantly try to sustain itself through the exclusion and subordination of "minority" elements and forces (469). Like majorities, minorities are not defined by how numerous they are. A minority may be relatively small, or it may itself constitute a numerical majority. It is instead defined "by the gap that separates" it from a given majoritarian ideal (ibid.). Both majorities and minorities are defined by their relationship to each other, as well as their relationship to the larger social body of which they are both a part. Conventional majoritarian politics[26] involves minorities trying to gain inclusion into the given majority standard; for instance, women trying to gain abortion rights, or racial minorities trying to gain the right to vote, or the Third World fighting for state autonomy from the First. Deleuze doesn't deny the potential value of such efforts, but instead defends a politics of "becomings," specifically a politics of "becoming-minor" (469–471). Rather than try to simply gain some inclusion relative to the majority standard, a true minoritarian politics[27] instead challenges the very values, axioms, parameters of normality, and boundaries of acceptable problematization of that majoritarian order. Like Rancière's politics of dissensus, it is not something that is sustained indefinitely. By solidifying into a new standard, it would by definition constitute a new majority with its own standards of normality, exclusion, and acceptable problems that one is allowed to seriously pose in relation to the prevailing order. It is instead a force that, in Rancière's terms, attempts to rearrange the distribution of the sensible. Minoritarian politics is productive in that it creates something new, but is distinguished by its disruption and destruction of the majoritarian status quo.

Both Deleuze and Rancière provide analyses that highlight the instability and contingency of prevailing ordering political images and their associated distributions of the sensible. Although they take different theoretical approaches and opt for different tools, they are remarkably similar in both their goals and conclusions pertaining to the nature of regimes of signs, the distributed notions of the sensible in a social field, and the ways that these help constitute political orders. They are also both keen on demonstrating the contingent and unstable character of any particular political order, and doing so by reference to their preferred weaponized concepts. For Rancière, the appeal to equality that undergirds his intervention serves as a challenge to the claims of naturalness associated with any political order's given stratified distributions of power, wealth, and social inclusion. It is always possible that a marginalized or subordinated person or group could challenge the unexamined consensus of the police order and introduce a new distribution of power and sensibility through dissensus. Rather than equality, Deleuze attempts to demonstrate the limits and contingency of official accounts of social and political order by appealing to difference. While equality of a particular sort certainly matters to Deleuze, it is the production of homogeneity and stasis that is his primary concern. Through the concept of becoming and its various manifestations (especially becoming-minor, becoming-revolutionary, and becoming-woman), Deleuze attacks the static image of Being, of stable unity, normality, and existence that are associated with a given political order, and which inevitably make up a part of its self-image. Understanding the artifice

Vertical Time-binding 113

behind the production of sensibility is important for our present purposes, while Deleuze's and Rancière's accounts of the nature of becoming and dissensus will be important for the final chapter of this work.

Their analyses converge on another point that will help us understand how vertical time-binding theories of obligation operate, and which also overlaps with Bergson's analysis of how spatialization works: constructing an ordering aesthetic entails manufactured blindness and deafness. The majoritarian systems of signifiance and subjectification in a social field maintain coherence not simply by sorting bodies, sensations, and sensibilities internally, and attempting to reter-ritorialize divergent elements, but also by masking and excluding them. The "parts who have no part," and the "minor" elements of a society aren't simply given a subordinated role in a general image of proper political life. Those who diverge significantly enough from the majoritarian ideal, or from the distribution of normalized political demands, questions, or behaviors may not figure at all within such an account, but may instead be ignored entirely, or allowed inclusion only by being cast as a contained, and manageably loathed or absurd, caricature.

The majoritarian aesthetic at work in a social order's legitimating representation of itself is as much an effort of vertical time-binding as the theories of our obligation apologists. That the first emerges without any definite author, while the latter is intentionally authored, makes no difference in terms of their desired temporal function, although they can clearly have very different magnitudes of actual influence.

Stratified Images of Obligation

It would be a mistake to suggest that the obligation apologists discussed here are identical in their arguments and projects. They are not. There are useful distinctions to be made in the normative and practical political implications of each. A Rawlsian natural duty theorist is not going to advocate the exact some conditions for obedience or desirable political and economic arrangements as a membership theorist. And yet, all of them are engaged in projects of vertical time-binding, and share in the assumption that such projects are valuable for the purposes of defending a representative (usually liberal democratic) account of how we ought to relate to the state and each other for the purposes of securing social order (and on my reading, temporal unity). When viewed from this perspective, the normative efforts of these apologists can also be interpreted, following Rancière, as engaging in little more than "rearrangements of the police order" of distribution and visibility. What defines and distinguishes the efforts of most of their positions is not, then, a deep disagreement on fundamentals. Rather, in encountering what they perceive to be the fragility and contingency of social and political order in modernity, they appear to diverge over which part of that order generates the most fear and anxiety when pondering its contingency and precarity, and imagining its collapse or absence. In order to secure that order and fend off anxieties about its impermanence, each apologist – in their own way, and with primary reference to their distinct principal values and fears – attempts to build

114　*Vertical Time-binding*

stratified images to seize and crystallize what they fear losing, reconstitute an effective cultural temporality, and arrest the flow of time. The maintenance of these constructs, however, comes at a cost.

As Bergson observes, building such spatializations has the benefit of providing a sense of continuity and stability, both collectively and through the construction of identities. It contributes to the intellectual, discursive, and moral architecture necessary for the maintenance of a "common" social and political order to which any sense of belonging is comprehensible. It also provides the conceptual reference points necessary for a political order to attempt to generate both the content and the standards of justification for itself, as discussed in the previous chapter. In order to stabilize this image and its attendant distribution of the sensible and give it any meaning at all, obligation apologists must generate an "outside" that falls beyond the boundaries of their account of who counts. In other words, in giving their image content and form, they are immediately compelled to exclude those elements of the world which would violate and tarnish that image; political structures bent out of shape, the wrong value sitting at the head of the table, and bodies disarrayed and not staying put, either in their place or out of sight. Each project of vertical time-binding not only attempts to striate and stratify the assemblages that it seeks to represent in a virtual image and distribution of sensibility, but must do so by also constructing a particularly threatening outside force – that which does not belong.

With this in mind, let us first reconsider the fairness theorists of obligation. I mentioned earlier, fairness theories occupy a curious, seemingly hybrid position between the political naturalists and anti-naturalists, and share a strong family resemblance to consent theorists. They still produce idealized strata, however, through their primary emphasis on the imperative to maintain one's promises and uphold agreements, though we must be careful here, because it is not the act of agreement in and of itself that produces an obligation for these theorists. Instead, they are primarily concerned with the importance of not abridging expectations generated through collective efforts, especially not for the pursuit of particularistic ends, because of a desire to avoid an *unfair distribution of costs and burdens*. Obligation is generated at the point of cooperative agreement, but by virtue of the principle of fair play and not because of the sanctity of the agreement as such (as it would be in consent theory). The imperative of fairness is attached to a particular image of proper mutual reciprocity. For fairness theorists, it is through a reliable and fair reciprocity of effort and burden that the benefits of social life become possible and the collective efforts that maintain both the benefits and social life itself become sustainable. By consolidating an isolated and idealized conception of reciprocity and its axiological guarantor – the principle of fairness – into one conceptual bundle, they elevate these concerns over those of competing obligation claims which emphasize a different set of prioritized slivers of social life, and different moral linchpins. These competitors pose a *challenge*, but most of them (especially other obligation apologists) are not a *threat*.

The threatening outside force for fairness theories is consistently portrayed as a particular conceptual personae – the shirker, or "free rider" (Klosko 2004, 37).

Vertical Time-binding   115

The free rider is someone who enjoys the benefits of collective effort without sharing in the burden. The free rider is not simply someone who acts unfairly but who is also largely ignorant of the consequences and costs of their actions. They are instead someone who generally recognizes the duties they would owe to carry their fair share of a collective burden, but who opts to try to get around them either partially or entirely. The free rider poses an absolute threat to fairness theories, because it simply negates all of the moral force that the apologist can bring to bear. It does not *oppose* that moral force, but instead simply moves around it, unconcerned with either its appeals to the imperative of fairness or the purported burdens place on others. The ideal free rider manifests self-derived and self-focused particularity in actions and concerns, without even the overt rejection and opposition offered by a proceduralist like Nozick. The free rider is terrifying for fairness theorists, because they imagine that if the free rider's self-focused behavior was universalized, necessary public goods and functions would not be met (Klosko 2004, 38).

This Kantian leap into universalization is the means by which the values and behavior represented by the free rider are contained and cast as absurd and illegitimate, because it is procedurally the same leap the fairness theorists make in order to elevate the significance of mutual reciprocity and project a foundation for it in the form of the principle of fairness. What is elided in this maneuver is that the ideal free rider makes no such universal appeals, and asks for no grounds for their actions. Whether we conceive of them in ideal terms (such as the betraying prisoner of game theory's Prisoner's Dilemma, or the rational maximizer of Hardin's Tragedy of the Commons), in an anecdotal way (the hell that is group projects during grade school, where credit was shared, but effort never seemed to be), or through historical cases,[28] free riders are engaging in a self-focused, particularistic endeavor that neither requires nor asks for justification. They are taking advantage of the actually existing concrete gap in obstacles to and countervailing force against their desires in particular circumstances, and, in a similar sense, inhabiting and taking advantage of the gap between a social order's ideal self-representation and reality. None of this is to say that free riding isn't potentially disruptive of social and political orders. At a critical mass, it certainly may entail the collapse of some collective endeavors, and, as Elinor Ostrom has observed, a variety of enforcement measures can be effectively brought to bear to counteract the desirability of free riding through both hierarchical and egalitarian forms of social and political institutions.[29] As time-binders focused on constructing comprehensive images of order, however, the fairness theorists have no means of internally accommodating a force that exists only by gnawing at the edges and gaps of that order and its representative images. They can only justify the coercion that will be applied by those who wish to counteract the efforts of the free rider (and preserve the image of fairness), and do so by subjecting the free rider to the same universalizing imperative they use to ground their own position, invariably (and predictably) finding it a wanting caricature.

The membership theorists develop idealized strata that elevate the importance of belonging and what we could call a principle of loyalty. There is some diversity between those who emphasize the social character of our associations

116 *Vertical Time-binding*

(especially in terms of our bonds with family and community) and those who emphasize our membership with the states that rule over us, or as in Gilbert's (2006) account, the way in which these become inextricably intertwined. Ultimately, though, the membership theorists ground themselves on a distinct form of projection. They accept an account of political subjectivity that affirms our ontological status as socially-embedded individuals, drawing important attention to the obligations we feel that we have in our day to day lives. Fearing social dissolution and the shredding of the web of relations that constitute our social lives and self-understanding, they project and defend a co-temporality to protect and sustain those relations. This projection contains both the minimal "homogenous, empty time" required for reifying and enabling the perception of belonging (as identified by Anderson in his discussion of nationalism) as well as a vertical axiology. This vertical axiology specifies the minimal co-temporality further by treating belonging itself as a virtue, and loyalty to the polity to which one belongs (and its legitimate authorities) as its political expression. Further specification of values and political behavior can be developed from this initial elaboration on minimal co-temporality, but the axiology of loyalty to one's co-temporal convergence and ensconcement with others is a bare requirement for membership theorists' vertical time-binding project.

In the spirit of Josiah Royce, the membership theorists not only uphold the virtue of loyalty to one's associations with others and membership in a particular polity, but also extol a "loyalty to loyalty" itself. Royce is deeply concerned with the individual pursuit of meaning and purpose:

> Human life taken merely as it flows, viewed merely as it passes by in time and is gone, is indeed a lost river of experience that plunges down the mountains of youth and sinks in the deserts of age. Its significance comes solely through its relations to the air and the ocean and the great deeps of universal experience. For by such poor figures I may, in passing, symbolize that really rational relation of our personal experience to universal conscious experience.
>
> (1995, 179–180)

He finds that it is not mere acquiescence to convention, but rather the intentional pursuit of a wider plan that can help us approach the depths of timeless and universal experience. A willful affirmation of one's fidelity to a larger cause allows them to sharpen and focus their life so that they can secure a stable, enduring sense of meaning. A truly isolated individual could not and does not manufacture such a plan. Instead, we experience a social world with ready-made plans and causes. By consciously joining with a community of others to advance a cause that requires collective cooperation and a pooling of individual wills, we forge a community defined by loyalty. The meaningful and morally enriched life, for Royce, is one that is embedded within a thick tapestry of loyalties. Loyalty to some set of other persons in a joint cause is morally insufficient, however, because that alone does not guarantee a *universal* ability to pursue loyalties. Some loyalties to a community or cause, after all, may infringe on the

Vertical Time-binding   117

ability of others to freely pursue their own loyalties, especially when that group or cause is advancing oppressive or "predatory" ends. "True loyalty," on the other hand, is a kind of loyalty that fosters the creation of new loyalties and communities, and thus a loyalty to loyalty itself:

> a cause is good, not only for me, but for mankind, in so far as it is essentially a *loyalty to loyalty*, that is, an aid and a furtherance of loyalty in my fellows. It is an evil cause in so far as, despite the loyalty that it arouses in me, it is destructive of loyalty in the world of my fellows.
>
> (Royce 1995, 56, emphasis in original)

Ideally, then, true loyalties build and expand upon each other, creating new circles of commitment and fidelity to others that can approximate universality.

While the membership theorists celebrate our cultivated loyalty to others, they also tend to go beyond the advocacy of a myopic loyalty to one's community alone. Similarly, they also oppose the predatory loyalty to a group whose actions are destructive to the ability of others to generate and maintain their own loyalties. While, as in the case of war or a draft, they may argue that a citizen's loyalties to their political community ultimately demand obedience, this is not usually the expression of loyalty they see as most desirable. Similarly, Royce recognizes that all actual communities contain predatory elements, and fall short of his ideal Beloved Community. Nevertheless, it is through fidelity to the "lost cause"[30] of this ideal community defined through loyalty to loyalty itself, he argues, that we are able to find meaning through the *pursuit* of this unactualizable ideal. The membership theorists prioritize the importance of our loyalties to a community as a precondition for the possibility of sustaining community as such, and consequently elevate the social dimension of loyalties and collective co-commitments into their primary axiological principle.

The threatening outside for the membership theorists is not represented by the stateless person or the immigrant. They may be outside of (or between) the bounds of fully recognized institutional roles or statuses within particular states, but they do not pose a fundamental challenge to the strata of the membership theorists. Their threatening outside is instead best represented by the egoist and the traitor. Although they do not appear explicitly in much of the membership theorists' work, the egoist and the traitor are figures that loom over them like the free rider does over the fairness theorists. Both find the principal concern of the membership theorists – the bonds, loyalties, duties, and intimacies of social and political life – to be expendable, and at best only instrumentally useful relative to other values and satisfactions. We don't need to limit our conceptualization of the egoist to that of the archetypal bourgeois rational maximizer of economists' fantasies. Like Max Stirner's (2005) egoist (which we will discuss in greater depth in Chapter 5), we don't need to specify their particular values or interests at all. What makes Stirner's egoist an egoist is instead its refusal to place any concept or ideal ("spooks" in his terminology) and its concomitant demands or prerogatives above the judgment and discretion of that particular person. The egoist in their concrete particularity is primary, and may use or dispose of

118 *Vertical Time-binding*

concepts and ideals without treating them deferentially, as sacred, or as unapproachable in their claims to truth. Trust and loyalties may be valued by the egoist, but loyalty (or any particular loyalty) is treated as provisional and instrumental at best, and disposable when it suits them rather than something to sacrifice oneself for without question. The egoist stance is the inverse of a Royceian true loyalty. The figure of the traitor also holds loyalties to be expendable, but may in fact do so by forging new loyalties (although not necessarily so, since one could also betray simply for money or spite). Where the traitor violates the axiology of the membership theorists is in rejecting the special value of obligation demands posed by the political order that one is a resident of or belongs to.[31] These figures can overlap in a single person, or briefly manifest at different periods in an individual's life or collectively in a period of social upheaval, but both fundamentally threaten the stability and coherence of the membership theorists' account of obligation.

Natural duty theorists like Rawls and Wellman develop strata that prioritize the importance of their respective conceptions of justice. While other theorists may certainly argue that a state must be a "reasonably" just one if their theories of political obligation are to be truly binding, the pursuit of justice itself is primary for natural duty theorists in their determination of what obligations we owe. Their vision of justice functions as a more far-reaching and specified regulative ideal when compared to other theories of obligation. Rather than isolating a particular element of social life in order to elevate and preserve it, natural duty theorists posit a more comprehensive set of moral principles and social arrangements that effectively define the standard of justice as an aggregate. Rather than attempt to isolate a core moral axiom that is best represented by a particular facet of social life, they develop an account of an ideal or necessary order contained within the concept of justice itself. In this sense, although contemporary natural duty theorists are relative newcomers in political obligation theory, their projects bear a much closer resemblance to those of the pre-modern religious political naturalists than their contemporary apologist counterparts.

Since natural duty theorists focus less on securing a particular fragment of social life, the threatening outside for their image is less clearly specified. Certainly, the kind of egoist described for the membership theorists would pose a threat. The Stirnerian refusal of subordination to spooks like Justice seems to pose a hard limit on the possibility of *any* natural duty theorist to universalize their particular vision. In this case, though, the egoist can be best understood not as (primarily) the manifestation of a challenge to the axiom of loyalty (or to the primacy of any axiom whatsoever), but as a reminder of the persistent gap between natural duty theorists' regulative ideal and existing conditions. Of course, one could argue that all existing conditions would necessarily appear like a pale, degenerate form of natural duty theorists' ideals, and thus could function as their threatening outside. There is certainly some truth in this, in that justice is a pure ideal that is striven for while always seemingly existing beyond our reach, something any natural duty theorist would plainly admit. As we have seen so far, however, the mess, complexity, and "deficiency" of the actually existing world is fairly easily (if unstably) folded into various kinds of spatialized

Vertical Time-binding 119

time-shelters[32] by obligation theorists. It is no difficult task to hitch the Real to the Ideal through the projection of a simple teleology of always-closer approximation. What the egoist can represent for us, though, is the irremediability of this deficiency. The flux and mess of reality, of duration, will always exceed the carefully trimmed hedges of natural duty theorists' ideals. The egoist is functionally a partisan for the unrepresentable and irreducible elements of this flux, the concrete particularity of individual beings at each moment, and a critical limit for any attempt to produce an over-arching image of order that attempts to neatly plug the world into allotted slots as components.

The multiple principles appeal is distinct from the other theories discussed in this chapter. As mentioned earlier, it is concerned more with questions of how justification and the success of obligation theories can be secured than with the particularities of those obligation theories. Theorists such as Klosko and Jonathan Wolff use it as a supplement to their preferred theories. More important and interesting though is their willingness to engage in the more overt instrumentalization of particular obligation theories. By elevating the importance of developing multiple theories for grounding obligations, the significance of the validity of any particular obligation claim is comparatively subordinated – but to what? Klosko defends the importance of the multiple principles approach by arguing that it is better equipped to respond to the complexities of modern life; people are differentially situated in terms of privileges and marginalization, problems operate at different scales, and some obligation demands are strong while others (such as stopping at a traffic light when no one else is around) are weak. Multiple principles are better able to ground the obligations of "all or virtually all citizens" (2005, 100), as well as justify a "presumption in favor of obedience" to a broad range of governmental functions (99–100). Through "cumulation," "mutual support," and "overlap," between different theories of obligation, the multiple principles approach is better equipped to incorporate and represent as much of political life as possible in grounding this presumption (101).

What we can see then is that the efforts of the multiple principles approach are oriented toward securing a more comprehensive representational coverage and coding of our behaviors and expected duties. It is an intensification of the underlying project of modern political obligation theory as such. It seems likely that the reason for this intensification is a consequence of the state of contemporary academic political obligation discourse itself, or at least what these theorists perceive to be the state of the discourse. As Klosko and others have claimed, there is a "widespread view that there is no satisfactory theory of political obligation" (99). Where individual apologist theories have failed, imbricating them and circling the wagons offers a greater hope of success. The emergence of this approach seems to be motivated by an elevated fear of representational slippage, with its advocates reaching for a kind of hyper-representation as a solution. Rather than any particular figure that represents a threatening Outside or minoritarian politics that doesn't fit within their visions of proper political life, the multiple principles project seems to fear the unrepresented or unrepresentable remainder itself.

120   *Vertical Time-binding*

If the effective axiological strata within the membership theorists' project is a Royce-inspired loyalty to loyalty, then its multiple principles counterpart can be usefully interpreted as an obligation to obligation. Whatever the value or persuasiveness of any particular content of distinct obligation theories, what is of vital importance for the multiple principles theorists is that obligation be defended. Like Royce's existential formalism (resorting to extolling loyalty to loyalty to secure guidance and meaning after being unable to convincingly defend any particular kind or target of loyalty without qualification) these theorists make a plea for the value of the form of obligation in spite of widespread doubts about the unassailability of any particular attempts to provide content to that form.

There appears to be an insoluble problem for our vertical time-binding obligation apologists of their own making. While all of these theorists can construct an idealized strata of obligations and values toward which their hopes and fears can find expression and temporal shelter, these constructs don't offer a stable solution. A principal point of rationalizing their value schemes is to give them a sense of solidity against the threat of loss and social dissolution. Yet, immediately upon producing what appears to be a solution to their fears, the coherence of that solution depends upon being counterposed against a new, potentially destabilizing threat from the outside (how can you understand what an obligation is without specifying what it isn't?). To be sure, the characters that are staged to represent these threats are themselves contained and managed in a variety of ways, usually cast as absurd, alien, or despicable figures. Even so, this threat persists like the ever-present and looming future of Nietzsche's eternal return, promising to dissolve these creations under the force of difference and time.

Conclusion: Divinity, Modernity, and the Great Chains of Being

In his archaeology of duty, *Opus Dei* (2013), Giorgio Agamben traces the influence and translation of the concepts of "liturgy" and "office" (*officium*) from their origins in the early Church to their general diffusion within Western ontology, ethics, and social and political life.[33] These terms designate (variously – their precise genealogy is not vital for us here) the production of a public work, service, duties, and within the Church, a praxis for priests in the fulfillment of their worship, and both their social and divine function. From their limited place as an early "paradigm of priestly praxis," he argues that the concepts of office and liturgy produced a distinct ontological transformation within the culture and philosophy of Western modernity, and made possible the introduction of "duty" into the sphere of ethics, politics, and practical sensibility in profound and, at this point, often "subterranean" ways (xii, 87). Classical ontology is an ontology of substance, and in it Being is defined as what one is. The paradigm of *officium*, however, ultimately enabled the ontological "transformation of being into having-to-be" (87) and thus into an ontology of "operativity" (118). In this paradigm, Being is defined not by one's substance, but by one's action, specifically

Vertical Time-binding 121

through carrying out one's duties. The priest, Agamben argues, is the figure that exemplifies this ontology, since

> the priest must carry out his office insofar as he is a priest and he is a priest insofar as he carries out his office. Being prescribes action, but action completely defines being.... The priest is that being whose being is immediately a carrying out and a service – a liturgy.
>
> (87)

This creates a circular relationship between being and having-to-be, wherein fulfilling one's liturgy (the carrying out of expected duties and action) becomes the mark of one's office, and that office is defined and made real by the carrying out of the liturgy. The slide from this into formal conceptions of the role of legitimate political subjects who are both actualized and defined by their expected behaviors and duties within a political order is not very far.[34]

Modern political obligation theorists tend to position themselves as distinct from the unabashedly interwoven metaphysical and axiological commitments entailed with the appeal to divine right or other forms of religious political naturalism. Insofar as an explicit appeal to God and a divine order is concerned, this distinction between the religious political naturalists and their more clearly modern counterparts can be maintained. Yet, was it ever really God as such that defined the character of the pre-modern political obligation theorists, or distinguished them from their modern counterparts? God may have ceased being an object of open reverence and source for political legitimation for most of our obligation theorists. If we follow Agamben's account of duty, however, it seems clear that the *function* God served as a despotic signifier for organizing and structuring temporalities and the social machines with which they are associated continues to be a recipient of their silent devotions. Our vertical time-binding theorists fulfill the dialectic of modernity by collapsing the character of political subjects (their Being-as-substance) into their active practice and fulfillment of their purported obligations in accordance with the stratified image of circumscribed values, behavior and social roles their theory entails. In this way, people can only be what they truly are by virtue of believing and acting in accordance with the set of behavioral and moral practices laid out by the theorist. In carrying out the liturgy of recognizing and affirming one's political obligations and enacting the appropriate form of compliance, we become what we are as political subjects. In approximating this performative ideal, we approach the desired threshold of universality and timelessness once represented adequately by God. Even with God's death the performance continues, sustained now through a collage of piecemeal representative surrogates and a lingering sense of the *mysterium tremendum et fascinans*[35] beckoning our obligation theorists to continue looking to the transcendent.

122 *Vertical Time-binding*

Notes

1 Obligation theories which rest on consent and variations on it, such as social contract theory, will be examined in Chapter 4. They depend upon a different process of time-binding than those obligation theories covered in this chapter.

2 Aristotle discusses the relationship between the naturalness of families, tribes, and the state throughout Book 1.2 of *The Politics*. See especially Aristotle (1996, 13–14).

3 Max Stirner identifies the continuation of God and the idea of the Holy in the thought of the Moderns, especially in their essentialist humanism, their concept of rights, and reified and universalized conception of Man (Stirner 2005). In *Political Theology* (1985), Carl Schmitt argues that

> All significant concepts of the modern theory of the state are secularized theological concepts not only because of their historical development-in which they were transferred from theology to the theory of the state, whereby, for example, the omnipotent God became the omnipotent lawgiver-but also because of their systematic structure.... The exception in jurisprudence is analogous to the miracle in theology.
>
> (36)

Friedrich Nietzsche identifies continuities between the ascetic ideals, moralism, and reach for universality intrinsic to Christianity, and the whole gamut of modern social developments and ideas: liberalism, rights, mass society, democracy, socialism, and equality (see Nietzsche 1967; 1974; 1982).

4 Romans 13:1–2.

5 Aquinas posits other reasons for the value of monarchy that are somewhat tangential here, including the tendency for other forms of government to (inefficiently) attempt to emulate the unified rule of one, and the greater possibilities of a wise and just monarch maintaining the polity as a community of virtue.

6 Filmer's patriarchalism grounds the authority of the monarch in the will of God, but the transmission of that authority is indirect. Rather than an appointment straight from God, the monarch (especially the Stuart monarchy of England) acquires the authority to rule through a repeated and contiguous process of inheritance – reaching back to biblical times – of the natural authority God granted Adam over his offspring.

7 Rawls distinguishes between "obligations" as things we voluntarily take upon ourselves, such as promises, and "natural duties" which apply to everyone generally, regardless of whether they have been voluntarily adopted (1999, 96).

8 Rawls' unique theoretical constructs left a powerful stamp on liberal theory in the last quarter of the twentieth century. While they had been subject to a flood of commentary and criticism, interest in them has waned considerably over the last decade. Nevertheless, their influence can still be felt in the way in which questions of justice, fairness, democratic procedure, and political obligations are conceived and addressed by philosophers and political theorists like Thomas Pogge, Amartya Sen, Michael Sandel, and Iris Marion Young.

9 See sections 55–59.

10 Contrary to Nozick, Thomas Nagel (1991) argues that Rawls' conception of distributive justice allows for *too much* inequality as a result of Rawls' concept of the "difference principle," which argues that increases in inequality are acceptable only if those increases benefit the least well-off. Iris Marion Young and Seyla Benhabib take issue (among other things) with Rawls' veil of ignorance, arguing that the impartial public rationality this veil purports to achieve is both highly gendered, and runs contrary to pluralism and a feminist ethic by attempting to subsume and eliminate difference and Otherness (Young 1990; Benhabib 1996). Michael Sandel (1998) provides a communitarian critique of Rawls' conception of personhood, arguing that it is inaccurate, and can have unpleasant normative implications if we imagine individuals as abstract beings separated from society who can pick and choose their commitments through a

Vertical Time-binding 123

detached form of public reason and choice. This is hardly a comprehensive list of even the major strands of critique, but it will serve our purposes for now.

11 It is worth noting the difference here between Samaritanism and fairness theories. While both approaches rely on the importance of public benefits delivered by the state, fairness theory argues that one must contribute their fair share because of the benefits that *they themselves* receive, while Samaritanism argues that it is the benefits received *by others* which are most important.

12 Political naturalism focuses on justifying obligations to a given community since political life is considered the default condition. Its counterpart, political "anti-naturalism," interprets political life as a form of human artifice (Simmons 2006, 253). Consent theorists, for example, are anti-naturalists because the polity is something justified through its construction or maintenance via individual agreements; the individual is considered to be prior. While fairness seems like a bit of a hybrid, appealing to both responsibilities to others and the generation of obligation via individual actions, I argue that it can best be understood as a form of anti-naturalism because it identifies obligations being derived from individual actions. It is not a form of horizontal time-binding or consent, however, because it still primarily rests on an appeal to the sanctity of promises and an ideal of reciprocity, not the act of promising or agreement as such.

13 John Rawls advocated a very similar version of Hart's position in his earlier works that he called a "duty to fair play" (1964), although he abandoned this in his later principle of "justice as fairness," which, name aside, would not be considered a form of fairness theory (1999).

14 Non-excludable benefits are benefits that cannot be denied to particular individuals in so far as they are publicly provided goods. Conversely, individuals cannot choose not to accept them; non-excludable goods are non-optional. Regularly cited examples include national defense, law and order, and pollution control. See Simmons (1979, 130) and Klosko (2004, 36–37).

15 Rule utilitarianism argues that the maximization of utility, happiness, or the greater good can be best achieved by supporting particular rules (rather than evaluating isolated individual acts) that can lead to these things.

16 Gans demonstrates, for instance, how both a Rawlsian natural duty approach and a communitarian approach can be combined in a complementary fashion. While the universality of Rawls' appeal to justice has left it open to criticisms regarding its applicability to any particular state, Gans argues that the addition of a communitarian approach can redress this weakness, rather than simply highlight it.

17 In social theorizing and analysis, honor is often reduced to masculinist caricatures of bravado and bloodshed. As Robert Oprisko (2012) demonstrates, honor is an unavoidable social fact that can't be swept away. It is the process through which value is conferred upon (or denied to) individuals by others, especially groups. Insofar as social groups affirm some values and decry others (which they always do), honor is in fact also necessarily unequally distributed. Its many facets – dignity, esteem, face, shame, and glory, among others – are thus powerful mechanisms for social binding, sorting, and rending from the smallest to the largest scales of human interaction.

18 Actionability is important because unlike the nation, political orders are far more dependent on the achievement of coordinated collective behaviors and activity in order for them to be maintained. A nation can persist through collective imagination alone far longer (though ritual and communal activity can certainly help sustain it) than a state could persist with everyone simply ignoring its laws and commands.

19 Deleuze discusses the function of these conceptual personae in more depth in *What is Philosophy?* (1994), especially Chapter 3. He argues that they are figures that can congeal and exemplify concepts, granting them force and clarifying their significance.

20 Thomas Christiano, for example, provides a defense of the legitimacy of rules derived from deliberative democratic procedures:

124 *Vertical Time-binding*

> Democratic discussion, deliberation, and decisionmaking under certain conditions are what make the outcomes legitimate for each person.... [W]hatever the results of discussions, deliberation, and decisionmaking ... they are legitimate. The results are made legitimate by being the results of the procedure.
>
> (1996, 35)

21 By "aesthetics," I am not referring to its narrow conception as pertaining to questions of "beauty" alone. Instead, I am applying it to broader questions of sensation, perception, and their boundaries and distributions, particularly as a way to suggest something more comprehensive about our sensory involvement than is suggested by either "semiotics" or "discourse" alone.

22 See Benjamin's *Illuminations* (1969, 217–251).

23 "Parts" can be understood both geometrically and economically, as in how much of the pie will be distributed to everyone who gets a piece, and in terms of theatrical parts and the special identities and roles one plays in a performance.

24 The reason for this is the uniquely flexible means by which capitalist axiomatics ground the capitalist system. If you will recall from the previous chapter, the territorial and despotic machines depend heavily upon a very rigid process of overcoding to maintain themselves. Because it rests on a bed of mass-deterritorialization (which tends toward the dissolution of conventionally rigid social strata, as with a Great Chain of Being), the stratifications that produce and reproduce group dominance and exclusions within a capitalist machine can be more flexible. What counts as normal in relation to a dominant segment of society can be altered over time without radically challenging the functioning of a capitalist machine overall.

25 Concerning the majority, "it is not a question of knowing whether there are more mosquitoes or flies than men, but of knowing how 'man' constitutes a standard in the universe in relation to which men necessarily (analytically) form a majority" (Deleuze and Guattari 1987, 291).

26 What Deleuze also calls "molar" politics in reference to molarity in chemistry, which pertains to the concentration of a solution.

27 In contrast to molar politics, Deleuze refers to this as "molecular" politics, and "becoming-revolutionary."

28 In the USSR, the criminal charge of "social parasitism" was leveled against people who refused to contribute to the well-being of the political body by working until the official retirement age. Nobel Laureate poet Joseph Brodsky, for instance, faced banishment from Leningrad for parasitism. His occasional odd-work and poetry were deemed an insufficient contribution to the "good of the motherland." The judge overseeing the trial that would land him in a labor camp asked him "Who has recognized you as a poet? Who has enrolled you in the ranks of poets?" Brodsky responded "No one. Who enrolled me in the ranks of the human race?" (McFadden 1996).

29 Ostrom argues for the importance of "polycentric systems" of social organization operating at different scales for solving collective action problems (especially in relation to commons resources), in contrast to the top-down regulatory model of solving the "tragedy of the commons" originally posed by Garrett Hardin. She argues that several key methods can be effective for disincentivizing free riding and maintaining a stable commons resource system, including clearly defined boundaries of members or users, effective monitoring and enforcement, rules that are adapted to local conditions, decision-making arrangements that allow users to participate in determining collectively-applied rules, and graduated sanctions for violators, among other things (see Ostrom 1990; 2010).

30 Royce considers this a lost cause in that it is not something that can be fully actualized, but he does not consider it a pointless or worthless cause. It is through the pursuit of this impossible ideal that we can actually sustain hope and cultivate purpose and our highest moral qualities.

Vertical Time-binding   125

31 Simmons refers to this idea of a special obligation to the political order of which you are a part as the "particularity problem" (1979, 31–32).
32 To borrow and somewhat modify a term of David Wood's (2007), who defines time-shelters as "local economies of time" that generate differentiated kinds of spatial and temporal organization, and thus contingent boundaries between a tenuously maintained interiority and exteriority in the world (26–27).
33 Philosophically, this occurred by way of Aristotle, Neo-Platonists, the early church Fathers, Latin and Medieval philosophers, Aquinas, and Kant, through to Heidegger, whose overall ontological project Agamben tries to offer completion.
34 This is an easier transition to understand when we keep in mind that the concept of office Agamben discusses is far less formal than the way in which we use it today, even though it is still "public" oriented in nature. It is a role defined by its actions and duties, but need not be housed within "official" positions in institutions like the state. The similarities are especially close with the Kantian conception of the subject wherein all particular individuals only exercise their autonomy as a subject through their recognition and carrying out of the universal moral law. Through this ontology, being is inextricably tied to a "pure" and "infinite debt." Modern ontology was formed, Agamben argues, through the tension between the ontology of substance and the ontology of operativity.
35 According to the theologian Rudolf Otto (1958), this "numinous" experience underlies all forms of religiosity and contains three parts. The *mysterium* refers to that which is "wholly other" than our ordinary, everyday experience, and which we thus respond to with wonder. The *tremendum* refers to the sense of awe, dread, and might this *mysterium* gives off, and the corresponding dependence and insignificance one feels when faced with it. Finally, this *mysterium tremendum* entails a *fascinans*, a fascinating attraction and charm given off both because and in spite of its alien and mysterious terror.

References

Agamben, Giorgio. 2013. *Opus Dei: An Archaeology of Duty*. Stanford, CA: Stanford University Press.

Aquinas, Thomas. 1981. *Summa Theologica*. Translated by Fathers of the English Dominican Province. Westminster, MD: Christian Classics.

Aristotle. 1996. *The Politics and The Constitution of Athens*. Edited by Stephen Everson. New York: Cambridge University Press.

Benhabib, Seyla. 1996. *Democracy and Difference: Contesting the Boundaries of the Political*. Princeton, NJ: Princeton University Press.

Benjamin, Walter. 1969. *Illuminations*. Edited by Hannah Arendt. New York: Schocken.

Bozeman, Adda. 1960. *Politics and Culture in International History*. Princeton, NJ: Princeton University Press.

Christiano, Thomas. 1996. *The Rule of the Many*. Boulder, CO: Westview Press.

Dagger, Richard. 2000. "Membership, Fair Play, and Political Obligation." *Political Studies* 48 (1): 104–117.

Deleuze, Gilles. 1994. *What Is Philosophy?*. New York: Columbia University Press.

Deleuze, Gilles, and Felix Guattari. 1987. *A Thousand Plateaus: Capitalism and Schizophrenia*. Translated by Brian Massumi. Minneapolis: University of Minnesota Press.

Dworkin, Ronald. 1986. *Law's Empire*. Cambridge, MA: Harvard University Press.

Edmundson, William A., ed. 1999. *The Duty to Obey the Law: Selected Philosophical Readings*. Lanham, MD: Rowman & Littlefield.

Gans, Chaim. 1992. *Philosophical Anarchism and Political Disobedience*. New York: Cambridge University Press.

126   *Vertical Time-binding*

Gilbert, Margaret. 2006. *A Theory of Political Obligation: Membership, Commitment, and the Bonds of Society*. New York: Oxford University Press

Glanville, Luke. 2010. "Retaining the Mandate of Heaven: Sovereign Accountability in Ancient China." *Millennium – Journal of International Studies* 39: 323–343.

Hart, H.L.A. 1955. "Are There Any Natural Rights?" *Philosophical Review* 64 (2): 175–191.

Horton, John. 2010. *Political Obligation*. Second Edition. New York: Palgrave Macmillan.

Klosko, George. 2003. "Samaritanism and Political Obligation: A Response to Christopher Wellman's 'Liberal Theory of Political Obligation.'" *Ethics* 113 (July): 835–840.

Klosko, George. 2004. *The Principle of Fairness and Political Obligation*. New York: Rowman & Littlefield.

Klosko, George. 2005. *Political Obligations*. New York: Oxford University Press.

Locke, John. 2003. "The First Treatise: The False Principles and Foundation of Sir Robert Filmer." In *Two Treatises of Government and a Letter Concerning Toleration*, edited by Ian Shapiro. New Haven, CT: Yale University Press.

MacIntyre, Alasdair. 1984. *After Virtue*. Second Edition. Notre Dame, IN: University of Notre Dame Press.

McFadden, Robert D. 1996. "Joseph Brodsky, Exiled Poet Who Won Nobel, Dies at 55." *The New York Times*, January 29.

McPherson, Thomas. 1967. *Political Obligation*. New York: Routledge & Kegan Paul.

Nagel, Thomas. 1991. *Equality and Partiality*. New York: Oxford University Press.

Nietzsche, Friedrich. 1967. "On the Genealogy of Morals." In *On the Genealogy of Morals and Ecce Homo*, translated by Walter Kaufmann and R.J. Hollingdale. New York: Random House.

Nietzsche, Friedrich. 1974. *The Gay Science*. Translated by Walter Kaufmann. New York: Vintage Books.

Nietzsche, Friedrich. 1982. *Daybreak: Thoughts on the Prejudices of Morality*. Cambridge: Cambridge University Press.

Nozick, Robert. 1974. *Anarchy, State, and Utopia*. New York: Basic Books.

Oprisko, Robert L. 2012. *Honor: A Phenomenology*. New York: Routledge.

Ostrom, Elinor. 1990. *Governing the Commons: The Evolution of Institutions for Collective Action*. New York: Cambridge University Press.

Ostrom, Elinor. 2010. "Polycentric Systems for Coping with Collective Action and Global Environmental Change." *Global Environmental Change* 20: 550–557.

Otto, Rudolf. 1958.*The Idea of the Holy: An Inquiry into the Non-rational Factor in the Idea of the Divine and its Relation to the Individual*. New York: Oxford University Press.

Rancière, Jacques. 1999. *Disagreement: Politics and Philosophy*. Minneapolis: University of Minnesota Press.

Rancière, Jacques. 2004. *The Politics of Aesthetics: The Distribution of the Sensible*. Translated by Gabriel Rockhill. New York: Continuum.

Rawls, John. 1964. "Legal Obligation and the Duty of Fair Play." In *Law and Philosophy*, edited by Sidney Hook. New York: New York University Press.

Rawls, John. 1999. *A Theory of Justice*. Revised Edition. Cambridge, MA: The Belknap Press.

Renzo, Massimo. 2008. "Duties of Samaritanism and Political Obligation." *Legal Theory* 14: 193–217.

Rockhill, Gabriel. 2009. "The Politics of Aesthetics: Political History and Hermeneutics of Art." In *Jacques Rancière: History, Politics, Aesthetics*, edited by Gabriel Rockhill and Philip Watts. Durham, NC: Duke University Press.

Royce, Josiah. 1995. *The Philosophy of Loyalty*. Nashville, TN: Vanderbilt University Press.

Sandel, Michael. 1998. *Liberalism and the Limits of Justice*. Second Edition. New York: Cambridge University Press.

Scheffler, Samuel. 2001. *Boundaries and Allegiances: Problems of Justice and Responsibility in Liberal Thought*. Oxford: Oxford University Press.

Schmitt, Carl. 1985. *Political Theology: Four Chapters on the Concept of Sovereignty*. Translated by George Schwab. Cambridge, MA: The MIT Press.

Simmons, A. John. 1979. *Moral Principles and Political Obligations*. Princeton, NJ: Princeton University Press.

Simmons, A. John. 2006. "Theories of the State." In *The Cambridge Companion to Early Modern Philosophy*, edited by Donald Rutherford, 250–273. New York: Cambridge University Press.

Stirner, Max. 2005. *The Ego and His Own*. Mineola, NY: Dover.

Wellman, Christopher Heath. 1996. "Liberalism, Samaritanism, and Political Legitimacy." *Philosophy and Public Affairs* 25 (3): 211–237.

Wellman, Christopher Heath. 2001. "Toward a Liberal Theory of Political Obligation." *Ethics* 111: 735–759.

Wolff, Jonathan. 1995. "Pluralistic Models of Political Obligation." *Philosophica* 56: 7–27.

Wood, David. 2007. *Time After Time*. Bloomington, IN: Indiana University Press.

Yonglin, Jiang. 2010. *Mandate of Heaven and the Great Ming Code*. Seattle, WA: University of Washington Press.

Young, Iris Marion. 1990. *Justice and the Politics of Difference*. Princeton, NJ: Princeton University Press.

4 Horizontal Time-binding

Consent holds a privileged place among theories of political obligation. At first glance, it seems to promise reconciliation between the antinomies of freedom and social order that have defined much of modern political thought, especially in the liberal tradition. Historically, we can find appeals to consent as a justification for political obedience and obligations extending at least as far back as Socrates. While primarily compelled by notions of piety and group membership, Socrates drank his hemlock with the deafening "echo" of reminders of his past commitments to his polity "resounding" in him, compelling him to acquiesce to his death sentence (Plato 2002, 53–57). Certainly, the staging of modernity has brought substantial changes of context and theoretical details for theories of consent. The rise of mass society, the modern state, the Enlightenment, liberalism, representative democracy, and capitalism, as well as the cornucopia of crises that each emerged from and contributed to, entailed tectonic shifts in the forms and conceptualizations of social and political relations. It is out of concrete circumstances of this tumult, for instance, that theories of "social contract" – a distinct form of consent theory – emerged as both a defense of political obligation, as well as a discursive tool against absolutist government. Hobbes, Locke, and Rousseau are the exemplary theorists of this conceptualization of contract and consent as a foundation for and justification of government, but the political salience of these ideas has extended well beyond their foundational tomes, both undergirding the authority of "legitimate" states and fomenting waves of revolutions from the seventeenth century until the present.

Modern political thought has also clearly elevated the importance of consent as a practical frame of reference in common political discourse and practical life. The conceptualization of political authority and obligations in terms of consent is not just a principally modern notion, but can be understood as one of the defining features of modern political thought. Harry Beran argues that it is far and away "the most commonly accepted theory of political obligation in the history of Western philosophy" (1987, 1), while A.J. Simmons argues that it is the most commonly and intuitively appealing basis for establishing political obligations in all of modern political theory (1979, 57). Consequently, perhaps it should come as no surprise that consent is appealed to by both (some) obligation apologists and their primary counterparts – the philosophical anarchists – as a means of supporting their respective positions. For the obligation apologists who accept it

Horizontal Time-binding 129

as a principle worth valuing, consent is seen as an especially attractive means of rendering one or another form of political rule legitimate. It provides a method of justifying obedience toward, and the enforcement of, certain kinds of social and political authority, while at the same time ostensibly respecting the will of the individual. For philosophical anarchists, consent serves much the same function. It still acts as a means of at least potentially sanctifying some arrangement of political authority, even while it delegitimizes existing states and the bulk of state claims upon the right to legitimately rule.[1] The normative motivations and technical standards of legitimation differ, but the structure and function of the concept of consent does not.

While both obligation apologists and philosophical anarchists contest the proper boundaries, political uses, and practical implications of consent, it is nevertheless generally taken to be a straightforward and sound concept. There are, certainly, some recognized problems and ambiguities. Hume's critiques of the social contract still inform many of the basic grievances reiterated by contemporary critics of consent theory. For the most part, though, these existing criticisms are seen as minor hiccups that do not threaten the overall essential cogency and value of the conventional conceptualization of consent, even among theorists who reject the primacy of consent as a ground for justifying political obligations. As Dudley Knowles observes, consent seems to exercise a kind of "moral magic" in liberal political theory and discourse, as well as in our practical lives (2010, 96).

Should we really be satisfied with this sense of intrinsic magic, or, what amounts to the same, an appeal to doxic intuition or common sense? The nature and force of consent may be considered obvious by most of its intellectual proponents operating within the liberal tradition, and commonsensical in wider political discourse. It is arguably because of its position as a keystone of modern liberal political discourse, though, that aspects of consent – especially those pertaining to its *disciplinary* functions within that discourse – remain undertheorized.[2] When viewed through a different theoretical lens, however, the presumed simplicity of the concept of consent is displaced by ambiguity and puzzlement.

In this chapter, I will provide a critical reassessment of consent and its place within theories of political obligation. While the concept of consent clearly intersects with many areas beyond the purview of political obligation, these are largely beyond our present scope. We will be especially concerned, as has already been implied, with how consent functions as a time-binding disciplinary construct within modern political obligation discourse. To this end, I will try to highlight what must be hidden as well as what must be imagined and perceived in order for the appeal to consent to serve this function, and will be specifically attending to its underlying processes of temporal structuration. In the previous chapter, I discussed the process of vertical time-binding as one common method that has been deployed – knowingly or not – by obligation theorists as a means of fulfilling the basic political dialectic of modernity. Appeals to membership, divine right, justice, or similar synthesizing images are examples of this method, and involve casting individuals as part of a wider vertical co-temporality; an image of stratified identities, roles, norms, and expectations cohering together

130   *Horizontal Time-binding*

within a shared imagined space. Horizontal time-binding is the second major method used to achieve this end, and it has been advanced almost exclusively through appeals to consent in one form or another. We will develop our analysis of consent, horizontal time-binding, and political obligation throughout the remainder of this chapter.

We will begin by reviewing the parameters of and basic divisions within theories of consent as they relate to debates over political obligation. In this, we will look at the origins of consent theory, theories of actual and hypothetical consent, and the social contract. We will also look at the primary articulations of philosophical anarchism, since they also base their arguments on grounds of consent. Finally, we will flesh out and apply our temporal analysis to the concept of consent, elaborate on how it functions as a form of horizontal time-binding, and draw out what the implications of this might be.

Theories of Consent

In the philosophical literature on political obligation, arguments from consent assert that political obligations to obey legitimate political authorities are generated through consent, either substantially or exclusively. Hugo Grotius, one of the foundational seventeenth century theorists of international law, expresses this aptly when he asserts that

> Neither is the Right which the Sovereign has over his Subjects to be measured by this or that Form, of which divers Men have different Opinions, but by the Extent of the Will of those who conferred it upon him.
>
> (Tuck 1993, 193)

The precise political implications derived from appeals to consent are as diverse as the consent theories that have mobilized them. Broadly construed, consent has been used as a justification for and against obedience to states, for *laissez-faire* capitalism, social democratic redistribution, and a variety of socialisms, and for and against representative democracy. When we discuss "consent theory," therefore, we should not take it to mean something that is uniform. A consent *theory*, following Don Herzog, is "any political, moral, legal, or social theory that casts society as a collection of free individuals and then seeks to explain or justify outcomes by appealing to their voluntary actions, especially choice and consent" (1989, 1).

While it has roots in both antiquity and medieval political thought, modern theories of consent emerged from the crucible of early Stuart England, especially in the tumultuous years surrounding the Civil War.[3] In 1642, Charles I raised his armies against those of Parliament after protracted struggles over royal and parliamentary power, finances, participation in the Thirty Years War, and religious policies, among other things. After an inconclusive series of battles and failed negotiations for an acceptable peace, Parliament turned to Scotland for aid, and the Scots obliged, citing religious and other grievances. After little change in their prospects for success, Parliament rebuilt their army, establishing

Horizontal Time-binding 131

the "New Model" army reforms. These reforms de-emphasized the significance of social rank and privileges, and raised the importance of skill and competence in determining positions within the army. It also provided the army with greater mobility and autonomy, by replacing its previous regional militia model with more independent professional soldiers. With the New Model Army, Parliament swept to victory against Charles I. Complications soon followed as many soldiers in the New Model Army had no wish to disband, and threatened to move against Parliament itself unless a shifting and uncertain set of demanded reforms were met. While one motive was surely that of securing their livelihood, the New Model Army was also both a magnet for and a seedbed of reformist and radical political ideas, often motivated by powerful religious conviction – the unforeseen consequence of the very autonomy and meritocratic egalitarianism that had made it a success on the battlefield.

At the Putney Debates within the New Model Army, the General Council met to make sense of a bewildering array of options, demands, and possibilities, and, more importantly, to act on them in a complex political situation. The old explanations and images of social order were faltering; appeals to the divine right of kings and the Great Chain of Being were insufficient, and the social, economic, and political exigencies of the time were producing new "masterless men" on a larger scale who did not fit easily into that feudal story (Herzog 1989, 39). As is evident in the transcripts of the debates, the delegates at the Council appealed to an eclectic combination of theoretical frameworks and conceptual artifacts in arguing their positions. In a period of extreme urgency and practical dangers, we nevertheless find highly philosophical appeals to social contract and consent, as well as the mythical "ancient constitution" of the English people, theories of republican virtue, and the natural rights of man. All of these were further enmeshed in religious appeals, themes, and convictions that cut across and informed their theoretical and political problems (35). As Herzog argues, these concepts were not dealt with lightly or as mere philosophical curiosities. Rather, they helped frame the nature of the problems they faced, and provided actionable guidance in a period of tremendous political stakes and social upheaval.[4] Consequently,

> [w]e should see the rise of consent theory as part of a drama involving social change. The emergence of masterless men in far-flung social settings made older conceptions of society increasingly baffling, increasingly opaque.... Through the lens provided by the older conceptions of society, that sort of society had to be disorderly, chaotic, anarchic, a pathological mess crying out for the reimposition of order. So if consent theory was in part a solution to the problems posed by social change, a more incisive map of the world, it also posed a new and profound problem: how is social order possible among a collection of free individuals?

(39)

The appeal to consent has thus historically involved a concern for the practical political utility of consent as an ordinance to be brought to bear in struggles over

132   *Horizontal Time-binding*

the boundaries and distributions of political power and institutional authority. To satisfy this concern, deference has been paid to the importance of what Beran refers to as the "defeating conditions" of contract and consent (1987, 6). Defeating conditions are those conditions that negate the validity or authenticity of an act of consent. There are few if any consent theorists who would argue that simply signing one's name or verbalizing one's consent is sufficient to make that consent "binding." Rather, consent must occur under conditions that consent theorists deem acceptably just.

Beran identifies three primary defeating conditions that tend to be commonly recognized among consent theorists: lack of freedom, lack of information, and lack of competence. The lack of freedom defeating condition involves consenting under conditions of objectionable influence, variously understood. Such objectionable conditions could include "coercion," "undue influence," "posthypnotic suggestion," or the exploitation of someone's predicament. The lack of information defeating condition involves the undesirable effects of ignorance, broadly understood. This can be an imposed ignorance through deception, an unintentional but misleading failure of communication, or a "gross misunderstanding" by consenting parties about fundamental elements of the agreement. Lack of competence involves a more thoroughgoing failure of the rational faculties of one or all of the parties to an agreement. This could include insanity, mental incapacitation (either temporary or permanent), or developmental immaturity (Beran 1987, 6–7). Each of these three major defeating conditions grows out of the concern for creating conditions for consent that approximate what the consent theorists consider to be an idealized operation of reason: an image of free and capable individual choice (and free individuals themselves) that can be considered essentially safe from fundamental criticism, and unproblematic within a liberal discourse of consent.

While these three defeating conditions are the most commonly listed, there are others. Knowles, for instance, argues that consent cannot legitimate certain social outcomes that are simply immoral, such as slavery or producing "evil" regimes. Other examples include compulsory self-destruction,[5] "voluntary euthanasia and extreme sadism" (Knowles 2010, 100). For Knowles and many other consent theorists, while consent can legitimate some political arrangements or choices, there are higher priorities, either consequentially or deontologically, which act as defeating conditions if consent curtails their fulfillment.

The meanings, proper application, and limits of these defeating conditions have been the subject of extensive disagreement between different branches of consent theory. There is, however, remarkably little analysis of the function of the defeating conditions as such for the maintenance of the stability of the concept of consent itself. Later in this chapter, we will attempt to provide an analysis of the functions of these defeating conditions in order to make sense of their significance.

It is important to understand the origins and basic motivations and priorities of theories of consent. It isn't entirely clear at this point, though, what we are discussing when we say "consent." As the concept of defeating conditions highlights, existing theories of consent seem to compress and collapse several distinct elements – such as rationality, intent, will, action, outcomes, and an array of competing values and limits – into a practically potent but philosophically ambiguous amalgam. What does it mean to talk about the transfer of one's "will" or "right," as if these were alienable properties or artifacts? How can such a transfer bind us at all across time? Are we really left with simply thinking of consent in terms of moral magic? What exactly is consent? Since these basic questions regarding the nature and function of consent will be reconsidered here, we must first sketch out the primary positions and points of contention among existing theories of consent. After this, we can reconsider consent in light of our temporal analysis, and evaluate the functions, strengths, and limits of existing conceptualizations of consent as a foundation for justifying political obligations.

In their efforts to defend consent as the proper ground for justifying political obligations, consent theorists have disagreed over two primary problems. The first problem is concerned with questions regarding what constitutes sufficient consent. This is primarily posed as an ontological question regarding the nature of rights and duties, how they may be given or transferred, and by which mechanisms. This line of questioning is usually understood in universalizing terms. The second problem asks under which circumstances consent can be considered genuinely given. This is primarily cast as a problem of practical politics. More specifically, this usually involves comparing the accepted universals established in response to the first question to particular circumstances, or at least somewhat less abstracted idealizations of particular circumstances.

Disagreement over these two basic problems has resulted first and foremost in a conceptual division between consent theorists as such and social contract theorists. Contract theorists can be understood as holding a particular, historically significant, form and application of consent theory. Their distinct and curious framing of the political situation, and the parameters of argument surrounding this frame, justify a separate consideration. Within each variant, there are further distinctions made between "actual" and "hypothetical" forms of contract or consent. Actual consent involves an active granting of consent (whether explicitly or implicitly), while hypothetical consent appeals to a hypothetical scenario of what representative actors should or would consent to in a given context. Actual contract identifies a source of political obligation in actively created social contracts (though not necessarily contracts enacted by living contractees), while hypothetical contracts use the social contract as a metaphor for framing our understanding of the nature and problems associated with social and political life, though at times the line between actual and hypothetical contract can become quite blurred. Although they share significant overlap with regard to their conceptual concerns, relevant theorists, and philosophical traditions, consent and contract theories are distinct in the ways they have been used and the particular kinds of criticisms that they have faced. It is important to note that although they mobilize their theories for different normative ends, both political obligation apologists deploying consent theory and the philosophical anarchists generally formulate their positions on consent within the parameters of this general typology. Consequently, both will be addressed in the remainder of this section, and both will be subject to many of the same basic criticisms.

134 *Horizontal Time-binding*

Forms of Consent

The category of "actual" consent refers to those forms of consent that are considered to be actively granted by some person or party. In this case, "actively" should not be taken to necessarily entail any particular gesture, articulation, or oath. Actual consent can involve both "explicit" and "implicit" ways of indicating that consent. One can imagine a scenario, after all, perhaps in an organizational or committee meeting, where simply refraining from comment or objection can be (for practical or expedient purposes) counted as consent. What is significant for theorists with affinities for actual consent is that some appropriate mechanism of justifying a transfer of powers or rights (appropriate meaning a mechanism that avoids some set of defeating conditions) must occur in order for political obligations to legitimately accrue.

Explicit consent is likely the most familiar and "common sense" notion of consent, both in relation to political obligation and more broadly. To explicitly consent is to overtly give a promise, swear an oath, recite a pledge, shake a hand, give one's word, sign one's name, or enact any of the countless varieties of rituals that have been and could be adopted to indicate consent. Consent is explicit here because of the overt nature of consent's indication, but the significance is not necessarily in any of the rituals themselves. Most consent theorists would consider an explicit consent ritual that occurs under a defeating condition to be null and void. The ritual is only significant in explicit consent insofar as it is seen as indicating a clearer mutuality in the recognition of an act of consent. Conventionally, explicit consent is also considered by many consent theorists to be the most argumentatively "rock-solid" means of establishing consent-based political obligations (Knowles 2010, 104). Implicit consent entails greater potential ambiguity and room for interpretation (and thus a greater potential illegitimacy of derived obligation claims), and, according to some critics, hypothetical consent isn't a form of consent at all. It may be granted by its defenders that perhaps explicit consent isn't terribly solid in its ability to bind *everyone* with political obligations. That is, in part, its appeal for philosophical anarchists after all. It is considered a practical certainty among most consent theorists, however, that those who genuinely and explicitly consent to some set of obligations acquire those obligations. One of the most glaring difficulties faced by explicit consent theorists who wish to appeal to explicit consent as a justification for political obligations is thus its starkly limited scope of applicability. "It may be well and good that explicit consent generates strong political obligations," a sympathetic consent theorist might say, "but what use is such a standard if it applies to only a relative handful of people?" After all, how many people have ever genuinely consented to the political order that they happen to live within? Adult immigrants who have freely chosen to take citizen oaths of loyalty under minimal duress might match the expectations of some of the more stringent explicit consent theorists, but not many others. Consequently, implicit consent has frequently served as an attractive alternative ground on which to base obligation claims.

Implicit or tacit consent is a form of actual consent that occurs (or at least is claimed to occur) even when one is silent, or otherwise not expressively explicit

Horizontal Time-binding 135

in consenting. Consent in this case, as mentioned earlier, could be registered through the silence itself as a form of expression, by refusing to register a contrary position. More controversially, however, implicit consent is also used to refer to the actions and choices of a person that are deemed to constitute consent and thus legitimize some set of political obligations, *even if they are not perceived as such by that individual.* Although elements of it appear in Socrates' defense of his compulsory suicide, the primary modern formulation of implicit or tacit consent is that of Locke, who asks "how far anyone shall be looked on to have consented, and thereby submitted to any government, where he has made no Expressions of it at all" (1980, §119). Locke's answers are multifaceted, but still define the major positions of contemporary appeals to implicit consent.

Locke first claims that an admission of tacit consent can be located in the continued *receipt of particular goods or benefits* from a government. He argues that "every man that has possessions or enjoyment of any part of the dominions of any government" is obliged to obey the laws of that government while receiving those goods or benefits, whether in perpetuity by possession of land passed down through family, a week's worth of lodging, or even for the simple duration of one's time spent using a highway (ibid.). Tacit consent, in Locke's account, is generated through an implicit appeal to a form of gratitude, fairness, or reciprocity, but also the suggestion of an actual kind of agreement. By taking the offered or non-excludable benefits secured by a government, one agrees to a silent exchange wherein the cost of those benefits is obedience. As the previous quoted section suggests, though, it isn't simply the receipt of benefits, but also the *continued* receipt that also establishes tacit consent. Locke argues that someone who is receiving benefits from a government and chooses to stay within that territory rather than emigrate has also registered their consent by virtue of their lack of disassociation and, by extension, lack of dissent. By continued acceptance of the implicit exchange of services between individual and government, consent is operative as a default. Extending Locke's line of reasoning, Peter Singer argues that if lack of dissent is sufficient to establish tacit consent, as is receipt of benefits, then active participation in the governing institutions of a decent state must also then be evidence of that consent (1973, 45–49).[6] Participation in voting and other institutions of governance, and generally acting *as if* the government one lived under was legitimate and that one consented to it is thus grounds for establishing consent. In benefiting from a government, acting as if its institutions were generally acceptable, and failing to indicate otherwise, Locke and his kindred successors identify consent through the character of and common expectations surrounding one's actions within a social context.

Hypothetical consent is a comparatively marginal position within consent theory as it pertains to political obligation,[7] but it is certainly one of the more controversial approaches. Some theorists, such as Beran, discuss John Rawls' hypothetical deliberations within the original position as a form of hypothetical consent. While this isn't without merit, I consider it more appropriate to discuss Rawls' ideas as a form of hypothetical contract put in the service of rationalizing a particular account of natural duty. Hypothetical consent involves postulating what an ideal rational or reasonable actor would do in certain conditions, and

136   *Horizontal Time-binding*

subsequently grounding the political obligations actual people should owe on what the ideal actor would do. Hypothetical consent is thus hypothetical because it removes the necessity of identifying any particular act as a legitimate instantiation of consent, and, indeed, removes the necessity of any particular person being a subject for consent at all. As Hanna Pitkin, one of the primary theorists of the hypothetical consent framework, puts it, "you are obligated neither by your own consent nor by that of the majority but by the consent rational men in a hypothetical 'state of nature' would have to give." Consent, for Pitkin, is thus not an act or mechanism that confers legitimacy upon a government, but rather something that is *owed* to the legitimate "government which *deserves* consent." A legitimate government "whose subjects are obligated to obey it, emerges as one to which they *ought to consent*, quite apart from whether they have done so" (Pitkin 1965, 999). The controversial status of hypothetical consent is, in part, a consequence of the apparent difference of its goals and of its formulation of the problem of political obligation from that of other voluntarist theories, specifically as a result of the displacement or removal of any concrete consenting subject from its theoretical lens (see criticisms from Horton 2010, 80–86; Knowles 2010, 117–120). While actual consent theorists seem thoroughly uncomfortable at the presence of hypothetical consent theories within their conceptual borders, it is worth questioning how justified that discomfort is. I will reconsider the nature of hypothetical consent in relation to other consent theories later in this chapter. For now we can ask: Is hypothetical consent so discomfiting to actual consent theorists because of how alien it is, or because of their inconvenient (if unrecognized) similarities?

Drawing Up the Social Contract

In part a reaction against the traditional methods of justifying political obligation by reference to divine right, modern social contract theory developed in the turbulent seventeenth and eighteenth centuries of Western Europe as a more secular justification for political obligation and the legitimacy of political authority. This certainly does not mean that it does not have deeply religious roots, or that the early users of social contract ideas generally intended the social contract to help usher in the death of God in social and political life; quite to the contrary. The language of the individuals at the Putney Debates was infused with religious imagery, scripture, and themes, and contained a sense of the immediacy of God as a reference point for developing their ideas and orienting their actions. Most modern justifications of political obligation that use the idea of a social contract are grounded in the classic social contract statements of this period, especially Thomas Hobbes' *Leviathan* and John Locke's *Second Treatise on Government*, as well as Jean-Jacques Rousseau's *The Social Contract*. Although later authors, such as John Rawls and Philip Pettit, employ the social contract in unique ways for their own normative theories, Hobbes, Locke, and Rousseau developed its most important and identifiable features.

In *Leviathan*, Hobbes tells us that prior to hierarchical social and political organization humans find themselves in a "state of nature." While individuals

Horizontal Time-binding 137

are unfettered and basically equal in this state of nature, they are also selfish and beset by an abiding and inborn fear and distrust of the potential motives and actions of others. Consequently, they are compelled by a "restlesse desire for power after power" (Hobbes 1987, 161) to assuage these fears of uncertainty. It is this consequent drive for the expansion of individual powers that leads to the odious condition of the "warre of every man against every man" (185). In order to escape this state of nature, individuals contract with each other to mutually forfeit certain individual powers (such as killing others, or stealing). These forfeited powers are in turn transferred to a sovereign who is then responsible for maintaining order and the possibility of society and political life, keeping each of the subjects "in awe" of its power (ibid.). The benefits of this transfer, for Hobbes, are the enhancement of security and the maintenance of reliable expectations regarding people's behavior, as well as a broadened scope of freedom for individual pursuits. While a particular sovereign may tend towards despotism, according to Hobbes the benefits accrued from this maintenance of social and political life outweigh the costs of returning to the anxieties and fear of the state of nature (186). In order to maintain this original covenant and the pursuant benefits from its inception, political obligations should be imposed by the sovereign upon a state's residents. Hobbes does not prescribe unconditional political obligations for subjects towards their sovereign, providing a defense of disobedience, self-defense, and defection in cases where the sovereign either fails to protect the security or life of the subject or intends to remove it through intentional punishment or persecution. In these circumstances, dissidents and defectors "but defend their lives," something no one, including the sovereign, can remove the right to do (270). Nevertheless, his understanding of the role of the social contract in justifying political obligations clearly tends towards justifying obedience to a sovereign by virtue of the ostensible benefits accrued within a particular image of collective security and stability.

Locke uses but modifies Hobbes' state of nature argument. For Locke, the state of nature is a noticeably less miserable state in which to be. While there is anxiety over the lack of security of one's rights and property in the state of nature, it is not, as with Hobbes', equivalent to a state of war. In the Lockean state of nature individuals remain obliged by the morality of natural law, which "teaches all mankind who will but consult it that, being all equal and independent no one ought to harm another in his life, health, liberty or possessions" (Locke 1980, §6). This equality of power and position also entails an equality of the right and responsibility of enforcement, of punishing wrongdoing, and being an "executioner of the law of nature" (§7–8). Such equality of enforcement is unstable and problematic, however, since humans are neither impartial nor dispassionate creatures when acting against those who have wronged them (§13). Thus, individuals still try to overcome the uncertain security (§123) and "inconveniences" of this condition, especially the possibility of it degenerating to a "state of war" through violations of the law of nature (§13). They achieve this by consenting to form a political society and government to ensure individual liberty and the establishment of a "common judge" who is above partial individual judgments and unequal enforcement (§18). For Locke, the act of explicit

138   *Horizontal Time-binding*

consent *or* the inference of tacit consent entails the acquisition of political obligations by subjects to a political order, and consequently confines one's ability to act legitimately against that order to exceptional cases.

Writing in the context of an emerging modern commercial society with its attendant social disruptions and unraveled cultural time, Rousseau modifies the basic ends of the social contract of Hobbes and Locke and applies it to understand his circumstances. Rousseau still argues that individuals pursue a social contract in order to advance their own freedom and security, but does so in a distinctly different way. In vesting their powers in the collective polity, the contracting individuals achieve their freedom by aligning the individual will with the aims of the general will of the group, "by means of which each, coalescing with all, may nevertheless obey only himself" (Rousseau 1998, 14). In doing this, Rousseau aims to establish neither the order and security-minded unitary Leviathan of Hobbes, nor the more classically liberal and constitutionally limited government of Locke. Instead he attempts to conceptualize a fully sovereign and undivided direct democracy that is finally capable of expressing the "general will" of sovereign society (a unity sacrificed with the emergence of modernity). Political obligations accrue from contractual consent for Rousseau, but he goes further by rendering the concept of both obligation and dissent unstable. His understanding of human nature and his assumptions regarding the possibility of harmonizable wills negating radical difference, can be read as precluding even the possibility of legitimate dissent within his idealized polity.

A common thread running through each of these attempts to establish a social contract theory is some idea of the "consent of the governed" justifying political obligations. Whether these theorists considered this consent to be actual or hypothetical is disputed, both between and within each.[8] David Hume is particularly critical of the ahistorical and problematic way in which consent and contract are understood by Locke, especially regarding the violent historical origins of states which Locke's state of nature tale glosses over, and the high costs borne by those who fail to consent to a government, a problem which raises questions about whether such choices can truly be considered uncoerced (Hume 1953). The problem of locating "original" consent, whether explicit or tacit (Locke 1980, §119), and establishing its relevance for justifying continued obligations are nevertheless major themes in each of the above works, and still powerfully undergird much of contemporary theorizing about political obligation. Consequently, Hume's criticisms have followed them and been joined by many others, indeed far too many to survey here. Carole Pateman and Charles Mills have critiqued social contract theory on the grounds that contract theorists' basic images of the contract-based organization of political life entail substantial discrimination against, and exclusion or concealment of, disempowered groups. For Pateman, social contract theories have conceptually entailed the exclusion of women through the gendered divisions made between domestic and public spheres of social life, while Mills argues that social contract theories entail substantial racist outcomes and the reinforcement of structural white privilege (Pateman 1988; Mills 1997; Pateman and Mills 2007).

Philosophical Anarchists and Consent

Within the literature on political obligation, the principal critics of political obligation as such – and the discussants who arguably lean most heavily on the concept of consent for their arguments – are the philosophical anarchists. Philosophical anarchism is distinguished from anarchism as a broader political tradition in that philosophical anarchism contains no explicit normative opposition to the existence of states or coercive institutional hierarchies as such. In considering the state to be illegitimate, philosophical anarchists simply "remove any strong moral presumption in favor of obedience to, compliance with, or support for" states (Simmons 2001, 104). States may or may not be desirable, according to philosophical anarchists, but regardless, they (meaning at least extant states) lack adequate justification for legitimately demanding obedience from their subject populations.

Contrary to what some political anarchist critics of philosophical anarchism have suggested, philosophical anarchism is not simply a "watered down" anarchism, separate from and at odds with the political anarchist tradition (even though particular philosophical anarchists may not consider themselves political anarchists). It is not a competing or distinctly alternative position to anarchism proper, because the two positions are not commensurable. Rather, philosophical anarchism can be more usefully understood as primarily an epistemological position peculiar to modern debates regarding the legitimacy of political obligation claims. It may be the case that philosophical anarchism lacks the normative bite and revolutionary injunctions of the political anarchist tradition, but then most of its main proponents do not seem to have intended to offer it as a competitor to or distinct school within this tradition in the first place.

Arguments in defense of philosophical anarchism consist primarily of two kinds: a priori and a posteriori. A priori philosophical anarchism argues that it is simply not possible to establish a general a priori obligation to obey the law or established authority. Robert Paul Wolff provided the theoretical foundation for this position in his 1970 essay, *In Defense of Anarchism*. A posteriori philosophical anarchism, on the other hand, does not argue that there could not theoretically be a satisfactory general defense of political obligation. Instead it maintains, following the reasoning of A.J. Simmons, that there have simply been no successful attempts to do so, primarily owing to the failure of actually-existing states and political circumstances to meet the proper requirements for justifying political obligations. These two theorists exemplify the general scope of the philosophical anarchist position, though at times there are ambiguous overlaps between them that complicate their distinction.

Wolff's arguments in defense of an a priori philosophical anarchism rest on moral grounds. Drawing heavily from Kant, Wolff argues that there cannot be a general political obligation to obey the law simply because it is law, because this would conflict with our "primary obligation" of autonomy (1970, 18). If we are to fulfill our obligation to be autonomous actors, then the law itself cannot legitimately command our obligation without violating this requirement. While one may accept the existence or need of a state, there can be no a priori justification

140 *Horizontal Time-binding*

for obedience to the commands of a state. Interestingly, Wolff does allow for political obligation in the case of a system of unanimous direct democracy. In such a hypothetically non-coercive, non-conflictual system, however, it is worth asking how the autonomously directed act of cooperation in agreement with others can meaningfully be considered an enactment of "political obligation," rather than simply an expression of the participants' convergent preferences and decisions in a particular circumstance. Wolff does not fully resolve the tension in this conceptual ambiguity.

Simmons' defense of a posteriori philosophical anarchism rests on a critique of existing conditions, specifically of the possibility of genuine consent being expressed in those conditions. While political obligation itself could be hypothetically derived from consent (Simmons 2001, 137), especially through institutional mechanisms that facilitate consent's explicit acquisition, the particular characteristics of all existing states are such that genuine consent is not possible (106). Until such standards of explicit and uncoerced consent are met, existing states fail to meet the burden of proof for establishing the legitimacy of their demands for political obligations. In a manner that is similar to the ambiguity identified in Wolff's unanimous direct democracy, the applicability of ideal conditions of consent for justifying obligations can be brought into doubt. If, hypothetically, Simmons' ideal conditions of consent under a radically un-coercive democracy were actualized, in what way would one be "obligated" rather than simply be choosing or accepting an action? Further, if one withdraws consent and is nevertheless still then "obligated," why do the conditions for the actual expression of consent suddenly lose their primary importance? How and why, again, does consent (even "ideal" consent) bind across time? These problems are not adequately redressed in Simmons' (and other consent theorists') work, in part, I argue, owing to an atemporal and inadequate theorization of the concept of "consent" itself, an inadequacy that cuts across both sides of the debates within modern political obligation discourse.

Theorization of consent within debates over political obligation remains bound within these general parameters. What, though, is the problem with this? In spite of its ambiguities, doesn't consent remain a useful concept for articulating demands regarding individual freedoms? If consent is disregarded, won't this lead to a trammeling of individual rights and liberties by authorities? Thinking beyond the bounds of political obligation, what about the implications for medical ethics, sexual violence, or other areas where consent plays an active role in framing discussion and contestation? We will re-examine the relationship between consent and freedom toward the end of this chapter and revisit these questions in more detail.

I offer for now an unintuitive set of claims regarding consent that we will develop throughout the remainder of this chapter. First, rather than simply suffering from peripheral and exceptional troubles, the concept as it is commonly used is irresolvably problematic at its core. The puzzles and conceptual blind spots it engenders are endemic, not incidental. Second, consent is not something one can give of oneself at all, either explicitly or implicitly. The traditional embodiment of consent (positing it as emanating from the will of an autonomous

Horizontal Time-binding 141

person) has deep roots within liberalism, but only serves to obfuscate its actual operations. Third, rather than being a bulwark of individual autonomy – as Wolff and Simmons and, indeed, nearly the whole of the liberal tradition imagines – consent actually serves a socially homogenizing and disciplinary function in its relationship to political obligation. Ultimately, these claims will culminate for our analysis in the argument that consent is a form of horizontal time-binding; it is a construct that binds individuals across time through a distinct process of temporal projection. This understanding of consent departs substantially and productively from its traditional theorization. Its implications, moreover, pose a fundamental challenge to those who attempt to justify or legitimate political obligations by way of consent, and consequently upturn much of both modern political theory and practical political discourse along the way.

Who Consents?

Recall Bergson's discussion of our doubled self. On the one hand, he argues, we experience ourselves as discrete bodies of flesh and bone in the world, encountering the flow of duration in each moment of the passing present – this is what I referred to as our "concrete self." On the other hand, we also have a "second self" that "obscures the first" (Bergson 2001, 138) – I referred to this as the "conventional self." Although this conventional self is only a refracted piece of the complex material and symbolic assemblages that make up our "self," we require it in order to live. The maintenance of a sense of enduring personal self with "well-distinguishing moments" through memory, the definition of that self through social roles, categories, and norms, the cultivation of a sense of personal meaning and life direction through the projection of a cohesive past, present, and future, and the direction of short and long term projects; the conventional self is both a practical product and facilitator of these efforts. We can't do without the creation of this conventional self or these illusory spatializations (as solid as they may appear to us in our day to day lives), Bergson says, but we can try to understand them, and in so doing perhaps keep ourselves from confusing "the real" for its "symbolical substitute" (139).

With this observation in mind, we can broach a neglected question in discussions of consent: who consents when consent occurs? By this I do not mean to ask "who *really* consents?" That is a common question that tends to fixate on the legitimacy or illegitimacy of someone's act of consent, perhaps by suggesting the existence of a defeating condition in some or even all circumstances, or by raising doubts about the status of tacit consent. It takes for granted, however, who is doing the consenting, from where consent is "emanating" or "originating" and the direction it travels. For those people living in contemporary liberal capitalist democracies and reared with the assumptions of liberal juridical and contractarian traditions, this might seem like an absurd question with an obvious answer (at the very least insofar as we are referring to explicit consent). This reaction is understandable. After all, you remember that it was you who gave your word, or signed that contract, or otherwise indicated agreement to a course of action with which you were confronted. Conversely, it appears quite obvious

142   *Horizontal Time-binding*

that it is you who has not consented when you feel the sting of being trampled upon roughshod by indifferent and capricious authority or power (whether of an official, warlord, boss, or schoolyard bully). What more is there that needs to be said?

It is here that the insight into our doubled selves can be useful. In using Bergsonian intuition, we see that norms, identities, conventions, and the roles we occupy and internalize in a social context are a product of spatialization. Social life itself require the maintenance of an illusory homogeneity and co-temporality – especially a sense of shared space, belonging, and commonality – and facilitates the production of our conventional self to interface with and navigate in that social field in our everyday lives. The radically unique particularity of our concrete selves is anathema to social life; we must be reduced to some common category or factor (e.g., citizen, human, person, etc.) to be intelligible subjects at all within a social situation. It is not our concrete, particular self of each moment that bears the attributed and inherited social categories and demands, then, but the virtual and refracted conventional self. We construct a sense of stable self by simplifying our radical heterogeneity and projecting time into a spatialization, but we do so in the context of, and in dialectical response to, the initial spatializations projected onto our conventional self throughout our development in social life. The processes of capture operating within the social machines in which we emerge and develop are irrevocably part of our constitution as particular beings. Our conventional self is, in part, a product of the majoritarian systems of signifiance and subjectification that make society possible. If it is this conventional self that bears the marks of social distinctions and sorting, that is the subject of actual claims made against a person by a social order, and is the fragmentary and representational aspect of ourselves that is considered legible in our interactions within any given discourses, communities, and institutions, then what are we to make of consent?

The traditional image of consent, at least when it is presented as a justification for political obligation, is that of an embodied yet alienable property. That image seems wholly inadequate when held against Bergson's account of our doubled selves. Without resorting to a Cartesian Cogito, Kantian transcendental unity, or other *deus ex machina*, there is no clear space for an alienable property like consent in our concrete self. Our concrete self cannot give consent, since it lacks a means for it to either bear or be bound by any spatialized abstraction beyond each particular moment. Or, if we follow Deleuze here, as larval subjects we are a contraction of many heterogeneous processes being created and rearranged anew at each moment. It is only through continuously renewed collective and individual fabulation that a stable Self – capable of being perceived as bearing responsibility, wielding authorship, and giving its word – can be superimposed on this assemblage.

How then can consent bind us across time and political obligations be acquired? We are left only with our conventional self. It explains nothing, though, to say simply that it is the conventional self that gives consent, since that puts us right back at square one. How does this purported consent through the conventional self "bind" the concrete self across time? If the conventional self is

Horizontal Time-binding 143

just that – a convention – and one that is formed within, by, and in response to the processes constituting a social situation, how can consent be borne by or emerge from within it as the traditional "embodied" conception entails? How can the authenticity of consent even be determined if this is the case? The traditional image of consent, it seems, leaves us with little more than aporias at its root. The traditional conception of consent appears to be a spatializing convention masking other temporalizing and disciplinary processes, both practically and conceptually.

What happens, though, if we invert this account of consent to better accommodate the implications of Bergson's intuition? Rather than emanating from within, I argue that Bergsonian intuition locates the origins of consent as coming from without, attributed onto our conventional self by the spatializations and temporal projections of others (people, institutions, discourses) in the social situation. Subsequently, the attribution of consent is borne by that individual's conventional self, and that conventional self is used to bind the concrete self across time. We can say, following this, that the individual subject of consent does not "give" consent at all. Consent is not something that *can* be given. The classical image of consent as a possessed, alienable property ultimately rests on and persists through a conflation of several hidden "movements."

In making this distinction we are left with a rather gaping theoretical hole and an obvious question. Even if it is granted that consent is externally attributed, what about the actions, intentions, and desires of the individual upon whom consent is being attributed? Do these now count for nothing? I don't believe that this is our only option, and needn't involve us stopping at a (caricatured) image of passively interpellated Althusserian subjects. On the contrary, it is only by distinguishing between the fictive constructs marshaled by the attribution of consent, and the concrete, embodied expressions, intentions, and lives of those being attributed that an adequately complex understanding of individual desire and action can be achieved.

Consent really involves an attribution from without onto oneself that is borne by the conventional self within a given institutional and discursive situation. In spatializing consent, consent theorists have conflated this process of attribution with the embodied expressions, rituals, and intent of the actual subjects of consent. They have collapsed these distinct movements of consent into one, and consequently have hidden the means by which consent is actually borne over time. In doing so, we have been left with a legacy of what Bergson refers to as "false problems," which arise by virtue of the "badly analyzed composites" that they are implicitly predicated on maintaining.

We can make a distinction between three distinct movements that are collapsed under consent's spatialization. The first movement of consent rests with the prior existence of the social situation itself, especially its institutional and discursive *bestowal* (or denial) of a recognized social identity and role set from which one can legitimately speak and act. This plays a part in the conventional ego's construction by setting the conditions under which a conventional self can exist, as well as the terms by which political obligations are acquired. In the traditional account of consent as an embodied and alienable property of the subject

144 *Horizontal Time-binding*

of consent, this initial movement is hidden entirely. Insofar as it makes an appearance, it is treated as an interloper arriving after and despoiling the ideal character of an act of consent; indeed, it becomes a "defeating condition" itself. The second movement is comprised of the individual's enactment (or not) of recognized rituals indicating their position regarding obligation claims. It is this second movement – that of *immediate expression* – that is the most visible in the traditional image of consent, because the actions and will of the subject are collapsed into the bestowed conditions and enforcement of consent claims. Rather than the act of consent being actual and most authentic in this movement, we can say instead that this second movement is comprised of an individual's immediate expressions of assent, dissent, or acquiescence in relation to political obligation claims. Distinguishing between the immediate acts of expression in themselves and the prior social bestowal of the conditions of consent is vital for dispelling the confusions surrounding consent's spatialization. Finally, the third movement involves the *binding* of an expression or a moment over time, through the conventional self and against the concrete self, which we can explore further in the next section.

Consent as Horizontal Time-binding

All conventions, identities, and social roles involve processes of spatialization, but we also need to look at the particular contours and details of that spatialization if we want to understand what it is framing, what it is masking, and what function it is serving for individuals, institutions, and discourses within a social and political context. Consent functions as a spatializing construct, but it is a construct of a particular type and shape, and its contours have implications for how it is experienced and how it operates as a conceptual and institutional artifact.

Based on our intuitional breakdown of the previously conflated movements involved in consent, we can conclude that consent is a construct that operates as a form of *horizontal time-binding*. In Chapter 2, we discussed the importance of placing the existing literature on political obligation within the context of the dialectic of modernity. The efforts of the participants in the Putney Debates to cobble together new images of and justifications for social order when faced with the crumbling of the Great Chain of Being are a concrete example of this effort. Within the modern dialectic, the appeal to consent is an attempt to reconstitute a temporality of social unity without abandoning the initial modern impulse towards radical individual separation from a pre-modern unselfconscious unity. In this context, time-binding is the process by which a temporality is structured and projected in order to secure an account of social order and restored unity, and through which concrete individuals are discursively disciplined, practically habituated, and conceptually bound toward the fulfillment of this dialectic.

In Chapter 3, we discussed the process of *vertical* time-binding as one method of providing this theoretical synthesis among political obligation theorists. Distinguishable from this, horizontal time-binding does not attempt to directly merge an individual's conventional self into an idealized or representational image of collective co-temporality or a more overtly imperative Ought. Rather, it attempts to

Horizontal Time-binding   145

bind a person *to* and *through* their conventional self across time. This is the third movement being masked by the conventional account of consent. We can break this movement down a bit further to clarify what it looks like. Horizontal time-binding attempts to extract and crystallize a moment from a person's life (in the case of consent, the recognized actual or hypothetical ritual expressions we saw in consent's second movement). This moment can be real or hypothetical. Regardless, even though it was only an ephemeral (or even fictitious) moment in that life, it is extended across time, persisting in a virtual fashion, and attributed to and borne by an individual's conventional self. Consequently, at the later moment in which political obligation claims are pressed, the ostensibly consenting party's conventional self (bearing the sanctity and recognized "legitimacy" of that past, virtually extended original moment) is turned against its concrete self in order to legitimate and secure the obedience that obligation demands.

Through this process of horizontal time-binding, consent theorists (tenuously) complete their modern dialectical synthesis. They reconcile the individuating break with unselfconscious unity by performing the theoretical maneuver that Rousseau attempted: reconciling the individual will with that of the general will in a harmonious fashion without reducing one to the other. Rousseau resorted to reifying humanity and the General Will as a harmonizing substitute for the lost "general will" of God attending the break with the old order. Modern consent theorists produce such a harmony by recognizing an individual's conventional self as their legitimate self, and then binding their concrete self across time according to the extended permission supposedly sanctified by the conventional self. As we have seen, it is by collapsing the three movements of consent into one and presenting the just-so story of consent as an alienable property that this process of horizontal time binding is rendered invisible, and sacrificed for the "requirements of social life."

The consequences of this reconceptualization of consent for existing consent theories are multifaceted, but the overarching effect is to render consent as it has been traditionally understood a theoretically untenable ground on which to build a defense of political obligation and correspondingly to legitimize political authority. This is, in part, a consequence of demonstrating that consent is not an alienable property of individuals that can be transferred at all, which is an observation that removes much of the initial moral luster of consent theories. Consent theorists will discover themselves performing nearly the same theoretical maneuvers that ultimately disregard the desires of concrete individuals as other political obligation apologists who couldn't care a whit about consent. More importantly, this contributes to our understanding of the problems, foundations, and limitations of the attempt to produce these kinds of "justifications" or "grounds" for political obligations at all, by recovering the actual phenomenological and discursive temporal processes that are necessarily quashed for the justifications' production and maintenance.

Following this, we can see that "actual" consent theory loses its moral magic, as well as the rock solid foundational status on which both apologists and some philosophical anarchists wish to ground their positions. If consent is always posited by powers and entities external to an individual, and carries conceptual

146 *Horizontal Time-binding*

force only by virtue of time-binding a conventional self against a concrete self (backed up in practice with the very real violence of a political order), then in no sense could it be said that actual consent allows for an uncoerced and free adoption and maintenance of political obligations. To the extent that individuals provide an immediate expression of assent or acquiescence to the obligations placed upon them, then there are simply no concrete conditions intruding upon a political order's justifying representations. The perceived obligations justified through an appeal to consent are not "in force" in any "deeper" or "truer" sense. Rather, they are simply being carried out by the "consenting" parties without resistance. Correspondingly, concerns for the defeating conditions of the authenticity of an act of consent are of dubious integrity. Rather than functioning as timeless guardians or an independent register against which conditions of consent may be measured, they seem to function as little more than roundabout, post hoc rationalizations for the boundaries of political obligation claims that a given consent theorist has already deemed legitimate (or, as has been the case historically, been forced to concede as legitimate after concrete political struggles redrew the map of thinkable and achievable political expectations).

Hypothetical consent, while shunned and harshly criticized by many other consent theorists, finds a new commonality with its brethren, though not in a way that its critics would be happy about. Knowles and Horton both argue that hypothetical consent has no place being considered as a consent theory of political obligation. This is in part on the grounds that hypothetical consent theorists like Pitkin replace the actual, particular judgments of concrete individuals with attributed hypothetical judgments corresponding to what an ideal rational or reasonable individual would do in order to act in accordance with their political obligations. Horton says that with hypothetical consent theories, consent's "role almost seems to be to provide us with reassurance that our obligation results from our voluntary choice even when it does not," going on to describe consent's role in hypothetical consent theory as little more than a "comforting subterfuge" (2010, 82–83). When viewed in terms of horizontal time-binding, however, there is no difference in kind between what occurs within the logic of hypothetical consent and any other consent theory. *All* theories of consent become "hypothetical" when it comes time to justify and enforce the authority claims that are the complement of an obligation, since all theories of consent depend upon horizontal time-binding and, in particular, the attribution of the virtual, temporally displaced will and judgment of a person's conventional self onto their later concrete self. There are differences of appearance, and potential differences of political implications, but no substantial differences in conceptual processes that undergird theories of actual and hypothetical consent.

What to make of the philosophical anarchists? While philosophical anarchists like Simmons and Wolff apply consent as a means of challenging political obligation claims and existing political authorities rather than justify them, they do so by simply holding to a more constrained and idealized threshold for putting political obligations into force. They do not actually move beyond the limits of the traditional conceptualization of consent that we have discussed. Both Wolff and Simmons, for instance, accept the hypothetical legitimacy of individuals assuming

Horizontal Time-binding 147

political obligations in the case of unanimous consent within a direct democracy. Thus, while both are critical of political obligation apologists, and make sure to enact strict defeating condition standards that make the conditions of legitimate enforcement of such obligations highly unlikely, they are both strictly limited in their ability to develop more foundational critiques of either political obligation or the way in which consent is used as a means of legitimating political rule.

Finally, following this analysis, the aporias or seemingly irresolvable ambiguities surrounding conventional conceptualizations of consent, such as those identified by Hume, are not then simply peripheral or minor problems of marginal significance to the integrity of the idea. Rather, they are endemic byproducts and necessary blind spots required for the conventional understanding of consent to be maintained at all. By bringing temporality back in through Bergsonian intuition and identifying the processes of horizontal time-binding at work in consent's function as a ground for political obligation claims, the traditional problems or paradoxes of consent evaporate. These traditionally recognized aporias can be shelved as unnecessary and redundant consequences of the false problems generated by conventional consent theorists. This should not be taken to mean, of course, that all practical social and political problems regarding assent, dissent, and other immediate expressions of preference and action are somehow resolved along with them. This approach simply makes it easier to recognize and assess the struggles and power dynamics involved in the social and political problems with which consent has traditionally been associated, primarily by removing consent theory's more mystifying elements. It is the consent theorists themselves who have so enthusiastically attempted to banish the complexities, struggles, and operations of power with which our lives as social beings are so indelibly stamped – politics itself – by displacing them beneath time-binding constructs.[9]

Conclusion: Consent and Freedom?

Revisiting the question posed earlier, how then can we understand the relationship between consent and freedom? When viewed through our temporal lens, we find that the common association of consent with autonomy and individual freedom is, at the very least, inadequate and incomplete. Instead of functioning as the standard for respecting individual autonomy vis-à-vis political obligation claims, consent in its traditional conceptualization is bound up and complicit in the justification and continuation of processes of social discipline, political control, and institutional habituation. It is also, as I have argued, crucially involved in the process of horizontal time-binding, which, while a dominant method for sustaining and justifying a particular notion of liberal political order in modernity, has dubious implications for any notion of freedom that isn't already tautologically hitched to a set of institutional commitments. While protests against hypothetical consent and Lockean-derived appeals to implicit consent are plentiful, our use of Bergsonian intuition demonstrates that even explicit consent theorists are susceptible to their own critiques. Consequently, even the most critical appeals to consent as formulated by the philosophical

148   *Horizontal Time-binding*

anarchists do nothing to save consent as a last bastion for the ostensibly non-coercive justifications of political obligation, except by either removing the possibility of consent itself ever legitimately occurring, or by positing a set of hypothetically acceptable institutional arrangements that lack political obligations (in any recognizable form) at all.

Are freedom and consent fundamentally at odds? It is beyond the scope of this chapter to more comprehensively reassess the concept of freedom as it relates to political obligation as such, or consent in particular. Part of this effort will be taken up in the next chapter. For now, we can ask what kind of accounts of freedom could function alongside this unorthodox account of consent and obligation.

The unavoidable spatializing processes that make social life possible entail profound and complex problems for accounts of freedom. The illusions and structured ignorance they cultivate and require, the practical habituation of our bodies and minds that they entail, and the disciplinary functions they serve make any simple or idealized notion of freedom as a "lack of constraint," or the achievement of some potentiality, or free choice within the boundaries of some "legitimate" institutional order extremely problematic, if not fundamentally flawed. Following theorists like Deleuze, Rancière, or Sergei Prozorov, however, perhaps an account of freedom as the transgression and disruption of tendentially ordering (and ossifying) temporal processes could meet our needs. If the spatialization of time and the organization of political rule go hand in hand, then perhaps contesting and disrupting those processes at their origin – at the level of time – can provide a new, more adequate ground for thinking about freedom. We will take up these and other questions in the final chapter.

Notes

1 Simmons, the exemplary a posteriori philosophical anarchist, and Robert Paul Wolff, the primary a priori philosophical anarchist, both accept the possibility of consensus direct democracy legitimately establishing political obligations.
2 As Bergson observes,

> The beliefs to which we most strongly adhere are those of which we should find it most difficult to give an account, and the reasons by which we justify them are seldom those which have led us to adopt them. In a certain sense we have adopted them without any reason, for what makes them valuable in our eyes is that they match the color of all our other ideas, and that from the very first we have seen in them something of ourselves.

(2001, 135)

3 Most of the general account of the English Civil War that follows is drawn from Don Herzog's *Happy Slaves* (1989).
4 Herzog notes,

> That ubiquitous pair of the canon, Hobbes and Locke, show how much one can do in building social contract theories. Their theories provided pointed political guidance: sign the Engagement and capitulate to Cromwell, even though the Puritans are contemptible; mount a revolution, if need be, to keep James II off the throne.

(1989, 34)

Horizontal Time-binding 149

5 Hobbes' position that an individual's claims to self-preservation can override an obligation to submit to destruction, even if he still believes that the Sovereign's will should be carried out in general, is an instructive example of this kind of concern.
6 Singer categorizes his position here as "quasi-consent," but the basis for this distinction is unclear and not very compelling.
7 It has a much more prominent role within issues of medical or bio-ethics.
8 For example, Hobbes seems to grant that the state of nature and the social contract were not actual events, while Locke uses the social contract in explicit, implicit, and hypothetical forms as he sees fit.
9 Bonnie Honig discusses the "displacement" of the political as a process that tendentially occurs, but that can be exacerbated or counteracted in different ways. Honig argues that most political theorists are actually quite hostile to the disruptions and conflicts entailed in political life. Theorists

> writing from diverse positions – republican, liberal, and communitarian – converge in their assumption that success lies in the elimination of dissonance, resistance, conflict, or struggle from a regime. They confine politics (conceptually and territorially) to the juridical, administrative, or regulative tasks of stabilizing moral and political subjects, building consensus, maintaining agreements, or consolidating communities and identities. They assume that the task of political theory is to resolve institutional questions, to get politics right, over, and done with, to free modern subjects and their sets of arrangements of political conflict and instability.
> (1993, 2)

These theorists then offer their preferred conception of subjectivity, order, or transcendent moral certitude as a means to secure *closure*, and soothe the ills of dissonance, conflict, pain, mess, and meaning (3).

References

Beran, Harry. 1987. *The Consent Theory of Political Obligation*. London: Croom Helm.
Bergson, Henri. 2001. *Time and Free Will: An Essay on the Immediate Data of Consciousness*. Mineola, NY: Dover.
Herzog, Don. 1989. *Happy Slaves: A Critique of Consent Theory*. Chicago: University of Chicago Press.
Hobbes, Thomas. 1987. *Leviathan*. Edited by C.B. Macpherson. New York: Penguin Classics.
Honig, Bonnie. 1993. *Political Theory and the Displacement of Politics*. Ithaca, NY: Cornell University Press.
Horton, John. 2010. *Political Obligation*. Second Edition. New York: Palgrave Macmillan.
Hume, David. 1953. "Of the Original Contract." In *David Hume's Political Essays*, edited by C. W. Hendel. Indianapolis: Bobbs-Merrill Co.
Knowles, Dudley. 2010. *Political Obligation: A Critical Introduction*. New York: Routledge.
Locke, John. 1980. *Second Treatise of Government*. Edited by C.B. Macpherson. Indianapolis: Hackett Publishing Company.
Mills, Charles W. 1997. *The Racial Contract*. Ithaca, NY: Cornell University Press.
Pateman, Carole. 1988. *The Sexual Contract*. Stanford, CA: Stanford University Press.
Pateman, Carole, and Charles W. Mills. 2007. *Contract and Domination*. Malden, MA: Polity.
Pitkin, Hanna. 1965. "Obligation and Consent – I." *American Political Science Review* 59 (4): 990–999.

150 *Horizontal Time-binding*

Plato. 2002. *Five Dialogues*. Indianapolis: Hackett.

Rousseau, Jean-Jacques. 1998. *The Social Contract*. Hertfordshire: Wordsworth.

Simmons, A. John. 1979. *Moral Principles and Political Obligations*. Princeton, NJ: Princeton University Press.

Simmons, A. John. 2001. *Justification and Legitimacy: Essays on Rights and Obligations*. New York: Cambridge University Press.

Singer, Peter. 1973. *Democracy and Disobedience*. Oxford: Clarendon Press.

Tuck, Richard. 1993. *Philosophy and Government 1572–1651*. Cambridge: Cambridge University Press.

Wolff, Robert Paul. 1970. *In Defense of Anarchism*. New York: Harper Torchbooks.

5 Chronarchy and Obligation

What are we left with of political obligation? Obligation apologists can provide a variety of creative constructs for justifying the necessity or reality of political obligations, offering appeals that speak to many people's deepest fears and needs. Yet, the success of these efforts depends upon doing violence to the complexity of ourselves, concealing the temporal processes and projections that undergird these constructs, and disciplining individuals into internalizing the rightness of their subordination in a manner that is indistinguishable from Stockholm Syndrome.[1] The philosophical anarchists can contest these efforts, raise the banner of individual autonomy to challenge the axiologies of the apologists, and warn of the gap between ideal and real states. Yet, even with their greater skepticism toward authority and different table of values, they leave much of the apologists' basic theoretical parameters for conceptualizing obligations intact.

One of the goals of this project has been to move beyond this ossifying theoretical impasse that has so thoroughly defined the parameters of this discourse, and to see what a shift in conceptualization and terms of debate might provoke. I don't expect the critique presented here to substantially shift the underlying normative commitments of most of the existing theorists of political obligation. Those attempting to crystallize political obligations into formal disciplinary constructs will likely continue to do so in their efforts to exert control in the Bergsonian sense (and otherwise). The crises of belief, atomization, and temporal disorientation that have accompanied modernity cut deeper into the psyche than any simple theoretical treatise is likely to reach. The philosophical anarchists who have rejected the existence of those obligation claims will likely continue to do so for many of the same deeply felt reasons, regardless of my critique of their conceptualization of autonomy, or of the limitations of consent as a defensible ground for defending freedom.

What conclusions can we draw about political obligations after the preceding critique? Where can the new lines be drawn? One potentially surprising claim that I would like to advance, and that I think necessarily follows from the perspective developed in this project is this: There *are* political obligations. The philosophical anarchists have been mistaken and dug themselves into a theoretical hole in attempting to contest the obligation apologists on the grounds of whether or not political obligations "exist." In doing so, they have

152 *Chronarchy and Obligation*

left themselves open to some withering (as well as some wanting) criticisms that they have been ill-equipped to contest.

Following the first rule of Bergsonian intuition, I will attempt to re-frame this problem. Rather than drawing a line in the sand over *whether* political obligations exist, we will instead ask *in what different ways* do political obligations manifest themselves, and *by what processes*? By focusing on whether political obligations are real, or truly exist, obligation apologists have conflated several distinct processes that need to be untangled. By accepting Being as a valid measure of the success of these political obligation claims, philosophical anarchists have reinforced this conflation, even while nominally contesting the validity of the apologists' conclusions. By shifting our measure to the question of becoming, and the processes by which both actually perceived and theoretically proposed political obligations are constructed and sustained, we can move beyond this trap.

Emergent and Formal Obligations

We are social creatures. What this means, apart from the obvious fact that humans generally associate with each other in groups and networks, is that each of us can only emerge as distinct individuals by virtue of our relationships with and dependencies upon others. The membership theorists are quite right to point out the significance of our social and political relationships for understanding ourselves and thinking about obligations. We are not only "thrown" into this world, as Heidegger would have it, but emerge out of it, through it, and ontologically as an inextricable part of it. We bear the indelible stamp of our origins as well as our unique developmental history in our bodies, memories, and the makeup of our conventional selves. In our earliest infancy, prior to the formation of any stable conventional self, we are in a state of utter dependence. Our continued biological existence depends utterly upon the willingness of others to respond to our primal cries of need. Beyond bare life, our sense of ourselves and the world is necessarily formed through an inheritance of materials provided by others. Before we can discover for ourselves some values or knowledge that might allow us to "walk with confidence in this life," we must be given such guidance and world-representations by others. Before we can consider Rawls' original position and the policies and principles one might rationally decide upon through veiled deliberation, we must go through our true original position of abject dependence and incompletion – a position to which we return in our moments of deepest despair, anguish, and emotional exhaustion.

We emerge as distinct individuals not only by the transmission of guidance, culture, and sustenance by others, but by the inevitable inability of those around us (and the world itself) to fulfill all of our tumultuously experienced demands and desires that have yet to be tamed.[2] At some point, the ever-present figure of the parent or guardian fails the child. Its demands go unanswered, and it is thrown back upon itself with its first glimmering and terrifying sense of its existence as a distinct entity.

Chronarchy and Obligation 153

The individual is baptized by fear in the universal ritual of betrayal. From the moment that we have been betrayed by those upon whom our life depends we lose our original continuity with others, never again to recapture it innocently. We realize that we cannot trust anyone absolutely.... Betrayal is the efficient or proximate cause of the conventional ego. It impels us to legislate for ourselves, in the first instance to lay down rules for avoiding future traumas, and later on to devise technical imperatives for taking advantage of others.

(Weinstein 1979, 60–61)

The relative prominence of care and kindness versus neglect or harm by caretakers can, of course, shape how much a person instinctively clings to methods of Bergsonian control and self-protection over openness and generosity of spirit, but this does not negate the foundational role of fear, vulnerability, and betrayal in the formation of individuality. We may eventually reject the norms and ideas instilled during our youth, or rebel against the care or violence of our guardians, but this in no way lets us escape from them as constitutive components of ourselves. We may not have true *tabula rasa* minds, but without others to bring us into existence there could be no "I" at all.

As we grow older and become more adept at consolidating a stable conventional self, we discover that the public situation in which we live and act is comprised of people and forces that can help, affirm, and empower us, and those that threaten, restrict, and alienate us.[3] We learn to navigate this field and interpret our relationship to it through a variety of strategies, patching them together into the piecemeal tapestry that constitutes our operative life philosophies. We exercise Bergsonian control to erect defensive fortifications against those people and circumstances we perceive as threatening. We learn to navigate the social and institutional hierarchies in which we find ourselves emplaced; perhaps we struggle to advance or defend our relative position within a system of honor and prestige, or master which ritual expressions and incantations will allow us to pass the gatekeeping efforts of a ponderous bureaucracy. Excepting the most traumatized, we are not simply trapped within such a siege mentality. We also open ourselves up to others. We relax our guard and expose some of our vulnerabilities in exchange for the comforts of intimacy and trust, and the potential fulfillment offered by the recognition and appreciation granted by others. Even in the face of new possible betrayals and harm, the hope that these moments offer are – with the exception of extreme cases of emotional and psychological trauma – usually sufficient to keep us alternating between these two poles of experience. As Judith Butler says: "Let's face it. We're undone by each other. And if we're not, we're missing something" (2003).

This ongoing social navigation leads us to create, destroy, and renew dense webs of dependencies, bonds, alliances, and battle lines, as well as expectations, memories – and, yes, obligations. The loyalties, trusts, promises, and implicit co-expectations that emerge and collapse through the interactions between individuals throughout our lives are what we can call "emergent" obligations. They are obligations in that we clearly perceive them as obliging us to act in particular

154 *Chronarchy and Obligation*

ways in relation to others, even when they are not explicitly spelled out. They are emergent in that they are created and sustained through the repetition of social interactions. My loyalty to my friends has emerged through a shared history of interactions that create a shared biography, as well as certain expectations regarding our relationship in the future. Once we cease recognizing and performing those obligations and the expectations that can engender them, however, they effectively cease to exist.[4] Shattered expectations and breaches of trust can cause us to resort to exercising greater control again, retreating and regrouping from the vulnerability we exposed to the other person, and modifying or ending the repetitions that had sustained that relationship's emergent obligations.

It is important for us to make a distinction between these emergent obligations and what we can call "formal" obligations, which include the kinds that have been defended by apologists of political obligation in the preceding chapters. Formal obligations are static, representational accounts of our relationships and expected duties, and exist independently of any actual, particular relationships and expectations generated between particular persons.[5] When considered through the lens of temporality, formal obligations appear as little more than rationalizing fictions and securitizing functions, motivated by constitutively deep-seated fears. I say this with both full analytically descriptive seriousness and a hint of sadness, rather than snide dismissal. Formal obligations offer a means to rationalize and codify the often messy and frayed relationships that many people treasure, pursue the collective aspirations and ideals they long for, and (in conjunction with other systems of rationalization) give one's life some whiff of direction and purpose. The security they offer is that of at least a partial shelter against time, against a precarious existence, and against uncertainty. While more recent obligation theorists have been woefully negligent in addressing this dimension, Rousseau, at least, offers us an honest appraisal of his experience of these fears and the hope he had vested in belonging, obligation, and social unity as an earthly deliverance from finitude.

Yet, it is impossible to separate the rationalization and securitization functions of formal obligations from their concurrent role as an aegis for state power.[6] The consolidated unity and direction given to the individual is premised upon its reflection of the self-image of the state. The insertion of that individual into a vertical co-temporality (through a convergence of disparate histories into a stable image of place, function, and belonging) entails the affirmation of the official histories and legitimating mythologies that all political orders produce to justify their existence and necessity. As time-binding constructs, formal obligations offer both a symbolic palliative for our fears, and weaponry for the police order and their philosophers of state.

It is certainly the case that in concrete social circumstances the distinction between these two kinds of obligation can become difficult to parse. The processes of machinic capture and systems of signifiance and subjectification act to ensure that one's sensibilities and desires are effectively intertwined with that of the wider social body. An appeal to formal obligations can thus suffuse an individual's sense of being and self, leading to at least a temporary

Chronarchy and Obligation 155

indistinguishability between the emergent, dynamic, and affective solidarities that serve as glue for much of interpersonal, familial, and social life, and the well-defined and representational formal obligations that function to rationalize the self-image of the dominant social and political order. For a nationalist or communitarian, love of family, neighbors, and friends may be inseparable from a general sense of belonging and duty felt toward a larger social body, as appealed to by membership theorists and reinforced by the political order itself. The emergent and the formal need not be conflated or reduced in order for each to color how the other is experienced. Consequently, they can often only be effectively separated by means of theoretical abstraction.

Both emergent allegiances, dependencies, and trusts, and the formal and official representations of socio-political relationships are instances of spatialization, time-binding, and Bergsonian control. Emergent obligations do not allow us to evade the tensions in our relationship with time and temporalization. If we think back to Nietzsche's field of force relations drawn upon by Deleuze (and keep in mind the expansive understanding of "force" entailed), the micropolitical relationships navigated by friends depend upon the operation and use of power no less than does the state, even if the scales, desirability, and outcomes of their operation can greatly differ. The promise given to a friend and the duties appealed to by the state can both serve to bind our conventional selves across time through the mobilization of memories, expectations, power, and fears.

The purpose of comparing these two forms of obligation is thus not to suggest that they are absolutely different in kind. Nor is it to unequivocally affirm emergent obligations and decry formal ones. Both can be potent in shaping and disciplining the direction, experience, and character of a person's life, and both can entail forms of self-creation and destruction. What this comparison can help us highlight are the processes of capture that can connect one to the other. These processes should be relatively familiar by now. Emergent bonds and obligations can be captured by being crystallized into and evaluated according to majoritarian norms. The personal bonds of particular families, for instance, may be judged according to how they measure up to a normalized conception of The Family. Official representations of order integrate and extol some kinds of political allegiance and behavior while criminalizing or marginalizing others, absorbing elements of sufficiently challenging kinds in order to reconstitute systemic stability.[7] This kind of capture is facilitated and sustained by means of social habituation and disciplinary practices, carried out through formal state institutions and dispersed sources of enculturation. In so far as this capture is successful, the ephemeral, emergent, and particular in individuals and their relationships with each other are brought into line with and interpreted through their rarefied representations, while this process of ordering is materially realized through the social production functions of the state machine. Obligation apologists contribute to this by defending the legitimacy of a discourse wherein this capture can seem reasonable and even necessary, and where their goal of creating a comprehensive justifying representation of legitimate rule by some and compliance by others can be framed as a vitally important problem – a problem whose solution lies in the creation of the most comprehensive and compelling justification for capture.

156 *Chronarchy and Obligation*

In concrete political circumstances, the tenuous stability of official narratives and representations of order, and their inability to perfectly capture all of collective life into stratified images and striated spaces leads to countervailing processes and moments of rupture and rationalization, deterritorialization and reterritorialization. The forces of capture function not to eliminate emergent obligations per se, but rather to minimize their ability to destabilize the form and representation of order being pursued. Emergent habits, bonds, relationships, obligations, and their ruptures are contained within a framework of order that is rationalized and supported through the processes of capture. They can thus become (imperfectly) captured, rationalized, and incorporated into formal patterns of domination, subjectification, social sorting, and distribution. Obligation apologists perform this maneuver by attempting to preserve and rationalize emergent obligations and prized components of or patterns in our social lives (reciprocity, assent, cooperation, etc.), subsuming them under their preferred time-binding representations of order (through appeals to fairness, consent, association, or a comprehensive account of justice). The formal obligations are then held to be morally (or even ontologically) primary, while emergent obligations and divergent behaviors and social practices are brought to heel or excluded entirely.

On this account, then, the theories of political obligation put forward by the obligation apologists clearly do exist – as formal images and crystallized representations of political order and a majoritarian image of social relationships. Consequently, while we can freely admit that the formal political obligations of philosophers' dreams do indeed exist – as time-binding mechanisms in the imagination of the obligation theorists, disciplinary constructs in the discursive regime of a political order, and a banner under which a variety of political goals may be fought – their existence need not carry any intrinsic moral force for us. They are, at bottom, simply historically contingent expressions of the human desire for Bergsonian control against fear and the anxieties produced through their encounter with time. Unfortunately, there is a general failure among obligation theorists to take seriously the temporality of their own positions. This is not to say that they have simply ignored history. It is not controversial among recent obligation theorists to recognize that the nature of political obligation claims has shifted between, say, ancient and modern Athens, or that social contract theory emerged out of a particular time and context in Europe. Rather, their commitment to implicitly build their theories of obligation as time shelters has also led them to temporalize history and the lessons they choose to take from it in ways that reinforce their projects.

Critical Freedom

We can now revisit the question of freedom in relation to political obligation that we broached in the previous chapter. As suggested there, attempts to pose strict dichotomies between freedom and political obligation, especially by appeals to autonomy and consent, run into a host of theoretical obstacles. The endemically power-infused ontology of social life and individual subjectification appears to

Chronarchy and Obligation 157

render any account of freedom as a stable achievement or condition highly dubious. Further, conventional conceptualizations of freedom and consent appear to be fully implicated in the processes of time-binding and temporal structuration entailed by theories of political obligation. The concept of freedom regularly appears constrained by prior commitments to particular institutions, discourses, or vertical images of ideal social forms. In his book on Foucault, Deleuze (1988) affirms the value of what he calls the "diagram" in Foucault's analysis of order and authority. A diagram is a historically specific and contingent kind of ordered space. It is ontologically a conjunction of particular regimes of truth, operations and distributions of power, and accounts of our subjectivity. As with Rancière's notion of the distribution of the sensible, residing within a diagram is what allows us to make sense of our world and selves, perceive a "common sense," make some things, ideas, or people visible or invisible, and orient our actions. To step outside of a diagram is to enter a condition of confusion and non-sense comparable to Bergson's description of what it would mean to experience pure duration. The diagram is thus comparable to Deleuze's conception of the social assemblage, as long as we remember that assemblages are material, semiotic, and discursive in character. Like the social assemblage, the diagram is machinic and reproduces a social order by virtue of sustaining a particular sense of the social and natural world, and fashioning people who are functionalized for and habituated to live within that world.[8] An important element of this reproduction is that ethics and behavior, as well as the concepts that represent them, are coded with certain judgments and valuations in terms of their appropriateness. Concepts like loyalty, justice, and freedom are themselves produced and functionalized to facilitate and deter different kinds of actions for different kinds of people at different locations in different power hierarchies within a taken-for-granted diagram.[9]

In so far as freedom is positively articulated as part of the successful operation of a diagram, it is not only implicated in but exhausted by the operations of power within that diagram. The neoliberal conception of freedom, for instance, extols the value of the institutions of capitalist property relations and market exchange. The subject is conceptualized as an autonomous individual with (first and foremost) property rights, as well as consumer preferences. Freedom is considered to be enhanced within a neoliberal discourse and governmental diagram in so far as these capitalist institutions are secured and expanded, even if this conflicts with the actual wishes of those who will live within these institutions. In spite of the apparent diversity (and incompatibility) of conceptions of freedom found in the history of philosophy, all conventional conceptualizations of freedom function as representatives for the successful operations of power and circumscribed behaviors of subjects situated within a particular discourse and its associated set of real or ideal institutions. Conventional freedom is a roundabout way of defining the parameters of our unfreedom.

Conventional freedom is not a timeless or universal value standing above the fray of political conflict and power struggles, but rather is functional and productive. It is functional in the sense that any positive[10] characterization of freedom affirms a range of acceptable values and behaviors within a given social diagram

158   *Chronarchy and Obligation*

while implicitly delimiting the introduction of alternatives. It is productive in that it both facilitates the production of particular kinds of political subjects, and enables the reproduction of the diagram as a whole. Conventional freedom appears, in other words, as little more than an auxiliary concept designed to reaffirm the presupposed social boundaries, political structures, characterizations of political subjects, and disciplinary requirements of a particular proponent and political discourse. While this formulation may be sufficient for modern obligation theorists, I find it entirely unsatisfying for developing a concept that ostensibly functions as the primary counterpoint against the demands levied by formal political obligations. How instead can we think about freedom beyond the confines of the diagram (what Sergei Prozorov refers to a "thinking freedom freely" (2007, 1)), and do so in a way that addresses our present concerns for thinking in terms of time?

If we are to salvage a conception of freedom that is cogent in the face of temporality, yet irreducible to a new set of time-binding exercises (including the positing of a unified, essentialist subject, the projection of a progressive or emancipatory teleology, or the evacuation of time through an appeal to a vertical image of co-temporality), and useful for informing political thought and activity, then it will need to be freedom of an unconventional sort. It will certainly need to be something more than philosophical anarchism with a wristwatch. The conception developed here will, following Paul Patton's commentary on Deleuze, be a kind of "critical" freedom.[11] By critical, I mean something more than simply that of negative criticism. It instead should be suggestive of the notion of critique as developed by Kant. The project of Kantian critique certainly entails its fair share of criticism, but it is not a blanket criticism, or a pure negation of something. Rather, it entails an affirmation of what is valuable in a concept, and an attempt to discover and overcome its limits.[12] Critical freedom does not negate the conventional conceptions of freedom, but rather affirms and works through them in order to lay bare their assumptions and limitations and transgress them. For Patton, "critical" should also be understood

> in the technical sense which relates to a crisis or turning point in some process. In these terms, a critical point is an extreme or limit case; a point at which some state or condition of things passes over into a different state or condition.
>
> (Patton 2000, 83)

Critical freedom is distinct for him, then, in that it allows us to think about the "conditions of change or transformation in the subject" (ibid.). Both of these senses of critical are pertinent to how we will use it here.

Critical freedom will have to go beyond the concept of negative freedom, as articulated by Isaiah Berlin (1969). Berlin defines negative freedom through a contrast with what he calls positive freedom. Positive freedom establishes a goal that must be achieved, such as a particular vision of social organization or idea of personal virtue. Freedom and truth become linked together whereby the achievement of freedom corresponds with the actualization of certain ideal or

Chronarchy and Obligation 159

required conditions. Negative freedom, on the other hand, pertains to the relative lack of obstacles to an individual's actions. When thinking in terms of negative freedom, we ask "what is the area within which the subject – a person or group of persons – is or should be left to do or be what he is able to do or be, without interference by other persons?" (121–122). In order to do this, we have to take several things as given. First, we must hold static the subject doing the acting and imagine it as something fully formed and stable, with given interests, characteristics, goals, and predilections. Second, we must imagine that constraints are external to this fully formed and given subject. An individual has given interests and desires, and the pursuit of some of those interests and desires in a particular circumstance might lead them to encounter resistance from others, such as law enforcement. The boundaries of this kind of resistance will vary over time and place, but, as Patton observes, the implication of this conception is that "freedom lies in between agents and the constraints upon their action" (2000, 84). Berlin is concerned with preventing "coercion" and advocates a form of pluralism to prevent abuses of power, but by virtue of his externalized conception of negative freedom, the manner in which subjects are produced and habituated within a society does not figure in his account. They are taken as more or less wholly formed, "normal" humans with a given conception of minimally necessary negative freedom that Berlin declares (with minimal argumentation) is "not artificially drawn" (Berlin 2002, 211). As Prozorov observes, in making this appeal to the natural and normal subject, Berlin is blind to the diagrammatic social production entailed in the fashioning of this universalized liberal subject, and ends up reproducing the same "manipulation of the definition of man" and conjunction of freedom with truth that he so thoroughly criticized in philosophers of positive freedom (Prozorov 2007, 49–50).

While Berlin's negative freedom is inadequate, defining critical freedom in terms of social belonging, self-actualization, or the achievement of a larger or distant project – positive freedom – has its own complications. Rousseau and Hegel are some of the primary defenders of this form of freedom, and it is no coincidence that they have also articulated some of the most comprehensive and totalizing visions of temporal structuration. For Rousseau, we must be forced to be free through our harmonization with the general will and a cultivation of our sense of patriotism and belonging in the service of a larger co-temporality. Hegel thought that freedom was to be found in *Sittlichkeit*, or "ethical life," which entails a bridging of individual feeling and desires with the institutions and morality of the society to which they belong, a collective harmonization achieved through a steadily perfecting (if often bloody and unpleasant) unfolding of the dialectic of history. Against Berlin's largely externalized spatial metaphor for freedom, Charles Taylor (1985) argues for a vision of positive freedom wherein subjects are able to redress internal obstacles to that freedom, such as "lack of awareness," "inner fears," and "false consciousness," while also considering the threat that external obstacles pose for this (212). In order to surmount these obstacles, we must be able to engage in self-evaluation in order to discriminate between our different motives. This will enable us to discover what truly and authentically matters to us and what is really essential to who we are "according

160   *Chronarchy and Obligation*

to our own pattern" (ibid.). If we are not able to do this, then we may end up being free to do what we like without external encumbrance, while nevertheless being unfree (215). For Taylor, being able to discover oneself requires that we recognize that we are not the final authority on the matter, since it is our own personal limitations and inner obstacles that are being struggled against. In allowing this, a possibility is opened for the necessary role of other people and particular social conditions, political programs, and even some restraining rules or external obstacles being an aid to the achievement of positive freedom.

Positive freedom depends on positing the content of freedom as something to be achieved, and evaluating the degree of freedom by how close we are able to get to that achievement. In the hands of Rousseau and Hegel, freedom is thick with demands of identification with a collective co-temporality, and with teleologies of both collective and individual progress. With Taylor, it requires a personal quest for the discovery of a stable, authentic, and true self (even though this personal quest may require aid from others). Ultimately, conventional articulations of positive freedom are oriented toward the construction and maintenance of stable temporalities at a variety of scales, and of time-binding doubled selves into these projections. Other normative evaluations of these projects aside, they too are undesirable as a means of conceptually developing a critical freedom.

Although attempts to ground and extrapolate theories of political freedom and obligation from an account of one's "basic" or "essential" human nature have rightfully taken a beating, especially over the last half-century, they are also still remarkably influential. The idea that freedom consists in the expression of our true nature has an ancient pedigree, providing the alluring possibility of living your life in accordance with the dictates or limits of what you really are. This offers a grounded sense of self, a validated individual and collective social project, and the temporal structures required to generate a sense of meaning and purpose. Contemporary appeals to human nature among theorists of freedom and obligation can take a variety of forms. The basic Hobbesian conception of individuals as essentially fearful and self-interested beings who require a sovereign in order to be over-awed into compliance and trust so that a sphere of free activity can be maintained is still widespread. So too are a variety of Kantian accounts emphasizing our capacity for exercising our basic abilities to reason, to use that reason to act in accordance with the demands of morality, and to progress individually and collectively. We can also interpret contemporary rational choice conceptions of subjects and their pursuit of given interests as defining freedom within a narrow account of human nature. Theories of freedom based on claims about the necessary demands of one's true nature are problematic for developing a critical freedom on two major points, each point involving its own distinct form of temporal structuration. These are not alternative points; the second follows from and presupposes the first, and the first depends upon the second for any meaning to be gleaned from it. While each point involves a distinct form of temporal structuration, they depend upon each other for the concept of human nature to have any force.

The first point involves a radical pruning of the ontology of the subject. Rather than the multiplicitous larval subject of Deleuze, we get a creature who is

Chronarchy and Obligation 161

presented to us with a select few dominant characteristics (fear, reason, self-interestedness, sociality, etc.). These characteristics are then treated as determinative of the subject's character, needs, and actions, as well as which kinds of actions are open to them in the present and future, while other aspects of their being are de-emphasized, suppressed, or hidden. The second point involves the projection of a teleology. This teleology can actually take two distinct forms, depending on the way in which human nature is being deployed for a particular account of freedom. The first type of teleology is what we can call a "positive" teleology. This includes the progressive moral arc of Kant and the dialectical spiral of Hegel. Positive teleologies lay out a distinct kind of path to be traveled – they are teleologies on rails. The second type of teleology is what we can call a "negative" teleology. By negative, I wish to suggest something closer to a film negative, entailing an inversion of a picture. This negative teleology does not simply place individuals on a clearly built (even if not always straightforward or absolutely determined) track, but rather uses the pruned ontology of human nature to rule out alternative pathways until only a highly constrained set of present and future options becomes possible. This is a teleology of hedgerows. By elevating our fearfulness and diffidence as our determinative characteristics, the realist freedom of Hobbes is the best example of this kind of negative teleology. Hobbes presents us with an account of freedom as a kind of contained civil sphere wherein we can carry out our lives, pursue commerce and culture, and live in relative security (relative, that is, to the war of all against all). He does not give us a progress narrative of the achievement of that freedom, but instead sweeps aside alternative ideal conceptions of and paths to freedom, especially the more optimistic appeals to the better angels of our nature. Flanked with either despair or daydreams as our alternatives to his account – and the state of war being the consequence in either case – we are left by default with the Leviathan as the only path to achieving that freedom.

A critical freedom will ultimately need to move beyond the conventional obligation/freedom dichotomy itself. Theories of political obligation are spatializing, time-binding constructs, but conventional theories of freedom are no different in this regard. Conventional conceptualizations of freedom contribute to both constraint within and the reproduction of particular discursive, institutional, and temporal parameters. They are the mirrored expression of the prohibitions and limits entailed within a diagram, but nevertheless do not go outside of that diagram. Even in a context of social transformation where a conception of conventional freedom might be functioning as a banner for change, it may, at most, contribute to the creation of a diagram with new features. Patton's account of a Deleuzian critical freedom provides an excellent conceptualization of a freedom that moves beyond any given diagram's limits. If, as Deleuze's approach invites us to, we think about them as different kinds of processes, then obligations function as molar, territorializing, consolidating processes of control on the one hand, while critical freedom functions as molecular, deterritorializing, dissolving processes of transgression on the other. In line with our project at hand, we can enrich this conception of critical freedom by reconsidering obligations and critical freedom as distinct processes of temporal structuration and dissolution.

162   *Chronarchy and Obligation*

Chronarchy and Anachronarchy

In order to develop this reconsideration, I propose thinking in terms of what we can call *chronarchy*. As the construction of the term suggests, the concept of chronarchy operates at the intersection between time (*chronos*) and rule (*archê*). It should not, however, suggest the "rule of time" as any kind of stable social or ontological condition. Chronarchy is not the political rule of the clock or the plan per se, nor is it the idea that time is the most important dimension for understanding existence. Instead, chronarchy represents the tendentially ossifying processes entailed in mechanisms of temporal structuration – the solidification of cohesive past-present-future projections, the consolidation of a teleology, the policing of the boundaries of a co-temporality, the maintenance of a time-binding disciplinary construct. In so far as each of these leads to the fortification of particular temporalities, they can be understood as chronarchic in nature. Chronarchy is not an achievable end-state, but is instead the virtual limit of total temporal structuration and spatialization toward which chronarchic processes converge. Any particular temporal process that contributes to its approximation can be said to be chronarchic.

If we can consider chronarchic processes to be those that contribute to the consolidation of temporalities and processes of temporal structuration, then critical freedom can be conceived of as a form of *anachronarchy*. If chronarchy is the virtual limit of processes of temporal structuration, then anachronarchy is the virtual limit of temporal decomposition. Like chronarchy, it is not something permanently and fully achieved, but is instead tendential. Anachronarchic processes are those that disrupt or transform given temporalities and chronarchic processes. They can be sudden and momentary or slow and decaying, but like Nietzsche's eternal return in Deleuze's third synthesis of time, they effectively haunt all chronarchic projects as reminders of their precarious existence and inevitable demise.

Anachronarchy corresponds more closely with Deleuze's concepts of deterritorialization, decoding, and becoming than it does with negative freedom. Rather than a stable state of being, each of these Deleuzian concepts suggests a process of transformation, of doing-otherwise, and of the disruption of a particular material, discursive, or conceptual assemblage along a particular "line of flight."[13] It would be a mistake, though, to consider them in any purely negative sense. Transgressive and molecularizing processes that loosen up or break apart a given assemblage can at the same time (though it isn't guaranteed) produce new semi-stable patterns and assemblages. For Deleuze, this connection with, and creation of, new assemblages is vital if transgression is to avoid simply dissipating into nihilistic destruction for destruction's sake. Since each of these concepts is highly spatial in its configuration and thus poses some obstacles for our ability to conceptualize the temporal dimension, thinking in terms of anachronarchy can help us get around this limitation. By thinking in terms of chronarchic and anachronarchic processes, we can also surmount the rigid political obligation versus (conventional) freedom dichotomy.

In *A Thousand Plateaus*, Deleuze and Guattari develop the concept of the "nomadic war machine."[14] This can be one of their more difficult creations, not

Chronarchy and Obligation 163

least of all because of the confusion generated by the traditional associations made with each of its terms. By "nomadic," they do not mean to suggest a phenomenon limited to the organizational mode or social practices of actual historical nomads. Deleuze and Guattari do discuss them, and allude to elements of actual historical nomadic groups that exemplify the idea of nomadism. They also, however, use nomad as an adjective, and refer to nomad music, nomad science, nomad games, and nomad sports.[15] By "war machine," Deleuze and Guattari are not talking about the state, or the military, or the military-industrial complex as such. In fact, they present the war machine as something at odds with the state, its military, and the wars they wage. While the state apparatus constitutes a form of "interiority," always attempting to close off, conserve, solidify, consolidate, sort, stratify, model, and control, the war machine is a form of "exteriority" that is "of another species, of another nature, of another origin" than the state (Deleuze and Guattari 1987, 354). It is a force for disrupting these interiorizations, and thus for bringing about transformation, decoding, deterritorialization, new heterogeneities, and the unexpected. Deleuze and Guattari argue that what distinguishes the state form and nomadism are the kinds of space they each produce. While the logic of the state form attempts to produce "striated" space that is sedentary, obeys an overarching logic, and has clear internal divisions, nomadism produces "smooth" heterogeneous space that facilitates variation, decentered and plural transformation, and open connections between points within it.[16] Nomadism and the war machine overlap, but as Eugene Holland argues, they are distinct.[17] As Patton argues, the nomadic war machine can be usefully understood as a "metamorphosis machine," which is a machine that "does not simply support the repetition of the same but rather engenders the production of something altogether different" (2000, 110). If lines of flight are the pathways on which change can possibly occur in a given situation, the war machine is a kind of assemblage that generates lines of flight. It is a machine from which "mutations spring," and is the source from which "all creation is brought about" (Deleuze and Guattari 1987, 229–230). This can be an insurgent minoritarian force for social revolution, an artist whose work moves or unsettles its viewers, or an idea that gnaws at you until, one day, you find that it has taken you far from who you were before.

In keeping with our temporal project, I would like to suggest an alternative to Deleuze's war machine: the time machine. Rather than deterritorialization, time machines help produce anachronarchy – disruptions of stable temporalities, obstruction of time-binding efforts, and the creation of new temporal projections that diverge from and upset a given chronarchy.[18] Like nomadic war machines, they can be operative at all scales. Individuals can use or be overcome by an experience or an idea that transforms how they understand their life trajectory and place or purpose in the world. Minority social forces can wield alternative historical narratives against the majoritarian histories that justify the dominant social order (and the exclusion of the minority). New paradigms and systems of belief can radically transform prior temporalities. The emergence of modernity (a time machine if ever there was one) that we discussed earlier entailed a profound anachronarchic disruption of the chronarchic structure of medieval

164   *Chronarchy and Obligation*

Christendom. Transformations in the material forces of social, economic, and technological production and circulation can also function as time machines, producing qualitative transformations of individual and collective temporalities through social acceleration and dislocation.

There are many examples of what we could consider forms of, or preludes to, anachronarchic thought, each of which rests upon the development of a particular conceptual time machine. Some of these examples are from theorists we have already discussed. Bergson's intuition, for instance, provides a method for looking behind the veil of custom and cultural givens in order to trace the temporal assumptions and transformations upon which they depend. By revealing the "act of the mind" required to transform heterogeneity into homogeneity and time into space, intuition demonstrates the contingency and artifice of all temporalities, including the chronarchic structurations that support political orders and their demands of obligation. The method of intuition is a time machine that specializes in revealing the movement of time in what had seemed to be solid and spatial, thereby weakening the givenness and stability of temporal structures through a particular kind of hermeneutics of suspicion. Given its importance for developing the theoretical framework of this project, it should be clear enough that Deleuze's work, even though it often emphasizes spatiality, is rich with anachronarchic thought and concepts that can be readily adapted to the task in ways we have already discussed.

As Deleuze has demonstrated, Nietzsche's eternal return can also be effectively mobilized as a way to challenge temporalities that stress continuity, unity, and the "return of the same." As a tool for cultivating the affirmation of that which is different, and as a motor for Nietzsche's project of transvaluing existing value systems and affirming one's own, the eternal return can be understood as a time machine of anachronarchic instigation. It encourages and facilitates both the transgression of existing constellations of meaning that structure our individual and collective lives, and the creation of new possibilities of behavior and sensibility through which we can exercise our power and transform our world. We can also use more conventionally existential readings of Nietzsche's eternal return, such as Lawrence Hatab's (2005), while still maintaining its value as a time machine. Hatab sees the eternal return as primarily an existential "test" and thought experiment that can help you evaluate your relationship with, and attitude toward, your own life. In other words, in the *Gay Science*, when Nietzsche's demon captures you and threatens you with having to live your own life exactly as you have live it in an eternal recurrence, you are meant to "suspend disbelief" and evaluate your own response (Hatab 2005, 99). Whether you curse the demon or perceive this as the greatest of all gifts will tell you whether or not you affirm your own life. In imagining yourself in this position, the eternal return forces you to evaluate the whole character of your life and whether it is something that you can positively embrace, or whether it is something that horrifies or disgusts you. If your response to living an eternity of your own life is negative, then the test is meant to compel you to re-evaluate your life and transform it into one you can affirm actually living. The existential reading of Nietzsche's eternal return can be understood as a time machine that uses

Chronarchy and Obligation 165

eternity in order to mobilize our concern for and affirmation of each passing present and "the eternal value of the temporal moment as such" (84). Practically, this can force a person to reconsider the value of conventional values and ways of living, and inspire them to fashion a new life and ways of relating to the world and themselves. We don't need to decide here whether the existential or Deleuzian reading of the eternal return is superior to see the significance of Nietzsche as a useful anachronarchist figure.

Max Stirner is a philosopher who is often associated with Nietzsche, and yet is – if possible – even more greatly misunderstood. We can also interpret Stirner as an anachronarchic thinker, engaging in a trenchant critique of all attempts to absorb individual uniqueness and particularity into an overarching representation, reductive essence, or imposed temporal projection, such as the dialectical teleology of Hegel. The time machine that Stirner provides is his concept of the Unique. The Unique is not simply his conceptualization of the subject, but is rather a tool to be used for critical self-reflection. It can also, I argue, be a powerful tool for cultivating anachronarchy at an individual level. His single major theoretical work, *The Ego and Its Own* (2005), has been regarded as one of the most biting works of political theory to ever exist (Huneker 1909, 350), and is at the same time quite marginal. Many of the concepts that are basic currency in philosophy, such as Rights, Society, Morality, and Freedom (among many others) are ejected or smashed in his epistemology as abstract unrealities that, to the extent they are taken seriously, occlude power and subject real "flesh and blood" individuals to violence (Stirner 2005, 13). Stirner describes the self as a "creative nothing" (5). As a creative nothing,

> I do not presuppose myself, because I am every moment just positing or creating myself, and am I only by being not presupposed but posited, and, again, posited only in the moment when I posit myself; that is, I am creator and creature in one.
>
> (150)

Stirner's creative nothing is "creative" in that it remains in a state of open-ended potential self-positing and reconfiguration, while it is a "nothing" in the sense of having no stable or fixed essence to which it is anchored. The self as conceived of by Stirner is also referred to as one's "own." One's own does not refer to juridical conceptions of property, but is rather a comprehensive account of everything under one's power and control, and "is my whole being and existence, it is I myself" (157).[19] It comprises a notion of the self that includes one's flesh, one's inner mental life, implicated power relations, capacity to affect the world, and unique developmental history.

Like Bergson, Stirner is sensitive to the power that language, categories, and other conceptual abstractions have over concrete individuals. Also like Bergson, the substance and importance of these ideas is only a conventional illusion. It is only when these "spooks of the mind" are treated as real (spatialized) that they begin to "possess" an individual, leading them to act in deference to the imagined abstraction (Stirner 2005, 43–45). They can find themselves subsumed in a

166　*Chronarchy and Obligation*

group's self-image, have their particularity lost, their worth denigrated or instrumentalized in the name of a "higher" cause, and their lives sacrificed in the name of any number of ubiquitously banal, yet still "sacred" or "fixed" concepts (what Stirner refers to as "spooks"). As such, he wants to avoid grounding his theoretical work in axiomatic abstractions. Instead, he offers the "extra-conceptual" tool of the Unique (De Ridder 2011, 157). As I have argued elsewhere, the Unique functions instead as a kind of placeholder that affirms the irreducible particularity of concrete individuals while refusing to subsume them under a fixed image of a larger abstraction (such as Mankind or Society), or reduce them to their supposed inner essence, true self, or human nature (Mueller 2015, 63). This placeholder is meant to be phenomenologically[20] occupied by the individual using Stirner's tools, primarily as a means to "get behind" the conceptual, linguistic, and cultural fog in which we find ourselves in modern society, in relation to each other and ourselves (Stirner 2005, 9). From within the position of the Unique, the user adopts an applied incredulity called "ownness"[21] towards all conceptual or symbolic spooks (spatializations) that might direct, absorb, compel, or coerce them, shedding them as rags and chains to be disposed of. Stirner doesn't say that you "must" or "ought to" accept the results of this approach and reject all concepts, language, or symbols – as with Bergson's spatialization, we arguably are not able to do so owing to the demands of practical life. Nor, then, could you necessarily use the Unique all of the time.

In terms of temporality, Stirner is best understood as a philosopher of what we could call a "critical presentism." By presentism, I am not referring to the school of thought within the philosophy of time which argues that only that which is in the present exists or is real. Stirner's presentism is deployed as a weapon, rather than an ontological proposition. His phenomenological position of the Unique is a time machine that produces a radical temporal rending. Once inside the position of the Unique, all collective co-temporalities evaporate, all teleologies derail, all attempts to time-bind former iterations of yourself appear as disposable disciplinary constructs, and any of your life projects or personal narratives appear as spooks that can be used or discarded. Whether kept, modified, or discarded, the temporalities that you use or find used against you are not approached as something toward which you automatically defer or treat as a given or sacred. Stirner leaves us only with ourselves, in our "nakedness and naturalness" (2005, 162) to ask ourselves what we as particular concrete beings (alone or alongside others) want and value in this world at a particular moment, and what will be required in order to achieve these things. It is not an overcoming, but an embrace, a deepening, and a radicalization of the "falling back into" the present initially created by the shattering of pre-modern cultural temporalities. While Hatab's existential Nietzsche uses eternity in order to challenge how we relate to the present and imagine alternative futures, Stirner weaponizes the present in a way that can expose the precarious and conventional nature of all temporalities.

Anachronarchic thinkers can generate tools that help us transform our encounters with time, and even inspire us to transform our lives. Anachronarchy is not something confined to the realm of theoretical reflection. As I have repeatedly emphasized throughout this project, our temporalities are intimately

Chronarchy and Obligation 167

intertwined with practical life and political possibilities. In an important sense, all social and political transformations that alter the way in which people relate to each other and understand themselves and their social world are anachronarchic in that they entail and require new temporalities. Challenges to the distribution of the sensible are necessarily challenges to the makeup of the temporal.

We can also identify a long history of practical and tactical interventions enacted by both individuals and groups to overtly and specifically transform the tempo, segmentation, pace, and organization of time in daily life and political struggle. The histories of labor and class conflict in particular are filled with struggles over the direct control of time. Fights for the eight-hour day, the weekend, vacation time, parental leave, and even overtime are struggles over not only survival and quality of life, but also over the segmentation, purpose, and uses of the time of our lives. Slow-downs, sabotage, work-to-rule, and strikes have been effective and direct tactical implementations of the power that workers have over the tempo and pace of their workplace, the reliable operability of the wider socio-economic assemblage in which their work and lives are integrated, and the relative costs imposed against the machinery of capitalist production and surplus value extraction for their lives being rendered as serviceable components to that machinery. When faced with the recognition that the wages we work for are hours of our lives exchanged for the means to live them, all struggles over conditions of work and the axioms governing the purpose and ends of work itself (up to and including its necessity at all) become deeply existential problems, as well as struggles over prevailing chronarchic processes.

Conclusion

By interpreting political obligation and freedom through their relationship to chronarchy, we can get around the traditional binary between the apologists and philosophical anarchists. This in turn lets us overcome the limitations that this binary creates for our attempts to understand the time-binding disciplinary processes that operate within theories of political obligation. We can admit and affirm the significance of the experience of emergent obligations in our relationships without accepting their formal counterparts, while at the same time recognizing that time-binding processes constitute each. We can affirm the value of freedom without imagining ourselves as self-contained, unencumbered autonomous actors who can brook no dependencies, vulnerabilities, or fear, or by limiting our ideas of freedom to those that are ready-made to reinforce our subjection.

In truth, most of us most of the time will vacillate between moments of control and openness, being and becoming, and chronarchy and anachronarchy throughout our lives. With roots deep in the project of modernity, the desire to produce a unified conception of ourselves is a desire to circumvent the tensions of this seemingly irreducible polarity in favor of the illusion of a stable, unified personal persistence across time. It is a desire to overcome our constitutive complexity, mutability, and mess, and substitute for it a rationalized, ordered existence that can endure in the face of time. We all engage in these substitutions, and we must if we are to survive. We need not become enamored with our own

168　*Chronarchy and Obligation*

creations, however, to such an extent that we forget their origins and the motivations behind their construction.

Future temporally-informed work on theories of obligation would certainly not make everyone an anarchist. It is entirely possible to recognize the temporal processes that support theories of obligation, while embracing time-binding explicitly as a desirable means of reconstituting some variation on Plato's Noble Lie, and using this to rationalize and justify the required methods of machinic capture until a preferred image of order or justice is approximated. Short of such explicit Napoleonic machinations, however, I consider a shift in the grounds of contest and inquiry to the hopes and fear, anxieties and prejudices, and deep values and formative experiences that lay occluded beneath the existing theories of obligation and philosophical anarchism to be far more preferable than the present impasse. At the very least, it would offer greater promise for the development of a theory of obligation that maintains fidelity to our complexity, and resists the urge to reduce us to little more than serviceable implements in a losing war against time.

Notes

1 Stockholm Syndrome is a colloquial term for the phenomenon whereby individuals held hostage come to empathize and identify with their captors. The name refers to a 1973 incident in Stockholm, Sweden, during which a duo of bank robbers held the bank employees hostage for six days. The employees began to identify with the robbers during their captivity to the point of resisting rescue, and continued to defend their captors after the incident (Graham, Rawlings, and Rigsby 1994, 1–11). Captives with Stockholm Syndrome exhibit a variety of related symptoms, including empathy and loyalty toward their captors, adopting their captor's beliefs and justifications, viewing their captors as their protectors and those trying to free them from their captors as threatening, and a failure to free themselves when it becomes possible (42–43). Graham argues that there are four conditions that enable the emergence of Stockholm Syndrome: 1. the captor poses a believable threat to the life of the captive; 2. the captive perceives the captor to be acting with some degree of kindness, although this kindness can amount to little more than a lesser degree of violence toward the captive; 3. the captive is isolated under the influence of the captor and is overwhelmingly exposed to the captor's perspective; and 4. the captive perceive themselves as unable to escape (33). If we refuse the obligation apologists' presumptive legitimacy of the state, their efforts begin to look like a complex exercise in rationalizing their captivity.

2 Through a powerful exercise in practical phenomenology, the child development specialist Daniel N. Stern has described the experience of a young child as a kind of serial "weatherscape" of sensory experience, bodily intensities, and "feelings-in-motion" where the distinction between internal and external sensation is still vague (1990, 14).

3 What George Santayana refers to as "powers" and "dominations" respectively:

> the distinction between Dominations and Powers is moral, not physical. It does not hang on the degree of force exerted by the agents but only on its relation to the spontaneous life of some being that it affects. The same government that is a benign and useful power for one class or province may exercise a cruel domination over another province or class. The distinction therefore arises from the point of view of a given person or society having initial interests of their own, but surrounded by uncontrollable circumstances: circumstances that will at once

Chronarchy and Obligation 169

be divided, by that person or society, into two classes: one, things favorable or neutral, the other, things fatal, frustrating, or inconvenient: and all the latter, when they cannot be escaped, will become Dominations.

(Santayana 1995, 1)

4 This does not mean that everyone is always on the same page regarding those obligations. A betrayal by a friend seems, by definition, to involve an unexpected breach of obligations and loyalties by one side of the relationship. It is a dead end (if still common) line of inquiry to ask whether the obligation still "truly" exists even when one party breaks the trust.

5 I refer to emergent obligations as emergent and not "informal" when being compared against "formal" obligations for a few reasons. One is that the formal-informal dichotomy tends to frame the informal as the immature or inferior predecessor to the formal. Like the order-disorder dichotomy that Deleuze identifies in *Bergsonism* (1991), it tends to elevate the formal as primary and more important or complete. The second is that I want to emphasize the kinds of processes at work within each. Emergent obligations are continuously being recreated, and are open to renewal or recension in that continuous recreation. They are more localized, immediate between persons, flexible, and emerge through interactions. Formal obligations are more static, representational, and are appealed to as possessing moral force independently of any particular individuals.

6 Even if a political obligation theory allows for rebellion or revolution in a given circumstance, it is only against a particular state that rebellion is permitted. Even then, it is only so that a more legitimate and proper authority may be better secured. Disobedience is allowed only insofar as it upholds the principle of authority.

7 The large-scale incorporation of labor unions into the apparatus of state governance after the Great Depression and the establishment of the National Labor Relations Board in the United States is one example of this operating on a large scale, and as a means of heading off the perceived threat of independent unions willing to disrupt the smooth operation of the social machinery in order to further their goals. The state's effective displacement of a competing internationalist class war narrative with that of a nationalist and racially-charged social contract narrative was vital for capturing union organization and redirecting its loyalties into a more manageable form. For more information on the racialized nature of the New Deal, see Ira Katznelson's *Fear Itself* (2013), and David Roediger's *The Wages of Whiteness* (1999).

8 It is one of the main goals of Foucault-inspired "governmentality" studies to trace the operations and technologies of power and discourse at work within a given diagram.

9 It bears repeating that this production does not require self-conscious intent. Although a diagram or social assemblage is produced at each moment through the repetition and reinforcement of its participants, it is not produced from scratch. The weight of habit, common sense, and collective mutual reinforcement carries the maintenance of a diagram or assemblage a long way. By acting within these confines, the functionalization and circumscription of concepts to fit within that diagram can be produced without bad faith on the part of individuals within that diagram.

10 Positive in the sense of being given particular content, specification, and definition.

11 Patton (2000) develops the concept of critical freedom by drawing from James Tully's (1995) use of the term. Patton contrasts critical freedom with the negative freedom of Isaiah Berlin and the positive freedom of Charles Taylor, arguing that both take the individual with their traits and interests as a given. A critical freedom emphasizes a person's capacity for diverging from what they have inherited and transforming themselves, what Patton refers to as the "conditions of change or transformation in the subject" (2000, 83). Deleuzian becoming is always a transformative process that disrupts sedimented patterns of being, and embracing critical freedom entails an affirmation of this becoming.

170 *Chronarchy and Obligation*

12 This basic element of the method of Kantian critique should be distinguished from his other concurrent projects, such as his desire to discover the universal conditions and rules of experience, morality, and knowledge.

13 The "line of flight" is Deleuze and Guattari's preferred term in *A Thousand Plateaus* for tracing, as Patton succinctly puts it, "the paths along which things change or become transformed into something else" (2000, 66). Owing in part to his encounter with Paul Virilio's critique of accelerationist theories of social transformation, Deleuze's treatment of lines of flight is ambivalent. On the one hand, he observes that "it is always on a line of flight that we create" (Deleuze and Parnet 1987, 135), while on the other hand, there is no guarantee that a break with the past, with prior assemblages and ways of being and doing will turn out well. Individually, we can fall into either renewal or crisis and suicide if we attempt to break from our past sense of self, while collectively a line of flight could fail to create a new assemblage, and instead lead to war and a transformation into the desire for pure destruction. Lines of flight thus also carry with them a danger, and "emanate a strange despair, like an odor of death and immolation, a state of war from which one returns broken" (Deleuze and Guattari 1987, 229).

14 See especially Plateau 12.

15 Deleuze's discussion of games is particularly instructive of the nature of nomadism. In comparing chess with the game Go, he says:

> Chess is a game of State, or of the court: the emperor of China played it. Chess pieces are coded; they have an internal nature and intrinsic properties from which their movements, situations, and confrontations derive. They have qualities; a knight remains a knight, a pawn a pawn, a bishop a bishop. Each is a like a subject of the statement endowed with a relative power, and these relative powers combine in a subject of enunciation, that is, the chess player or the game's form of interiority. Go pieces, in contrast, are pellets, disks, simple arithmetic units, and have only an anonymous, collective, or third-person function.... Go pieces are elements of a nonsubjectified machine assemblage with no intrinsic properties, only situational ones. Thus, the relations are very different in the two cases. Within their milieu of interiority, chess pieces entertain biunivocal relations with one another, and with the adversary's pieces: their functioning is structural. On the other hand, a Go piece has only a milieu of exteriority, or extrinsic relations with nebulas or constellations, according to which it fulfills functions of insertion or situation, such as bordering, encircling, shattering. All by itself, a Go piece can destroy an entire constellation synchronically; a chess piece cannot (or can do so diachronically only). Chess is indeed a war, but an institutionalized, regulated, coded war, with a front, a rear, battles. But what is proper to Go is war without battle lines, with neither confrontation nor retreat, without battles even: pure strategy, whereas chess is a semiology. Finally, the space is not at all the same: in chess, it is a question of arranging a closed space for oneself, thus of going from one point to another, of occupying the maximum number of squares with the minimum number of pieces. In Go, it is a question of arraying oneself in an open space, of holding space, of maintaining the possibility of springing up at any point: the movement is not from one point to another, but becomes perpetual, without aim or destination, without departure or arrival. The "smooth" space of Go, as against the "striated" space of chess. The *nomos* of Go against the State of chess, *nomos* against *polis*. The difference is that chess codes and decodes space, whereas Go proceeds altogether differently, territorializing or deterritorializing it (make the outside a territory in space; consolidate that territory by the construction of a second, adjacent territory; deterritorialize the enemy by shattering his territory from within; deterritorialize oneself by renouncing, by going elsewhere...). Another justice, another movement, another space-time.
>
> (Deleuze and Guattari 1987, 352–353)

Chronarchy and Obligation   171

16 It is important to note here that the logic of the state form versus the nomadic war machine is a binary that Deleuze applies to a wide variety of different arenas: the structured nature of classical music versus the free form of jazz, the universalized geometry of royal science versus the practical differential calculus of nomad (or "minor") sciences, the architecture of Romanesque cathedrals versus that of the Gothic, etc.

17 Holland argues that the object of nomadism is a "distinctive composition of social relations occupying smooth space" (2009, 220), while the war machine is a particular "reactive" expression of nomadism (219). It is reactive, because it is only through opposition to the State form in a particular context that nomadism transforms into a war machine that treats the State form as an "enemy" and "obstacle" (ibid.).

18 Like new assemblages, a new temporality can be both a force for transgression and a force for consolidation at the same time, depending on the vantage point we adopt and the particular relationships between assemblages or temporalities that we are considering.

19 This understanding of one's "own" is similar to Jose Ortega y Gasset's understanding of the nature of the self as "I and my circumstances."

20 I mean "phenomenologically" in a broad sense here, rather than in the narrow delineation of the formal phenomenology instigated by Husserl. While the formal phenomenology of Husserl contains a universalizing dimension in its categories and structure, the phenomenological application of the position of Stirner's Unique is always particular to the position of the unique individual by whom it is being used.

21 As observed by Kathy Ferguson, ownness is "a way of being oneself, of having oneself within one's power" (2011, 169).

References

Berlin, Isaiah. 1969. *Four Essays On Liberty*. Oxford: Oxford University Press.

Berlin, Isaiah. 2002. *Liberty*. New York: Oxford University Press.

Butler, Judith. 2003. "Violence, Mourning, Politics." *Studies in Gender and Sexuality* 4 (1): 9–37.

De Ridder, Widukind. 2011. "Max Stirner: The End of Philosophy and Political Subjectivity." In *Max Stirner*, edited by Saul Newman. New York: Palgrave MacMillan.

Deleuze, Gilles. 1988. *Foucault*. Translated by Sean Hand. Minneapolis: University of Minnesota Press.

Deleuze, Gilles. 1991. *Bergsonism*. Translated by Hugh Tomlinson and Barbara Habberjam. New York: Zone Books.

Deleuze, Gilles, and Felix Guattari. 1987. *A Thousand Plateaus: Capitalism and Schizophrenia*. Translated by Brian Massumi. Minneapolis: University of Minnesota Press.

Deleuze, Gilles, and Claire Parnet. 1987. *Dialogues*. New York: Columbia University Press.

Ferguson, Kathy. 2011. "Why Anarchists Need Stirner." In *Max Stirner*, edited by Saul Newman, 167–188. New York: Palgrave Macmillan.

Graham, Dee, Edna Rawlings, and Roberta Rigsby. 1994. *Loving to Survive: Sexual Terror, Men's Violence, and Women's Lives*. New York: New York University Press.

Hatab, Lawrence. 2005. *Nietzsche's Life Sentence: Coming to Terms with Eternal Recurrence*. New York: Routledge.

Holland, Eugene. 2009. "Affirmative Nomadology and the War Machine." In *Gilles Deleuze: the Intensive Reduction*, edited by Constantin Boundas. London: Continuum.

Huneker, James. 1909. *Egoists: A Book of Supermen*. New York: Scribner's Sons.

Katznelson, Ira. 2013. *Fear Itself: The New Deal and the Origins of Our Time*. New York: Liveright.

172 *Chronarchy and Obligation*

Mueller, Justin. 2015. "This Flesh Belongs to Me: Michael Weinstein and Max Stirner." In *Michael A. Weinstein: Action, Contemplation, Vitalism*, edited by Robert L. Oprisko and Diane Rubenstein, 55–76. New York: Routledge.

Patton, Paul. 2000. *Deleuze and the Political*. New York: Routledge.

Prozorov, Sergei. 2007. *Foucault, Freedom, and Sovereignty*. Burlington, VT: Ashgate.

Roediger, David. 1999. *The Wages of Whiteness: Race and the Making of the American Working Class*. Revised edition. New York: Verso.

Santayana, George. 1995. *Dominations and Powers: Reflections on Liberty, Society, and Government*. New Brunswick, NJ: Transaction Publishers.

Stern, Daniel N. 1990. *Diary Of A Baby: What Your Child Sees, Feels, And Experiences*. New York: Basic Books.

Stirner, Max. 2005. *The Ego and His Own*. Mineola, NY: Dover.

Taylor, Charles. 1985. *Philosophical Papers: Volume 2, Philosophy and the Human Sciences*. Cambridge: Cambridge University Press.

Tully, James. 1995. *Strange Multiplicity: Constitutionalism in an Age of Diversity*. Cambridge: Cambridge University Press.

Weinstein, Michael A. 1979. *Structure of Human Life: A Vitalist Ontology*. New York: New York University Press.

Index

a posteriori anarchism 139–40, 148n1
a priori anarchism 5, 139, 148n1
acceleration 59, 88n1, 164, 170n13
Adorno, Theodor 61
aesthetics 98, 108–10, 124n21; *see also*
  Deleuze, Gilles; Rancière, Jacques
Agamben, Giorgio 120–1, 125n33, 125n34
Ages of Man 21
Aion 52n53
alienable property 133, 142–3, 145; *see
  also* consent
Al-Saji, Alia 44–5
amnesia 16, 80; *see also* forgetting
anachronarchy 9, 162–7; *see also*
  chronarchy; freedom (critical)
anarchism 4–5, 7, 9–10, 11n11, 12n12,
  65–7, 83–4, 86, 91n27, 91n33, 92n47,
  93n52, 93n54, 107, 128–30, 133–4,
  139–40, 145–6, 148, 148n1, 151–2, 158,
  167–8 (*see also* a posteriori anarchism;
  a priori anarchism); philosophical 4–5,
  7, 9, 11n11, 65–7, 83–4, 86, 91n27,
  91n33, 92n47, 93n52, 107, 128–30,
  133–4, 139–40, 145–6, 148, 148n1,
  151–2, 158, 167–8; "political" 9, 11n11,
  12n12, 67, 93n54, 139
Anderson, Benedict 12n13, 27, 107, 116
Angelus Novus 22
Anscombe, Elizabeth 68
Anti-Oedipus 72
apartheid: South African 2
Apocalypse 89n10; *see also* End of Days;
  eschatology
apologists 4–5, 10, 25, 65–70, 81, 83, 86,
  91n27, 92n47, 93n52, 97, 107, 113–15,
  118–20, 128–9, 133, 145, 147, 151–2,
  154–6, 167, 168n1; *see also* association;
  consent; fairness; membership; natural
  duty
appreciation 32, 153; *see also* control;
  expression; Weinstein, Michael

Aquinas, Thomas 98–9, 122n5, 125n33
Arendt, Hannah 2
Aristotle 70, 98–100, 122n2, 125n33
assemblage 43–4, 52n61, 73–5, 79, 81,
  86–7, 111, 114, 141–2, 157, 162–3, 167,
  169n9, 170n13, 170n15, 171n18; *see
  also* machine
assent 2, 144, 146–7, 156
association 11n1, 72, 85, 99, 103–4,
  115–16, 152, 156; *see also* membership
Athens 65–6, 156
Augustine 93n54
authority 1–4, 12n12, 21, 42, 57, 64, 66–8,
  70–1, 83–4, 86, 88n7, 90n20, 90n22,
  90n25, 90n26, 93n54, 98–100, 102,
  122n6, 128–9, 132, 136, 139, 142,
  145–6, 151, 157, 160, 169n6
autonomy 5, 7, 33, 40–1, 65, 67, 70,
  91n27, 91n32, 112, 125n34, 131,
  139–41, 147, 151, 156–7, 167; *see also*
  Kant, Immanuel; Wolff, Robert Paul
axiom 78–9, 92n46, 112, 118, 124n24,
  166–7

Bachelard, Gaston 37
Badiou, Alain 52n58
badly analyzed composite 27–8, 31,
  49n26, 143; *see also* false problem
Baron, Ilan Zvi 90n19
Bauman, Zygmunt 88n1
becoming 36–8, 43, 46, 51n47, 51n50, 73,
  80, 111–13, 124n27, 152, 162, 167,
  169n11; becoming-minor 112;
  becoming-revolutionary 112, 124n27;
  becoming-woman 112; *see also* Being;
  difference
Being 27, 34, 36, 80, 112, 120–1, 152, 167
belonging 11n6, 12n13, 61, 63, 98, 100,
  104, 107–8, 114–16, 142, 154–5, 159
Benhabib, Seyla 122n10
Benjamin, Walter 22–3, 27, 38, 109, 124n22

174   *Index*

Bentham, Jeremy 4
Beran, Harry 90n24, 128, 132, 135; *see also* defeating condition
Bergson, Henri 6, 8, 10, 12n13, 15–16, 23–30, 32–40, 42–7, 48n16, 49n17, 49n19, 49n20, 49n21, 49n22, 49n24, 49n27, 50n28, 50n31, 50n32, 50n33, 50n37, 51n43, 51n45, 51n49, 51n51, 52n55, 53n65, 57, 64, 73, 80, 85–8, 90n14, 90n18, 97, 113–14, 141–3, 147, 148n2, 151–3, 155–7, 164–6; and Deleuze, Gilles 27–47, 49n24, 49n25, 49n27 (*see also* duration; memory); metaphysical pragmatism 44; method of 'intuition' (*see also* intuition; second self; spatialization)
Bergson and Modern Physics 48n16
Bergson–Deleuze Encounters 44; *see also* Moulard-Leonard, Valentine
Bergsonism 27, 82, 169n5
Bergsonisms 47
Berlin, Isaiah 158–9, 169n11
Berman, Marshall 58
betrayal 32, 67, 115, 118, 153, 169n4
Birth, Kevin 48n9
Borges, Jorge Luis 41
Boundas, Constantin 53n64
Bourdieu, Pierre 23, 56, 81
Brief History of Time, A 17
Brodsky, Joseph 124n28
Brown, Wendy 50n38
Bryant, Levi 19–20
Buchler, Justus 46; *see also* summed-up-self-in-process
buggering method 44–5, 53n63
Burke, Edmund 60
Butler, Judith 153

calendar 14–15, 19, 21
Čapek, Milič 48n16
capital 72–3, 77–8, 92n41, 92n42, 92n44
capitalism 58–9, 71–3, 75, 77–9, 88n1, 88n5, 92n39, 92n44, 92n46, 107, 111, 124n24, 128, 130, 141, 157, 167; *see also* machine (capitalist)
Capitalism and Schizophrenia 79, 109; *see also* Anti-Oedipus; *Thousand Plateaus, A*
Capitalism and Slavery 88n5
capture 35, 44, 74–7, 79–82, 87, 111, 142, 154–6, 164, 168; *see also* assemblage; coding; machine; Stockholm Syndrome
change 7, 10, 16, 18–19, 23–4, 26–9, 35–7, 39, 41, 45–6, 51n45, 51n47, 53n65, 58–9, 62, 71, 88n1, 89n13, 90n26,

92n46, 100, 107, 128, 130–1, 158, 161, 163, 169n11, 170n13
chess 170n15
Christendom 4, 22, 58, 91n37, 164
Christianity 34, 59, 88n3, 89n8, 99, 122n3
Christiano, Thomas 123n20
chronarchy 9, 151, 162–4, 167; *see also* anachronarchy; freedom (critical); time-binding
Chronos 52n53
Church, the 4, 21–2, 89n10, 100, 120
Cinema 53n65
City of God 93n54
civilization 61, 75, 77; *see also* machine (capitalist)
clock 6, 14–15, 24, 26, 162; clock time 26
code *see* codification
codification 72–8, 108, 157, 170n15; *see also* decode; flow
Cogito 35, 40, 61, 142; *see also* Descartes, René
communitarian 70, 91n27, 122n10, 123n16, 149n9, 155
community 2, 11n7, 12n13, 22, 48n4, 57, 66, 69–70, 99, 103–5, 116–17, 122n5, 123n12
Comte, Auguste 24
conceptual personae 108, 114, 123n19
concrete self 28, 32–3, 87, 141–6; *see also* conventional self; second self
Confucius 98–100
Connolly, William E. 51n50
consciousness 15, 22–3, 25–6, 28–32, 38–9, 41, 45–6, 49n19, 51n44, 62, 74, 106, 116, 159, 169n9; *see also* time-consciousness
consensus 104, 110, 112, 148n1, 149n9
consent 3–5, 7–8, 11n7, 83, 91n27, 91n37, 102, 105–6, 114, 122n1, 123n12, 128–48, 149n6, 151, 156–7; actual 130, 133–6, 145–6 (*see also* alienable property); explicit 133–4, 137–8, 140–1, 147, 149n8 (*see also* time-binding (horizontal)); hypothetical 130, 133–6, 138, 145–7, 149n8 (*see also* immediate expression; movements of consent); tacit 134–5, 138, 141
consistency 25, 73–4, 76, 85–6, 91n35
continuity 1, 6–8, 11n8, 12n12, 14, 21–3, 26, 28, 30, 34–41, 45–6, 56–7, 59–60, 62, 64–6, 73–4, 77–8, 91n34, 91n37, 92n44, 98, 108, 114, 121, 122n3, 135, 138, 142, 147, 153, 164, 169n5; *see also* discontinuity

Index 175

contract 3, 4, 8, 10, 60, 69, 100, 102, 105,
122n1, 128–31, 132–3, 135, 136–8, 141,
148n4, 149n8, 156, 169n7; actual 133;
hypothetical 133, 135; *see also* social
contract
contraction 37–40, 46, 142
control 5, 8, 10, 32, 52n57, 64, 67, 72–4,
76, 79, 104, 123n14, 147, 151, 153–6,
161, 163, 165, 167, 168n3
convention 5–10, 14–16, 23, 25–8, 30–2,
35, 38–9, 42–4, 46–7, 48n10, 50n34, 62,
64, 67, 72–3, 87, 90n22, 91n37, 108,
110, 112, 116, 124n24, 129, 134, 141–7,
152–3, 155, 157–8, 160–2, 164–6; *see
also* conventional ego; conventional
self; practical viewpoint
conventional ego 30, 143, 153; *see also*
conventional self
conventional self 8–9, 31–2, 50n34, 87,
108, 141–6, 152–3, 155; *see also*
concrete self; conventional ego; second
self
Copernican revolution 19
co-temporality 87, 97, 107–8, 116, 129,
142, 144, 154, 158–60, 162, 166;
minimal 107–8, 116; vertical 87, 97,
107–8, 116, 129, 154, 158
Creative Evolution 53n65
creative nothing 165; *see also* Stirner, Max
Critique of Practical Reason 48n7
cultural time 28–9, 50n34, 56–9, 61–2,
64–5, 79, 88n2, 97, 114, 138; *see also*
Weinstein, Michael

Dagger, Richard 104
death 3, 4, 14, 19–21, 32, 35, 47n1, 47n2,
48n12, 59, 62, 121, 128, 136, 170n13;
see also God (death of)
debt 77, 91n38, 92n42, 125n34
decode 77, 170n15; *see also* codification
defeating condition 132, 134, 141, 144,
146–7; *see also* Beran, Harry
DeLanda, Manuel 52n61
Deleuze, Gilles 6, 8, 10, 12n13, 15–16, 20,
23–4, 27, 33–47, 49n24, 49n25, 49n27,
50n36, 50n37, 50n39, 50n40, 50n41,
51n42, 51n43, 51n45, 51n47, 51n48,
51n51, 51n52, 52n53, 52n54, 52n55,
52n56, 52n57, 52n59, 52n60, 52n61,
52n62, 53n63, 53n65, 57, 65, 72–80, 82,
86–7, 91n34, 91n36, 92n39, 92n40,
92n43, 92n44, 92n45, 92n46, 98,
109–13, 123n19, 124n25, 124n26,
124n27, 142, 148, 155, 157–8, 160–4,
169n5, 170n13, 170n15, 171n16 (*see*

also aesthetics; assemblage; axiom;
becoming); and Bergson 27–47, 49n24,
49n25, 49n27, 53n65 (*see also*
codification; difference; dogmatic image
of thought; flow); and Guattari 12n13,
44, 52n62, 72–5, 77–9, 91n34, 92n39,
92n44, 92n45, 92n46, 109, 111, 124n25,
162–3, 170n13, 170n15 (*see also*
Guattari, Félix; line of flight; machine;
majority; minority; molarity; molecular;
nomad; nomadic war machine; rhizome;
significance; socius; state, the;
subjectification; syntheses of time;
territorialization; transcendental
empiricism)
democracy 3, 9–10, 12n13, 47, 66, 69, 71,
83, 88n1, 91n30, 92n39, 113, 122n3,
122n8, 123n20, 128, 130, 138, 140–1,
147, 148n1; direct 3, 91n30, 138, 140,
147, 148n1; liberal 9–10, 47, 66, 69, 71,
83, 113, 128, 141
Derrida, Jacques 23; *see also* eschatology;
Messianicity
Descartes, René 15, 24, 31–2, 40, 61–2,
65; Cartesian 35, 40, 142; *see also*
Cogito
despotic signifier 91n37, 93n58, 121
deterritorialization 78–9, 92n43, 124, 156,
161–3, 170n15; *see also*
reterritorialization; territorialization
diachronic 6, 28, 30, 38–9, 44, 170n15
diagram 15, 50n33, 79, 157–9, 161, 169n8,
169n9
Dialectic of Enlightenment 61
dialectic of modernity 97–8, 107, 121, 129,
144
dialectical materialism 73
difference (Deleuze) 33–7, 40–1, 44, 46,
50n40, 50n41, 51n43, 51n48, 66, 73–4,
80–1, 111–12, 120
Difference and Repetition 34, 38, 46,
50n39, 50n41, 52n53
discipline 2–3, 5–6, 8–10, 42, 52n60,
64–5, 87–8, 90n16, 98, 108, 110–11,
129, 141, 143–4, 147–8, 151, 155–6,
158, 162, 166–7; *see also* disciplinary
construct
Discipline and Punish 52n60
disciplinary construct 5–6, 8, 10, 64–5, 98,
129, 151, 156, 162, 166
discontinuity 35, 37, 42, 45, 51n45, 98; *see
also* continuity
disloyalty 1
disobedience 1, 3–4, 8, 64–6, 70, 99, 101,
103, 137, 169n6; *see also* obedience

176　*Index*

disorder 49n25, 49n26, 82, 131, 169n5
displacement of the political 149n9
displacement of time 6, 58, 79, 146
dissensus 110, 112–13
dissent 1, 135, 138, 144, 147
distribution of the sensible 109–10, 112, 114, 157, 167; *see also* Rancière, Jacques; sensibility
distrust 137
divine right 90n23, 97–100, 121, 129, 131
divinity 4, 11, 25, 51n46, 57, 88n3, 89n8, 90, 97–100, 120–1, 129, 131, 136; *see also* divine right
dogmatic image of thought 15
domain limiting principle 83
domination 19, 24, 43, 45, 48n12, 100, 111, 156, 168n3
doubt 18–19, 31–2, 48n4, 49n21, 50n35, 61–2, 84, 86, 88n7, 120
doxa 56, 80–1, 86, 93n51, 129
Dumézil, Georges 1–2
duration 6, 14, 24–33, 35–8, 40, 49n17, 49n20, 49n24, 49n27, 51n45, 51n49, 53n65, 57, 73, 80, 90n14, 119, 135, 141, 157
durational economy 63
durée see duration
duty 2, 59, 77, 91, 101–3, 105, 120–1, 123n13, 155; *see also* natural duty
Dworkin, Ronald 104
dysteleology 19, 37; *see also* teleology

ego 33, 35, 37–8, 117–19; *see also* conventional ego; transcendental ego
Ego and Its Own, The 165
egoist 117–19
Egoumenides, Magda 11n11
Eichmann, Adolf 2
élan vital 33, 37, 42
embodied self 9, 28; *see also* concrete self
embodiment 142–3
emergent obligation 152–6, 167, 169n5; *see also* formal obligation; political obligation
Empires of Speed 88n1
End of Days 21, 59; *see also* Apocalypse
English Civil War 130, 148n3
Enlightenment, the 58–61, 89n13, 100, 128
epistemology 25, 59, 61, 67, 139, 165
eschatology 21, 23; *see also* Messianicity
Essays on Deleuze 50n36
eternal return 36, 40–1, 51n46, 51n47, 51n48, 120, 162, 164–5; *see also* Deleuze, Gilles; Nietzsche, Friedrich

eternity 4, 60, 92n45, 99, 112, 164–6; *see also* eternal return
Europe 1, 3, 21–2, 31, 57–61, 75, 77, 89n13, 93n54, 98–100, 108, 111, 136, 156
excision 80–1, 92n47
existential 10, 19, 34, 61, 62, 64, 120, 164–6, 167; existentialism 34, 64, 120, 164–6, 167
expectation 3, 14, 23, 25–6, 29–30, 32–3, 39–40, 47, 47n1, 52n56, 56, 59, 63–4, 67, 71, 82, 99, 105, 114, 119, 121, 129, 134–5, 137, 146, 153–5, 163, 169n4
expression: ritual expression 134, 143–4, 153; *see also* immediate expression
expression (Weinsteinian) 32; *see also* appreciation; control; Weinstein, Michael
extensity 26, 49n21
exteriority 125n32, 163, 170n15

fairness 4, 8, 11n7, 69, 91n28, 97, 101, 104–7, 114–15, 117, 122n8, 123n11, 123n12, 123n13, 135, 156, 158
false problem 27, 82, 143, 147; nonexistent problem 27, 49n25, 49n26; *see also* badly analyzed composite; badly stated problem 27
family 2, 56, 90n22, 90n26, 103–4, 116, 122n2, 135, 155
fascism 34, 60
Faulkner, Keith 52n57
Fear Itself 169n7
Fechner, Gustav 24
Ferguson, Kathy 171n21
feudalism 58, 100, 131
Filmer, Robert 90n23, 99, 122n6
finitude 16, 28, 77, 154; *see also* infinity
Finnis, John 69
First Treatise of Government 99
flow 6, 18, 21, 26, 28, 35, 49n23, 64, 72–5, 77–9, 81, 91n34, 91n35, 92n39, 92n43, 111, 114, 116, 141
force 1–3, 6, 12n12, 16, 21, 23, 26, 35, 37, 40–3, 46, 52n59, 53n65, 62, 66, 68–9, 71, 74, 76–80, 83, 89n13, 92n41, 92n42, 93n58, 100, 106, 110, 112, 114–15, 120, 123n19, 129, 146, 153, 155–6, 159–60, 163–5, 168n3, 169n5, 171n18; active 43 (*see also* assemblage); bodies 43; reactive 43; relations 42–3, 52n59, 74 (*see also* threatening outside force)
forgetting 16, 27, 31, 39, 42, 80, 168; *see also* amnesia

Index 177

formal obligation 152, 154–6, 158, 167, 169n5; *see also* emergent obligation; political obligation
Foucault, Michel 10, 52n60, 74, 157, 169n8
fragging 2, 11n2
free rider 102, 114–15, 117
freedom 9, 11n6, 16, 30, 35, 41, 59, 61, 65, 88n7, 91n27, 102, 117, 128, 130–2, 134, 137–8, 140, 146–8, 149n9, 151, 156–62, 165, 167, 168n1, 169n11; conventional 157–8, 160–2; critical 9, 158, 160–2, 169n11; positive 158–60, 169n11; negative 158–9, 162, 169n11
French Revolution 60
Freud, Sigmund 33, 41
Friedman, David 91n33
friend 3, 69, 90n26, 99–100, 103, 104, 154–5, 169n4
future 6–7, 12n13, 14–16, 18–19, 21–4, 27–32, 38–41, 45, 47n2, 48n6, 48n15, 50n28, 50n32, 51n47, 52n53, 52n54, 56–7, 59–63, 65–6, 72, 81, 87, 88n2, 90n14, 90n16, 120, 141, 153–4, 161–2, 166; immediate future 29
Future and Its Enemies, The 88n1
Futures Past 59

Gans, Chaim 106, 123n16
Gay Science, The 51n46, 164
general will 63–4, 91n37, 138, 145, 159
Gilbert, Margaret 85, 93n55, 116
Go (game) 170n15
God 2, 4, 11n5, 20, 40, 51n46, 57, 59–60, 62, 77, 88n3, 89n8, 91n37, 93n54, 93n58, 98–9, 121, 122n3, 122n6, 136, 145; death of 4, 20, 59, 62, 121, 136
Godwin, William 12n12
Gorgias 81
governmentality 169n8
Great Chain of Being 4, 20, 22, 58, 88n3, 120, 124n24, 131, 144; *see also* Lovejoy, Arthur
Great Depression 169n7
Great Recession 92n42
Great Transformation, The 88n4
Green, T.H. 11n3
Grosz, Elizabeth 53n64
Grotius, Hugo 130
Guattari, Félix 10, 12n13, 44, 52n62, 72–9, 91n34, 92n39, 92n44, 92n45, 92n46, 109, 111, 124n25, 162–3, 170n13, 170n15; *see also* Deleuze, Gilles
Guerlac, Suzanne 24, 45

Habermas, Jürgen 12n13
habit 1, 6, 11n7, 14, 16, 23, 25, 30, 37, 39–40, 42, 46, 48n6, 50n29, 74, 76, 111, 144, 147–8, 155–7, 159, 169n9
habitus 23
Hallward, Peter 52n58
Happy Slaves 148n3
Hardin, Garrett 115, 124n29
Hart, H.L.A. 104–5, 123n13
Hassan, Robert 88n1
Hawking, Stephen 17
Hegel, Georg Wilhelm Friedrich 4, 23, 33–4, 36, 50n36, 52n59, 70, 75, 91n36, 159–61, 165
Heidegger, Martin 22–3, 38, 47, 48n15, 125n33, 152
Herzog, Don 130–1, 148n3, 148n4
Hesiod 21
heterogeneity 6, 24, 26–7, 31, 33–4, 37, 45, 52n62, 73–4, 110, 142, 163–4
hierarchy 5, 7, 12n12, 57, 76, 88n3, 99–100, 108, 115, 136, 139, 153, 157
history 8, 11n6, 16, 19, 23, 36, 45–6, 48n3, 50n36, 53n63, 56, 59–61, 63–4, 66, 72, 74–81, 87, 89n10, 92n40, 92n45, 93n49, 93n58, 102–4, 107, 115, 122n3, 128, 131, 133, 138, 146, 152, 154, 156–7, 159, 163, 165, 167; stages of 75, 92n5; universal 74–5, 92n40
Hobbes, Thomas 4, 68–70, 82, 89n8, 100, 102, 108, 128, 136–8, 148n4, 149n5, 149n8, 160–1
Hodges, Matt 53n64
Holland, Eugene 12n13, 163, 171n17
homogeneity 6, 8, 15–16, 18–20, 24–8, 33, 41, 46, 49n19, 49n21, 49n22, 68, 73, 86–7, 107, 112, 116, 141–2, 164
Honig, Bonnie 149n9; *see also* displacement of the political
honor 65–6, 108, 123n17, 153
hope 18, 23, 61, 63, 119–20, 124n30, 153–4, 168
Horkheimer, Max 61
Horton, John 12n12, 69, 85, 90n25, 103–4, 136, 146
Hoy, David Couzens 11n10, 17, 19, 47
Huemer, Michael 91n33
human nature 64, 68, 70, 90n16, 138, 160–1, 166
Hume, David 39, 50n37, 129, 138, 147
Husserl, Edmund 171n20
Hyppolite, Jean 33

identity 26, 31–6, 41, 50n40, 51n48, 52n62, 56, 63, 86, 108, 143

178 *Index*

ignorance 15, 27, 33, 60, 71, 101–2, 115, 122n10, 132, 148
Illuminations 124n22
image 6, 8–9, 15, 21, 24, 28, 33–5, 38, 41, 45–6, 48n7, 51n42, 52n56, 66, 74, 82, 87, 89n10, 97–8, 104, 107–15, 118–19, 121, 129, 131–2, 136–8, 142–4, 154–8, 166, 168; diachronic 6, 28, 38 (*see also* dogmatic image of thought; self-image); stratified 87, 97, 107–9, 113–14, 121, 129, 156; vertical 157–8; virtual 45, 114
Imagined Communities 27
immediate expression 143–7; *see also* consent; expression
In Defense of Anarchism 139
In Search of Lost Time 51n45; *see also* Proust, Marcel
In The Meantime 88n1
individual 2–3, 5–7, 10, 14, 16, 20–2, 27, 32–3, 40, 42–3, 45–7, 48n7, 49n22, 50n39, 52n57, 56–7, 61–6, 68, 70, 74, 77, 83, 86–7, 88n2, 88n7, 90n25, 90n26, 91n27, 99–102, 104–8, 110–11, 116, 118–19, 122n10, 123n10, 123n14, 123n15, 123n17, 125n34, 129–32, 135–8, 140–7, 149n5, 151–7, 159–61, 163–7, 168n1, 169n5, 169n9, 169n11, 170n13, 171n20; (*see also* identity); individuality 17
infinite debt 77, 125n34
infinite doubt 84
infinity 17, 28–9, 36, 39, 51n47, 77, 84, 108, 125n34; *see also* eternity; finitude
Innerarity, Daniel 88n1
insurrection 65
interiority 125n32, 163, 170n15
intuition 6, 23–5, 27–8, 33, 35, 46, 49n17, 49n24, 53n65, 88, 129, 142–4, 147, 152, 164; *see also* Bergson, Henri

James, William 1, 47
Joan of Arc 22
jurisprudence 12n13; *see also* law
justice 2, 11n6, 23, 47, 57, 69, 85, 93n54, 101–2, 107, 118, 122n8, 122n10, 123n13, 123n16, 129, 156–7, 168, 170n15; *see also* natural duty
justification 3–5, 7, 9–10, 49n18, 57, 65–7, 69, 71, 80, 82, 85–8, 90n26, 91n33, 91n37, 93n51, 93n56, 93n57, 97–100, 103–8, 110, 114–15, 119, 123n12, 128–30, 133–4, 136–42, 144–8, 148n2, 151, 154–5, 163, 168, 168n1

Kafka, Franz 66

Kālachakra 21
Kant, Immanuel 4, 15, 18–19, 22–6, 34, 40–1, 48n7, 50n37, 51n52, 58–9, 70–1, 88n7, 91n32, 92n48, 125n33, 139, 158, 161 (*see also* Copernican revolution); Kantian 19, 24, 33, 49n26, 115, 125n34, 142, 158, 160, 170n12 (*see also* transcendental ego; transcendental idealism; unity of apperception)
Katznelson, Ira 169n7
Kierkegaard, Søren 41, 50n34
Klee, Paul 22
Klosko, George 68, 70–1, 90n24, 90n25, 91n28, 91n33, 103, 105–6, 114–15, 119, 123n14
knowledge 51n45, 69–70, 101, 152, 170n12
Knowles, Dudley 83, 85, 93n53, 129, 132, 134, 136, 146
Kojève, Alexandre 33
Koselleck, Reinhart 22, 59–60, 89n10
Krishna 98
Kropotkin, Peter 12n12

lack 70–1, 77–8, 80
Latour, Bruno 59–60, 89n8, 89n11, 89n12
law 1–3, 11n7, 48n7, 62, 66–9, 84, 89n8, 93n54, 93n58, 98–9, 102–3, 105, 122n3, 123n14, 123n18, 125n34, 130, 135, 137, 139, 159 (*see also* jurisprudence); international law 130 (*see also* natural law); rule of law 3
Lefebvre, Alexandre 12n13, 53n64
legitimacy 2–5, 7, 12n13, 21, 57, 64–6, 70, 82–6, 88n7, 91n27, 91n37, 93n50, 93n58, 98–102, 107, 110, 113, 115–16, 121, 123n20, 128–30, 132, 134–6, 138–41, 143, 145–8, 148n1, 154–5, 168n1, 169n6
Lepre, George 11n2
Leviathan 89n8, 108, 138, 161
Leviathan 136
liberalism 98, 100, 122n3, 128, 141; *see also* democracy (liberal)
line of flight 10, 43–4, 162–3, 170n13
linear time 21, 37–9, 52n56
Liquid Modernity 88n1
liturgy 120–1
lived present (Bergson) 29–30, 50n30; *see also* living present; present
Livesey, Graham 73
living present (Deleuze) 38–40, 52n54; *see also* lived present; present
Locke, John 4, 68, 90n19, 99–100, 128, 135–8, 147, 148n4, 149n8

Index 179

Logic of Sense 52n53
Lovejoy, Arthur 88n3
loyalty 2–3, 11n6, 65, 93n50, 115–18, 120,
134, 153–4, 157, 168n1, 169n4, 169n7;
see also Royce, Josiah; true 117–18
Luther, Martin 59, 89n10

Maat 57
Machiavelli, Niccolò 1, 108
machine 36, 43, 46, 57, 66, 74–9, 91n37,
92n39, 92n44, 92n46, 111, 121, 124n24,
142, 155, 162–7, 169n7, 170n15,
171n16, 171n17; capitalist 77–9, 92n39,
92n44, 92n46, 124n24; despotic 76–9,
124n24; (*see also* machinic; nomadic
war machine); social 46, 57, 74–6, 78–9,
91n37, 121, 142, 169n7; territorial 75–7,
124n24
MacIntyre, Alasdair 91n31, 104
MacIver, R.M. 15, 47n2, 57, 90n18
McPherson, Thomas 85, 93n56, 104
Maistre, Joseph de 1, 11n1
majority 71, 110–13, 124n25, 142, 155–6,
163; majoritarian 110–13, 142, 155–6,
163; *see also* minority
Mandate of Heaven 99–100
market 58, 72, 77, 88n1, 89n13, 91n33,
92n41, 92n44, 157
Marsilius of Padua 98
Marx, Karl 58, 72–3, 75–9, 91n36, 92n44
Marxism 34, 73, 75, 91n36
Matter and Memory 33, 87
meaning 10, 14, 16, 25, 28, 33, 41, 56, 58,
60–2, 64, 72–3, 75–6, 84, 88n2, 105,
111, 114, 116–17, 120, 132, 141, 149n9,
160, 164 (*see also* purpose);
transpersonal 33, 56, 61–2, 64, 88n2
medieval 3, 21–2, 61–2, 98–100, 108,
125n33, 130, 163
membership 4, 8, 56, 63, 67, 69, 75, 85,
91, 97, 99–100, 103–4, 113, 115–18,
120, 128–9, 152, 155; member 7, 11n7,
21, 57, 85, 93n56, 105, 124n29
memory 14, 18, 23, 30–1, 33, 37–40, 42,
44–5, 50n33, 63, 87, 141; cone 50n33;
pure memory 30, 37
Mencius 100
Merleau-Ponty, Maurice 44, 47
Messiah 23
Messianic power 23; *see also* Benjamin,
Walter
Messianicity 23; *see also* Derrida, Jacques
metaphysical pragmatism 44
Middle Ages (Europe) 31, 57, 59
Milgram experiments 12n12

Mill, James 4
Mill, John Stuart 4
Mills, Charles W. 138
minority 111–13, 119, 163, 171n16; *see
also* majority
Mintz, Sidney 88n5
mnemonic synchronization 14
modern(ity) 2–4, 8–10, 11n3, 11n6, 11n8,
11n11, 12n12, 12n13, 17–18, 20–2, 27,
31, 33, 42, 46–7, 48n10, 49n18, 50n29,
52n61, 56–71, 73, 75–6, 78–81, 83–4,
88n1, 89n8, 89n11, 89n12, 89n13,
91n28, 93n58, 97–8, 100, 104, 107, 113,
119–21, 122n3, 125n34, 128–30, 135–6,
138–41, 144–5, 147, 149n9, 151, 156,
158, 163, 166–7; *see also* dialectic of
modernity; pre-modern temporality
molarity 10, 124n26, 124n27, 161; *see
also* molecular
molecular 92n43, 124n27, 161–2; *see also*
molarity
moment 9, 11n1, 22, 25–35, 38, 46, 47n1,
50n30, 51n46, 56, 58, 60, 63, 80, 87,
90n18, 92n45, 103, 107, 119, 141–2,
144–5, 152–3, 156, 162, 165–7, 169n9;
three moments of the dialectic of
modernity 60; *see also* time-binding
money 72, 76–7, 103, 118
Moral Principles and Political Obligation
84
morality 70–1, 80, 83, 91n32, 92n48, 137,
159–60, 165, 170n12
Moulard-Leonard, Valentine 19, 24, 44,
51n45
movements of consent 143–5; bestowal
143–4; *see also* immediate expression;
time-binding (horizontal)
multiple principles 97, 106–7, 119–20; *see
also* apologists
multiplicity 6–7, 26, 35–6, 41, 46, 87, 160
Mumford, Lewis 74
mysterium tremendum et fascinans 121,
125n35; *see also* numinous experience;
Otto, Rudolf
mystic 77

Nagel, Thomas 122n10
narrative 7, 21–4, 30, 56, 60, 79, 89n13,
98–9, 156, 163, 166, 169n7;
metanarrative 56; nationalist 98;
progress 23–4, 161
nation 2, 27, 107, 123n18
nation-state *see* state, the
National Labor Relations Board 169n7
nationalism 27, 107, 116

180   *Index*

natural duty 4, 8, 69, 97, 100–2, 104, 113, 118–19, 123n16, 135; *see also* apologists
natural law 89n8, 99, 137; *see also* law
nature 4, 21, 48n12, 52n61, 59, 89n8, 89n11, 98, 137; *see also* human nature; state of nature
necessary function 68–9, 71–2, 80–1, 102
New Model Army 131
newness 6, 26, 28, 31–5, 37, 41, 47, 60, 73, 112, 142, 163; *see also* becoming; duration; difference
Nietzsche, Friedrich 4, 34–6, 38, 40–3, 48n3, 50n37, 51n46, 51n47, 51n51, 52n59, 52n60, 59, 76, 98, 108, 120, 122n3, 155, 162, 164–6; blonde beast 108; *see also* eternal return; will to power
Noble Lie 168; *see also* Plato
nomad 12n13, 43, 52n62, 162–3, 170n15, 171n16, 171n17; nomadism 12n13, 163, 170n15, 171n17; *see also* nomadic war machine
nomadic war machine 43, 162–3, 171n16, 171n17
non-excludable benefits 105–6, 123n14, 135
nonlinear time 21
nostalgia 18
Nozick, Robert 90n19, 91n29, 102, 106, 115, 122n10
Numa 1–2
numinous experience 125n35; *see also* *mysterium tremendum et fascinans*; Otto, Rudolf

obedience 2–4, 7–9, 11n7, 12n12, 64–5, 67–8, 70, 79–80, 82, 84, 87–8, 93n56, 97, 99, 102–7, 113, 117, 119, 128–30, 135–40, 145, 63
Objects of Time 48n9
obligation 1–10, 11n6, 11n7, 11n8, 11n9, 11n11, 12n12, 12n13, 24–5, 32–3, 42, 44–7, 49n18, 56–7, 63–72, 79–88, 90n25, 90n26, 91n27, 91n28, 93n50, 93n56, 97–108, 113–14, 116, 118–21, 122n1, 122n7, 122n8, 123n12, 125n31, 128–30, 133–48, 148n1, 149n5, 151–8, 160–2, 164, 167–8, 168n1, 169n4, 169n5, 169n6 (*see also* anarchism; apologists; emergent obligation; formal obligation); political obligation as a problem 2–4, 8, 16, 49n25, 49n26, 63, 66–7, 83, 86, 104, 136; theoretical failure 5, 65, 139

obligation apologists *see* apologists
Ochoa Espejo, Paulina 12n13
office (*officium*) 120–1, 125n34
ontology 1, 6, 22, 25–6, 35–6, 38, 46, 52n55, 59, 63, 76, 81–2, 89n11, 116, 120–1, 125n33, 125n34, 133, 152, 156–7, 160–2, 166; of operativity 120, 125n34; of substance 120–1, 125n34
oppression 100, 104, 110, 117
Oprisko, Robert 123n17
Opus Dei 120
order 1–6, 8–9, 11n1, 11n6, 11n9, 15, 18, 21–2, 24–6, 33, 37, 42, 46, 48n16, 49n25, 49n26, 56–8, 62–5, 68, 72, 75, 77, 79, 81–2, 84, 86–7, 88n3, 89n13, 90n16, 98–102, 105, 107–15, 118–19, 121, 123n14, 123n18, 125n31, 128, 131, 134, 137–8, 142, 144–8, 149n9, 154–7, 163–4, 167–8, 169n5
original position 71, 101–2, 135, 152; *see also* Rawls, John
Ortega y Gasset, Jose 171n19
Ostrom, Elinor 115, 124n29
Otto, Rudolf 125n35
outside *see* threatening outside force
ownness 166, 171n21

Parekh, Bhikhu 4, 11n7, 69–70
Parliament (English) 130–1
particularity requirement 85
past 6–8, 14–15, 18, 21–3, 27–32, 37–40, 44–5, 48n6, 50n28, 50n30, 50n32, 50n33, 51n45, 51n47, 52n53, 52n54, 56–7, 59–63, 66, 72, 87, 88n2, 89n12, 90n14, 128, 141, 145, 162, 170n13; immediate past 29; pure past 37, 40
past-present-future 32, 56, 60–1, 72, 162
Pateman, Carole 4, 12n12, 65–6, 83, 138
patriotism 64, 90n16, 104, 159
Patton, Paul 10, 43, 79, 158–9, 161, 163, 169n11, 170n13
perception 1, 6–8, 10, 15–22, 24, 26–7, 29, 31, 35, 37, 42, 45–7, 47n1, 49n21, 49n22, 49n25, 50n31, 50n32, 51n45, 56, 59–60, 67, 73, 82, 87, 89n11, 90n21, 98–9, 102, 105, 107–10, 113, 116, 119, 124n21, 129, 135, 142, 146, 152–3, 157, 164, 168n1, 169n7
philosophy/philosopher 1, 3–7, 9–10, 15–19, 22–5, 33–8, 44–7, 48n3, 48n7, 48n16, 50n36, 50n39, 52n53, 52n55, 52n61, 53n63, 53n65, 57, 60–3, 65–7, 83–7, 90n23, 91n27, 91n33, 92n47, 93n52, 102, 107, 109–10, 120, 122n8, 125n33, 128–31, 133–4, 139–40, 145–7,

Index 181

148n1, 151–4, 156–9, 165–8 (*see also* anarchism (philosophical)); Continental 34; French 24, 34; life 36, 153; process 46; of state 1, 87, 154; of time 16–19, 22–3, 25, 37–8, 52n53, 52n55, 53n65; Western 19, 34, 45, 120, 128
piety 3–4, 66, 128
Pitkin, Hanna 3, 84, 93n58, 136, 146
Plato 1, 3, 15, 34, 36–7, 48n3, 52n62, 58, 81, 108, 125n33, 128, 168
pluralist (theory) 4, 106; *see also* apologists; multiple principles
Pogge, Thomas 122n8
Polanyi, Karl 88n4
police, the (Ranciere) 110–13, 154
polis 65, 170n15
political anti-naturalism 114, 123n12; *see also* political naturalism
political naturalism 8, 98–100, 104, 114, 118, 121, 123n12; (*see also* political anti-naturalism); religious 8, 98–100, 118, 121
political obligation *see* obligation
Political Theology 93n58, 122n3
Politics (Aristotle) 122n2
politics (Ranciere) 109–10, 112; *see also* dissensus
polycentric systems 124n29
positivism 24, 33
practical life 16, 30, 48n16, 86, 128, 166–7
practical viewpoint 25–7, 30, 42; *see also* conventional self
pragmatism 20, 44, 47
pre-modern 8, 11n8, 20–2, 27, 48n10, 57, 64–6, 118, 121, 144, 166; *see also* pre-modern temporality
pre-modern temporality 8, 21–2, 27, 48n10, 57, 64–5, 166; atemporality 21; circular 21; cyclical 21; *see also* *Kālachakra*
present 6–7, 14–15, 21–3, 26–32, 37–41, 44–5, 47, 48n6, 50n28, 50n30, 50n31, 51n45, 51n48, 52n53, 52n54, 56, 60–3, 66, 72, 87, 90n14, 120, 128, 141, 152, 161–2, 165–6; ideal present 29; *see also* lived present; living present; presentism
presentism 166; critical 166
primitive communism 76
Prisoner's Dilemma 115
process 1, 6–9, 16, 18–20, 26–8, 30–1, 33, 36–44, 46–7, 49n22, 49n27, 50n32, 51n44, 51n52, 52n55, 52n59, 57–60, 64, 72–6, 78–81, 87–8, 89n13, 90n18, 91n35, 97, 107–8, 110, 122n1, 122n6, 123n17, 124n24, 129, 141–8, 149n9,

151–2, 154–8, 161–2, 167–8, 169n5, 169n11; of capture 44, 74–7, 79–81, 87, 111, 142, 154–6, 168; philosophy 46; *see also* spatialization; structuration; time-binding
production 1, 19, 29, 35–7, 40–3, 51n45, 58, 73–8, 81, 87, 92n45, 97–8, 109, 111–13, 120, 142, 145, 155, 157–9, 161, 163–4, 167, 169n9; of change 29, 37; of concepts 51n45; of consistency 73–4; of desire 1; of difference 36, 41; of experience 19; of images 97–8, 109; social 74–5, 77, 87, 155, 159; of times 42; of unities 75
progress 14, 21, 23–4, 40, 45, 59, 61, 75, 79, 92n45, 158, 160–1
projection (temporal) 6–7, 9, 15, 28, 30–2, 40–2, 45–6, 50n32, 56–7, 60–1, 66, 72–3, 80–2, 87, 88n2, 92n47, 113–19, 141–4, 151, 158, 160–3, 165
property 69, 76–8, 90n17, 90n19, 102, 137, 157, 165 (*see also* alienable property; capital; capitalism); rights 78, 90n19, 102, 157
Proudhon, Pierre-Joseph 67
Proust, Marcel 35–6, 38, 40–1, 50n37, 51n45
Prozorov, Sergei 148, 158–9
Pufendorf, Samuel von 4
purpose 6, 8, 15–16, 22, 28, 30, 33, 44–6, 48, 56–8, 61, 65, 76, 78, 83, 86, 113, 116, 124n30, 134, 154–5, 160, 163, 167; *see also* meaning
Putney Debates 131, 136, 144

qualitative 12n12, 22, 25–6, 28, 35, 111, 164
quantitative 26, 28, 52n59

Rancière, Jacques 98, 109–10, 112–13, 148, 157; *see also* aesthetics; consensus; dissensus; distribution of the sensible; police, the (Ranciere); politics (Ranciere)
rationality 20, 46, 48n4, 49n19, 58, 61, 64–5, 70–1, 75, 79, 80–1, 91n32, 108, 115–17, 120, 122n10, 132–3, 135–6, 146, 152, 154–6, 160, 167–8, 168n1; instrumental 61; rational actor 108, 146; rational choice 160; rational maximizer 115, 117
Rawls, John 69, 71, 97, 101–2, 113, 118, 122n7, 122n8, 122n10, 123n13, 123n16, 135–6, 152; *see also* original position; veil of ignorance

182 *Index*

reality 6, 15, 18–19, 25–8, 31, 33, 34, 37–8, 44, 46, 49n20, 51n45, 59–60, 66, 73, 81–2, 87, 89n10, 93n54, 110, 115, 119, 121, 141, 145–6, 151
Reformation, the 60, 89n10
religion 2, 8, 23, 57, 59, 89n13, 98–101, 107, 118, 121, 125n35, 130–1, 136; *see also* Christendom; Christianity; Great Chain of Being; modernity; secularism; Zen Buddhism
Renzo, Massimo 103
repetition 35–6, 40, 51n48, 80, 154, 163, 169n9
representation 5–6, 8, 14, 23–4, 28, 30–1, 34–7, 41–2, 44, 46, 49n20, 50n33, 51n42, 51n48, 52n62, 64–5, 71, 87, 101, 108, 113, 115, 119, 121, 128, 130, 133, 142, 144, 146, 152, 154–7, 165, 169n5
reterritorialization 78–9, 92n43, 113, 156; *see also* deterritorialization; territorialization
Reuleaux, Franz 74
"Reveries of a Solitary Walker" 62–3
revolution 18–19, 23–4, 59–61, 92n46, 112, 124n27, 128, 139, 148n4, 163
rhizome 44, 51n62
rights 4, 68, 91n27, 98, 100, 102, 112, 122n3, 131, 133–4, 137, 140, 165; *see also* property (rights)
Robespierre, Maximilien 59
Roediger, David 169n7
Rome 1–2, 89n10
Romulus 1–2
Rosenberg, Julius and Ethel 2
Rousseau, Jean-Jacques 12n13, 62–5, 80, 90n14, 90n15, 90n16, 90n17, 91n30, 128, 136, 138, 145, 154, 159–60
Royce, Josiah 16, 48n4, 116–18, 120, 124n30; *see also* loyalty
rule 1, 3–4, 7, 9, 30, 57, 65–8, 75–6, 79, 82–3, 86, 88n6, 90n22, 93n54, 93n58, 98–100, 102–4, 107–8, 111, 116, 122n5, 122n6, 129, 147–8, 155, 162; *see also* law (rule of)
rule utilitarianism *see* utilitarianism

sabotage 167
Saint Paul 99
Samaritanism 68, 90n26, 102–3, 123n11
Sandel, Michael 91n31, 122n8, 122n10
Santayana, George 168n3
Sartre, Jean Paul 47
savage man (Rousseau) 62–3
Savonarola, Girolamo 22
Scheffler, Samuel 103

Schmitt, Carl 93n58, 98, 122n3
science 4, 17, 24, 48n8, 48n16, 58–9, 89n8, 90n20, 163, 171n16
Second Scientific Revolution 24
second self 28–30, 141; *see also* concrete self; conventional self
Second Treatise on Government 136
secularism 59, 71, 93n58, 98, 100, 122n3, 136
security 1–2, 4, 26, 30, 32, 46, 57, 59–60, 63–5, 68–70, 78, 86, 92n46, 97, 100–2, 106, 113, 116, 118–20, 131, 135, 137–8, 144–5, 149n9, 154, 157, 161, 169n6
self 6, 8–9, 11n7, 16, 18, 26, 28, 30–3, 40–1, 46, 50n34, 51n46, 56, 58, 60–3, 87, 90n14, 103, 107–8, 115–16, 118, 132, 137–8, 140–6, 149n5, 152–5, 159–61, 164–7, 170n13, 170n15, 171n19, 171n21; *see also* concrete self; conventional self; embodied self; individual; second self
self-image 46, 112, 154–5, 166; of the state/social order 154–5, 166
Sen, Amartya 122n8
sensibility 25, 31, 51n42, 109–10, 112–14, 120, 164; *see also* distribution of the sensible
Shakerley, Jeremy 60
Sharma, Sarah 88n1
significance 110–11, 113, 142, 154; *see also* subjectification
Simmons, A. John 5, 82–5, 91n33, 98, 106, 123n12, 123n14, 125n31, 128, 139–41, 146, 148n1
Singer, Peter 135, 149n6
Sittlichkeit 159
slow-downs 167
Smith, Daniel 50n36, 72–3
Smith, M.B.E. 106
social cartography 43
social contract 3, 4, 8, 10, 100, 105, 122n1, 128–31, 133, 136–8, 148n4, 149n8, 156, 169n7; *see also* consent; contract; Hobbes, Thomas; Hume, David; Locke, John; Mills, Charles W.; Pateman, Carole; Rousseau, Jean-Jacques
Social Contract, The 91n30, 136
social machine *see* machine
social man (Rousseau) 63
society 1, 11n1, 16, 33, 47n2, 56–7, 60–1, 63–4, 68, 70, 72, 74–5, 78, 81, 89n8, 90n26, 91n28, 91n35, 93n56, 105, 110–11, 113, 122n3, 122n10, 124n24, 128, 130–1, 137–8, 142, 159, 165–6,

168n3; eternal 60; modern 63, 68, 91n28, 138, 166

socius 73–7, 79, 91n35; *see also* machine

Socrates 3, 66, 128, 135

sovereignty 1–3, 10, 70, 76–7, 79, 84, 86, 89n8, 91n30, 91n37, 93n58, 98, 130, 137–8, 149n5, 160

space 5, 6, 8, 10, 14, 18, 20, 24–8, 43, 45, 48n4, 49n21, 49n26, 49n27, 58, 77, 88, 130, 142, 156–7, 163–4, 170n15, 171n17 (*see also* amnesia; forgetting); smooth 163, 170n15, 171n17; (*see also* spatialization); striated space (*see also* striation)

spatialization 5, 26–8, 31, 33–4, 42, 45–6, 49n20, 64, 73, 80, 85–7, 90n18, 92n47, 97, 108–9, 113–14, 118, 141–4, 148, 155, 161–2, 165–6

Spencer, Herbert 24

Spinoza, Baruch 35, 42, 50n37

spook 117–18, 165–6

Stagoll, Cliff 36

state, the 1–5, 7, 11n7, 12n12, 12n13, 34, 43–4, 57, 64–72, 74–84, 86–7, 88n6, 90n19, 90n26, 91n27, 91n28, 91n30, 91n33, 92n39, 92n41, 92n44, 92n45, 92n46, 92n47, 93n49, 93n53, 93n54, 93n58, 97, 102–7, 110–13, 116–19, 122n2, 122n3, 123n11, 123n16, 123n18, 125n34, 128–30, 135, 137–40, 151, 154–5, 163, 168n1, 169n6, 169n7, 170n15, 171n16, 171n17

state of nature 62–3, 68–9, 82, 102, 105, 136–8, 149n8

Stern, Daniel N. 168n2

Stirner, Max 59, 89n9, 98, 117–18, 122n3, 165–6, 171n20

Stockholm Syndrome 151, 168n1; *see also* capture

strata 10, 108, 114–15, 117–18, 120, 124n24

striation 10, 43, 73, 114, 156, 163, 170n15

strikes 167

structuration 46–7, 57, 71–2, 87, 107, 129, 157, 159–62, 164; *see* temporal structure

subject 7, 11n7, 20, 22, 40, 46, 61, 70–1, 80–1, 85, 99, 125n34, 136–7, 139, 142–4, 157–60, 165, 169n11, 170n15; larval 46, 142, 160

subjectification 110–11, 113, 142, 154, 156, 170n15; *see also* significance

subjectivity 5, 19, 22, 36, 45–6, 52n55, 70, 81, 116, 149n9, 157

summed-up-self-in-process 46

surplus value 77–8, 167

Surrealism 34

Sweetness and Power 88n5

synchronic 6, 28, 30, 38, 45, 56, 87

syntheses of time (Deleuze) 23, 37–42, 51n51, 51n52, 52n53, 52n54, 52n57, 162; first 38–9, 52n54; second 39–40, 51n51; third 40–2, 51n51, 162

tabula rasa 153

Taine, Hippolyte 24

taxation 67, 76–8, 88n6, 90n19, 103

Taylor, Charles 91n31, 159–60, 169n11

technology 59, 88n1, 107, 164, 169n8

teleology 21, 23–4, 37, 39–40, 52n59, 61, 71–2, 75, 79–81, 91n36, 92n47, 119, 158, 160–2, 165–6 (*see also* dysteleology); negative teleology 161; positive teleology 161

telic 15, 71–2, 79–80, 100

telos 23, 60

temporal structuration *see* structuration

temporal structure 6, 16, 19, 64, 70, 92n47, 160, 164; *see also* chronarchy; structuration

temporality 6–10, 12n13, 15–23, 27, 30–3, 37–8, 40, 42–5, 47, 48n6, 48n8, 48n10, 50n38, 51n50, 53n65, 56–7, 59–65, 69–72, 79–80, 82, 86–7, 90n15, 90n16, 90n17, 90n18, 92n47, 93n49, 97, 107–9, 113–14, 116, 120–1, 125n32, 129–30, 133, 140–8, 151, 154–68, 171n18; *see also* co-temporality; linear (*see also* linear time); modern temporality; nonlinear (*see also* nonlinear time); pre-modern temporality; temporal structure/ structuration; time

tendency of the rate of profit to fall 92n44

tense 21–2; *see also* future; past; present

territorialization 10, 43, 79, 92n43, 161, 170n15; *see also* deterritorialization; reterritorialization

Theory of Justice, A 71, 101

thinking in time 45–6; *see also* Guerlac, Suzanne

Thousand Plateaus, A 162, 170n13

threatening outside force 114, 117–20

Tilly, Charles 93n54

time 4–9, 12n13, 14–47, 47n2, 48n6, 48n8, 48n10, 48n12, 49n19, 49n20, 49n26, 49n27, 50n29, 50n34, 50n38, 51n45, 51n46, 51n51, 52n53, 52n55, 52n57, 53n63, 53n65, 56–66, 70, 73, 79–81, 86–8, 88n1, 88n2, 89n10, 89n13, 90n14, 90n18, 97–100, 103–4, 107–9, 113–16, 119–21, 122n1, 122n6, 123n12, 124n24,

184 *Index*

time *continued*
 125n32, 129–31, 133, 135, 138–48,
 154–68, 170n15, 171n18; "as measured"
 15 (*see also* cultural time); invisibility
 of 14–16; "lived" experience of *see*
 temporality; masking of 5–6, 15–16, 25,
 42, 46, 143–5; multiplicity of 17, 26, 38,
 41, 87; perception of *see* temporality;
 pre-modern temporality; spatialization;
 syntheses of time; tense; time-binding;
 time machine; universal 17–20, 22,
 48n8; untimeliness
Time and Free Will 33, 49n17
time machine 163–6
time-binding 7–9, 43, 57, 65, 86–8, 97–8,
 107–9, 113–16, 120–1, 122n1, 123n12,
 128–30, 141, 144–7, 154–8, 160–3,
 166–8; horizontal 8–9, 87, 108, 123n12,
 128, 130, 141, 144–7; vertical 8, 43, 87,
 97–8, 107–9, 113–14, 116, 120–1, 129,
 144
time-consciousness 45
tool 6–9, 20, 23, 25, 33, 43, 45, 66, 88,
 112, 128, 164–6
toolbox 10, 87
totalitarianism 34, 61
tragedy of the commons 115, 124n29
Tragic Sense of Life 31
traitor 117–18
transcendental ego 19, 46, 142
transcendental empiricism 44, 73
transcendental idealism 18, 40, 142
transcendental illusion 35, 51n42
Trobriand Islanders 21, 50n29, 91n38
trust 39, 118, 153–5, 160, 169n4
truth 15–16, 27, 48n3, 49n20, 51n45, 81,
 85, 111, 118, 157–9
Tully, James 169n11
Two Sources of Morality and Religion, The
 10, 33

Unamuno, Miguel de 31–2, 50n34, 50n35
Unique, the (Stirner) 165–6, 171n20
United States 2, 92n42, 169n7
unity 1, 8, 14, 18–19, 22, 24–5, 33–8,
 40–3, 46, 49n23, 51n44, 52n62, 57–8,
 60–4, 73–5, 77–8, 80–1, 90n16, 112–13,
 138, 142, 144–5, 154, 164; *see also*
 unselfconscious unity
unity of apperception 19; *see also* Kant,
 Immanuel

unselfconscious unity 22, 60–1, 64, 144–5;
 see also pre-modern
untimeliness 34, 50n38
Urstaat 78–9, 92n45
USSR 2, 124n28
utilitarianism 105–6, 123n15

veil of ignorance 71, 101–2, 122n10; *see
 also* Rawls, John
Vietnam War 2, 11n2
Virilio, Paul 170n13
virtue 1, 3, 62, 65, 67, 100, 104, 116,
 122n5, 131, 158
voluntarism 65, 83, 103, 122n7, 130, 136,
 146

Wages of Whiteness 169n7
Wahl, Jean 33
war machine *see* nomadic war machine
Weber, Max 66, 84, 93n50
Weinstein, Michael A. 32, 56, 60–1, 88n2,
 153; *see also* cultural time
Wellman, Christopher 68, 102–4, 118
West, the 89n10, 89n13, 100
Western 19, 24, 34, 45, 50n29, 59, 71,
 90n22, 120, 128, 136
What is Philosophy? 123n19
Whitehead, Alfred North 47
Widder, Nathan 37, 40, 52n57
will to power 42, 52n59
Williams, Eric 88n5
Williams, James 38, 41, 52n53
Wolff, Jonathan 106–7, 119
Wolff, Robert Paul 5, 67, 90n24, 139–41,
 146, 148n1
Wong, Mabel 12n13, 63, 90n15, 90n16,
 90n17
Wood, David 16–17, 125n32
"Work of Art in the Age of Mechanical
 Reproduction, The" 109; *see also*
 Benjamin, Walter
work-to-rule 167
Works and Days 21
World and the Individual 48n4
World of Becoming 51n50

Young, Iris Marion 122n8, 122n10

Zen Buddhism 25, 90; *satori* 25; *zazen*
 meditation 26
Zimbardo experiments 12n12